THE CENTENNIAL HISTORY
OF THE
AMERICAN BIBLE SOCIETY

THE MACMILLAN COMPANY
NEW YORK · BOSTON · CHICAGO · DALLAS
ATLANTA · SAN FRANCISCO

MACMILLAN & CO., Limited
LONDON · BOMBAY · CALCUTTA
MELBOURNE

THE MACMILLAN CO. OF CANADA, Ltd.
TORONTO

ELIAS BOUDINOT
President of the American Bible Society, 1816

The Centennial History

of the

American Bible Society

BY

HENRY OTIS DWIGHT

VOLUME I

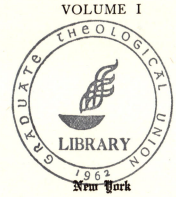

New York

THE MACMILLAN COMPANY

1916

Copyright 1916
By THE MACMILLAN COMPANY
Set up and electrotyped.   Published, April, 1916

PREFACE

In dealing with so serious and significant a subject as the effort of a Society to increase the circulation of the Holy Scriptures in the world the point of view has been that of an humble servant acknowledging that success in the effort can proceed only from the guidance and help of Him to whom these ancient writings belong.

The plan of this book has excluded many things which may have been expected to appear in a review of labours covering a whole century of the world's progress. Its aim was to make a book to be read by the people rather than a manual of reference for the student.

It is natural, then, for this Centennial History to seek in every chapter the glory of God. The pervasive, living power of the word of God is emphasised by the facts of distribution in many lands, and these facts suggest praise and thanksgiving on the part of all who have shared in the development and progress of the Bible cause.

The author would frankly confess his obligation to the Rev. Dr. William I. Haven and the Rev. Dr. John Fox, his colleagues as Secretaries of the Society, for kindly criticism of the manuscript, much to its advantage.

In publishing this record of the first hundred years of the labours of the American Bible Society we would suggest that it is only the beginning of a story which, please God, will continue until the knowledge of the Lord shall cover the earth as the waters cover the sea. The future is impenetrable to the vision of the present writer as it was to the men who founded the Society a hundred years ago and bravely set forth on unknown paths. Many things clearly ought to be done in the years immediately before us. In the meantime all may look forward with yearning and pray with the beloved disciple, that the Lord Jesus Christ may hasten His coming.

CONTENTS

INTRODUCTORY

CONTENTS

FOURTH PERIOD 1841-1861

FIFTH PERIOD 1861-1871

LIST OF ILLUSTRATIONS

VOLUME I

CENTENNIAL HISTORY

INTRODUCTORY PERIOD

CHAPTER I

THE BIBLE THE BOOK OF THE NEW WORLD

THE beginning of the story of the American Bible Society is found in those providences of God which made the Bible the book of the American Colonies.

Had there been no endeavour in the seventeenth century by European kings and rulers violently to control intellects and consciences awakened by the Reformation, there might have been no American Bible Society. It is not necessary to speculate upon this point. There is, however, occasion to call to mind, sometimes, the extent to which early settlers of the American Colonies now forming part of the United States had emigrated from their homes because they were lovers of the Bible. The Dutch and Swedes, who settled in New York and on the Delaware River, came out of the turmoil of religious wars, and brought their Bibles with them. The settlers of New England emigrated in order to secure liberty of conscience. They not only brought the Bible over on the *Mayflower,* but in the period from 1620 to 1640 they called about them some 20,000 people from the old country, who, like themselves, had suffered for the sake of this charter of their liberty. In 1689 the Friends had well established their " Holy Experiment " in Pennsylvania. To New York, Maryland and South Carolina Huguenots fled, Bible in hand, from France after the revocation of the Edict of Nantes. Like them were the German Mennonites and Palatines, who escaped from religious oppressors in their home land, and became rooted in Pennsylvania. The Presbyterians from Ulster, who took refuge in the Carolinas and in Georgia, were plain God-fearing people, who made the Bible the guide not only of their politics, but of their lives. The Virginia Colonists of 1607 may have included mere gold-seekers; but, under Captain John Smith, Jamestown was early provided with a church, and the Bible became a source of instruction to many of the settlers.

So, of almost all of the early immigrants to America, it might be said as the Roman Catholic Brunetiere said of the Huguenots, when speaking of the paralyzing effect of the revocation of the Edict of Nantes upon moral progress in France: " It drove into exile the people who called themselves men of the Bible, and who carried their morality, faith, and intelligence everywhere. . . . Louis XIV cut the nerve of French morality for the metaphysical satisfaction of having God praised only in Latin."

Stephen Charnock, the old Puritan of Cromwell's time, noted as a result of his observation that " all God's providences are but his touch on the strings of the great instrument of the world." That these men, the American Colonists of the seventeenth and eighteenth centuries, had been driven from their homes by religious persecution, was grievous; but, in truth, this emigration was simply a turning of the wrath of man to the glory of God.

These men loved the Bible. It may seem a little singular, perhaps, that if we leave out of account Eliot's Version of the Bible in the language of the Massachusetts Indians, and some Bible portions which Spanish Friars printed in Mexico in the end of the sixteenth century, we find the first Bible printed in America to be German, published in Philadelphia in 1743, by the enterprising Christopher Sauer, in order to supply the large German population who demanded the Word of God.

Bibles in English were a monopoly of the king's printers in England and Scotland at this time; but the monopoly existed to insure the text rather than to give wealth to the printers. A small nonpareil Bible, at the beginning of the eighteenth century, could be had for a shilling, or at most for a shilling and sixpence. With such prices American printers could not compete; so American readers depended upon the king's printers, too.

With all the other upheavals which the Revolution brought to the colonies it suddenly stopped Bible sales. Connection had been severed with the London printing houses. In 1777 a famine of Bibles was one of the many ills which a distracted Congress was called upon promptly to remedy at one of the Pennsylvania towns where it was able to meet in security. Dr. Allison, one of its chaplains, petitioned Congress to order the printing of at least twenty thousand Bibles. The lack of suitable paper, and even of sufficient type, in all the thirteen States for such a work negatived the scheme; but Congress voted by seven States against six to import twenty thousand Bibles from Holland, and this plan was set in execution.

Six States voted against the proposition. These were: Maryland, Virginia, North Carolina, South Carolina, Delaware, and New York. The seven States which considered scarcity of Bibles a concern of national importance were: Georgia, Massachusetts, New Hampshire, Connecticut, Rhode Island, Pennsylvania, and New Jersey. Let us note, by the way, that the vote of New Jersey in that Congress was cast by Elias Boudinot, one of the Trustees of Princeton University, eminent as a lawyer, who was afterwards President of the Congress, and later the first President of the American Bible Society.

About the time that Congress was making its provision of Bibles Robert Aitken, of Philadelphia, printed the first English Bible which came from an American press. The enterprise nearly ruined him, for almost as soon as the book was ready, peace with Great Britain was signed. Cheap Bibles from England appeared in the bookshops again, and the Aitken Philadelphia Bible lay dust-gathering on the shelves of the book-sellers. It is worth noting that the Bible which fed the soul of Abraham Lincoln in the Kentucky log cabin of his boyhood, was one of those cheap little Bibles imported from London.

The records of Bible printing in America show that many souls were being fed in those days by the wonderful words of life. In the later years of the eighteenth century, Bibles were printed not only in Philadelphia, New York and Boston, but in Trenton, New Jersey; Worcester, Newburyport, and Northampton, Massachusetts; at New Haven and Hartford, Connecticut; at Albany, New York; and at Wilmington, Delaware, etc. The Bible had become the book of the New World.

God's book had become man's book, since need to know themselves and their God everywhere impels men to read, ponder and absorb its teachings. The book so becomes to lovers of the Bible a groundwork for their activities, habits and character. In the Bible we all have found high and inspiring ideas of God, answering every yearning of the needy soul. There we all have been won over to noble conceptions of right, purity and service, have acquired certainty that life is more than meat or raiment; and Bible axioms have been taken up so as to become a part of our very nature. From the Bible the people have gained that enthusiasm for high attainment which ennobles the humblest man or woman and brings success, in some degree, to every effort permeated by a will to follow the leading of the Divine Master. It is this nurture in the Bible which has built up in our people a breadth of vision, and a deep consciousness of duty sure to show itself in good will to the less favored, such as appears in the widespread impulse to aid missionary and Bible Societies established for the sake of God.

Bible distribution among those who have it not used to spring from what scoffers called a mere theory; that is, from a belief that the book has the same living power to change men of every race which it has shown among those of our own race. But the idea is exploded which regards this as a theory. The Bible is to-day in the hands of tens of thousands of people, speaking several hundred different tongues, and belonging to all the races of mankind. After one hundred years of labor, the belief which led men to begin missionary enterprises has become absolute certainty. In every land those changed through the living and pervasive power of the Bible gain, and transmit to their children, some tendency to a nobler life. Bible readers thus influence permanently the community, or the nation, or the race, of which they are factors.

In the thirteen American Colonies large groups of choice souls were more or less hidden from sight by another sort of settler, who cared nothing for the Bible; had no use for any rule or any theory that did not result in some way in gaining fields, or harvests, or more precious valuables which can be weighed, and counted, and jingled. Nevertheless, generally speaking, the influential men and leaders of the colonies were apt to be found among the religious sections of the people.

To use the words of an anonymous writer in the old *Panoplist:*[1] "In no other country that ever existed was less restraint put upon men with regard to their religious or moral sentiments and behaviour. Here (in America) if a man is corrupt in his religious sentiments, there is nothing to obstruct his publishing them to others, beyond the restraint which he feels from the opinions and frowns of the virtuous, or the superior deference which the truth always challenges from falsehood. Here, if anywhere, men speak and act for themselves. Yet in no other country did Christianity ever command more respect from the people at large, or exhibit a greater influence on the minds and conduct of men taken in a mass. . . . Let not the writer be understood to mean, by the foregoing remarks, that the great body of the people of the United States, or that a majority of them, are Christians in the most important sense of that term. What he intends is that the proportion of such Christians is comparatively large, and that the influence of Christian doctrine and example over the great mass of the people is such as to warrant all that he has said."

Dwellers in that half-mastered wilderness noted in their midst shining lights, seemingly small and insignificant as the firefly flashes of a summer night. But amid the toil and murk which were the lot of that people, those little lights became beacons for wanderers, because they had been kindled from the great light for the feet of men — the Word of God.

[1] A religious magazine founded by Rev. Dr. Jedidiah Morse and published in Boston.

CHAPTER II

THE MISSIONARY IMPULSE IN AMERICA

In each of the American Colonies, before any large expansion took place, a policy had to be adopted toward the Indians. They were curious, suspicious, and often hostile to the pushing white strangers. Even inanimate nature opposed the advances of the Colonists upon its hidden treasuries. The forests resisted the intruder with their silent mystery and isolation; with their heavy undergrowth here, and tangled ropes of the wild grape there; and now and then with a broad abattis of huge trunks, twisted by a cyclone as though intended to bar, by acres of interlaced and jagged branches, access to some hidden, great prize. Mountains hindered any advance, walling in the land beyond with steep, rocky heights, or bewildering adventurers by offering them dark glens, and deep gulches that led to nothing more than another line of walls. Rivers forbade progress, with their deep, dark, unfeeling waters that could not be passed. And so it was fully a hundred years after the earlier landings before the colonists made any great advances away from the coast.

Meanwhile the great rivers of the Atlantic coast had become friendly helpers to those who explored northern New York and the broad interior of Pennsylvania. Before the Revolutionary War, too, adventurous hunters from Virginia and the Carolinas had found passes through the mountains into Kentucky and Tennessee, and had let the Kentucky, Tennessee, and Cumberland Rivers carry them, with their families, far westward toward the Mississippi. In 1792 Kentucky was admitted to the Union as a state, and in 1796 Tennessee. Pennsylvania was the least thinly populated of the states; and at the end of the eighteenth century groups of settlers were scattered in meadow land and along

6

river banks as far to the westward and northward as the Indians would permit.

About the same time the breezes brought from England to the eastern colonies of America unwonted voices. Where doubts and scoffings had filled the air, at the end of the eighteenth century stirred by the Wesleyan revival, the call to teach all nations rang out clear and positive. The appeals of William Carey in England had led to the establishment of the Baptist Missionary Society in 1792. His ideas had aroused the churches to such an extent that the London Missionary Society was formed in 1795, with the aim of evangelising those South Sea Islands described to the world by Captain Cook; the Church Missionary Society, with an eye to reaching Africa, in 1798; the London Religious Tract Society in 1799.

A pleasing circumstance which appears on examining the American religious periodicals of the opening years of the nineteenth century is the quickness of the healing of the wounds left by the Revolutionary War. One ancestry, one faith, one language, may permit petty misunderstandings, such as might spring up between husband and wife; yet such ties are too strong to be permanently broken. Noble impulses in one must naturally react upon the other. The English religious press was often quoted in those early American publications; and there was little or nothing to suggest that but a few years earlier friendly relations with England constituted a crime. In England there was a Society for the Propagation of the Gospel in Foreign Parts, and a Society for the promotion of Christian Knowledge—both formed in the seventeenth century. The Massachusetts Society for the Promotion of Christian Knowledge among the Indians was established in 1803. Following the establishment of a Religious Tract Society in London, a Connecticut Religious Tract Society was established in New Haven in 1807. The Massachusetts Missionary Society had already been established in 1800. The New Hampshire Missionary Society began in 1804 " to oppose that torrent of errors which threatens to deluge our infant settlements." The same impulse which had stirred British Christians, awakened among the feeble American Colonies quick response, as though the command to teach the world had now first been spoken.

In 1803 the purchase of " Louisiana " from the Emperor Napoleon added to the American domains an enormous tract of wilderness west of the Mississippi River, whose boundaries were then inconceivably distant, since they included one-third of the entire area of the present United States. This purchase of a wilderness, ridiculed at the time even more than Mr. Seward's purchase of Alaska was, gave the United States unchallenged ownership of the lower Mississippi, and had the effect, at the time unexpected, of increasing among the states of the Union still in the embryo stage, with little real solidarity, a broader aspiration and a stronger sense of nationality. This was a fitting prelude to the strong outburst of feeling among religious people which followed information of the establishment of the British and Foreign Bible Society in 1804.

The suggestion of the Reverend Joseph Hughes, when a few men were discussing the formation of a Bible Society for the supply of Wales, had the effect of an electric shock to quicken men's faculties. At the thought of a Bible Society, Mr. Hughes had remarked: " And if for Wales, why not for the whole world? " No one could nor would any one wish to put that question out of mind. It led to the founding of the British and Foreign Bible Society; and when, a few years later, the latent power in that remark had been proved by experience, the same question led to the establishment of many Bible Societies in the United States.

The first was the Philadelphia Bible Society, organised in December, 1808. It adopted a constitution differing somewhat from that of the British and Foreign Bible Society, but specifying that the Bibles which the Society should publish must be without notes; copies being distributed in all languages calculated to be useful, whenever this seems to be necessary. Some thought that the Philadelphia Society ought to design to serve the whole country. It was, however, the feeling of the founders of the Society that this would not be wise. A general Society, extending throughout the United States, would be unwieldy, they thought, and would languish in all places excepting the centre of its operations. It appeared to them that if similar societies were established in the principal cities of the Union, they might, by corresponding with each other, and occasionally uniting their funds, act with more vigour and greater effect than the one general Society. " If no similar Society should be formed in any part of this country," the Managers said, " then it will be the duty of this Society to extend its arms from Maine to Georgia, and from the Atlantic to the Mississippi."

They immediately sent circulars to leading persons in the different religious denominations throughout the United States urging them to establish Bible Societies on a similar basis.

The good people in Connecticut next moved to organise a Bible Society (in May, 1809). Then came Massachusetts with its Bible Society in July of the same year. New York followed in November, 1809, and New Jersey in December. Within six years time more than one hundred Bible Societies had been organised in the United States, with the simple purpose of providing Bibles for the poor who had no means of supplying themselves. Almost every one of the new Societies had in its Constitution provision for extending its benefactions when possible to heathen lands.

The British and Foreign Bible Society sent hearty congratulations to each of these new Societies; and realising that such societies would need tangible help in beginning their operations, it made grants of from Three Hundred to Five Hundred Dollars to each of the state Societies. In the masterly history of the first hundred years of the British and Foreign Bible Society, Mr. Canton remarks [1] that by the end of 1816 that Society had presented to sixteen American Bible Societies 3,122 pounds sterling.[2]

It is not a matter for surprise that those connected with the American Societies frequently expressed their affection

[1] Vol. I, p. 248.

[2] The donation of five hundred pounds which it made to the American Bible Society upon its organisation is not included in this amount; nor is a donation of one hundred and fifty pounds to the Bible and Common Prayer-Book Society, which hardly stands in the same general category as the interdenominational Bible Societies.

for the British Society under the title, " Venerable Parent."
A little later than this, a speaker on the Bible cause in New
York expressed his feeling in fulsome language, as follows:
" With the profoundest veneration I bow before the majesty
of the British and Foreign Bible Society. This illustrious
association (its history is recorded in Heaven, and ought to
be proclaimed on earth) has been instrumental in distributing
a million and a half of volumes of the Word of Life, and
has magnanimously expended, in a single year, near four
hundred thousand dollars for the salvation of man. This
transcendent institution is the brightest star in the constella-
tion of modern improvements, and looks down from its
celestial elevation on the diminished glories of the Grecian
and Roman men." [1]

A true missionary impulse leads Christians who wish to
tell the glorious facts to those who do not know Jesus
Christ " to begin at Jerusalem." This is the natural order;
but men at home who are stubbornly refractory may not
bar others from hearing the message of Jesus Christ; so
the impulse to tell facts to all will not tolerate sitting still
until the last inhabitant of the home city has surrendered.

A plain, rather bashful student in Williams College,
Samuel J. Mills, musing on this subject, felt the need of our
own frontiersmen. He also pictured the ignorance of the
wild barbarians beyond, and then questioned whether poor,
dark Africa must wait until all in America have consented
to drink of the water of life. In his diary is one sentence,
which, to him, was the conclusion of the whole matter:
" Though we are very little beings, we must not rest satisfied until we have made our influence extend to the remotest
corner of this ruined world." With unfailing persistence
Mills held that doctrine up to the very end of his short life.

The first public work to which Mills put his hand was to
go with some like-minded students in Andover Theological
Seminary to some of the leading clergymen of his acquaintance. The students announced to the astonished pastors
that they were ready to give their lives to work as foreign

[1] See the address of George Griffin, Esq., at the ratification meeting held in behalf of the American Bible Society at City Hall, in
New York, May 13, 1816.

missionaries; and they wished to know whether Christian people would support them in this enterprise. This was early in 1810. The quiet earnestness of Mr. Mills' question impressed the good ministers, and they took the matter seriously in hand. The formation, in September, 1810, of the American Board of Commissioners for Foreign Missions followed. The despatch to India of five of the devoted volunteers as missionaries of the American Board was the first step taken by that great Society toward extending its influence " to the remotest corner of this world."

Mills was not one of the five chosen to go abroad. Perhaps he was disappointed; but he was soon called to missionary work at home which, as we shall see, was destined closely to connect him with the organisation of the American Bible Society. It is a little singular, by the way, that the man who drafted the constitution of the British and Foreign Bible Society in 1804 was also a Samuel Mills, for forty-three years a member of the directing " Committee " of that Society. The extent of the territory added to the United States by the purchase of " Louisiana " was so great, and current knowledge of its people so little that the Massachusetts Missionary Society in October, 1812, appointed Reverend J. M. Schermerhorn as one of its missionaries, in co-operation with the Connecticut Missionary Society, to explore the West and Southwest. Mr. Samuel J. Mills was selected as a companion to Mr. Schermerhorn on this adventurous journey.

Five months were allotted to the young men for their work; this would be mainly occupied in travel, much of the time through pathless forests. It was a happy alleviation of the strain of such a journey that the two young missionaries were introduced to General Andrew Jackson at Nashville, Tennessee, then on the point of starting for Natchez with fifteen hundred soldiers; the war with Great Britain having just commenced. General Jackson liked the young men, and invited them to go as far as Natchez on his steamer; which they were glad enough to do. It was something of a descent from this high level of comfort as guests of the general commanding the army, when the two men engaged passage on a flat-boat from Natchez to New

Orleans; preferring this discomfort to an expenditure of six times as much money for the sake of going on a steamer.

The return journey from New Orleans was still more painful. The two missionaries were just one month going from New Orleans overland to Nashville, a distance of five hundred miles through heavy forests, thick canebrakes and bridgeless rivers, so remote from human habitation that wolves and bears and rattlesnakes were ready to dispute the right of way.

When the explorers returned from this long expedition, they made a moving report of the extraordinary situation which they had found. Almost as soon as they had passed Pittsburg, the story became monotonous; the little settlements were without religious privileges. Again and again they found districts where fifty thousand or more people were without opportunity to hear preaching, and almost entirely without the Bible for their own comfort or for the bringing up of their children.

Mr. Mills was so moved by the prevailing destitution that at every opportunity he gathered people together and induced them to form a local Bible Society; for there were plenty of good people who, when brought together, found that they could work with some prospect of success. In this way the Ohio State Bible Society, the Indiana Bible Society, the Illinois Bible Society and the Nashville, Tennessee, Bible Society were formed. The Kentucky Bible Society at Lexington was reorganised, and stirred with new hope. A new Bible Society was established at Natchez, Mississippi; and finally, after consulting with the Roman Catholic clergy of New Orleans, the New Orleans Bible Society was organised; the Roman Catholic Bishop saying that if the books circulated were the translations favoured by the Roman Catholic Church, he would contribute to the Society's funds.

The two explorers had been furnished by the New York Bible Society and the Philadelphia Bible Society with a certain number of Bibles, with which they rejoiced the hearts of those responsible for the work of the new Bible Societies which they left on their trail.

In 1814 the Massachusetts Missionary Society appointed

Mr. Mills to make another tour over practically the same ground which he had examined two years before; this time to preach and distribute religious literature, seeking to encourage the different communities to organise for the support of pastors at least a part of the year. The Rev. Daniel Smith of Georgia was appointed to be Mr. Mills' companion on this journey.

After visiting various points from Steubenville to Marietta, they urged the Missionary Society to establish a river mission; the preacher to go in a boat along the Virginia and the Ohio shores, stopping at eight or ten stations, so that the people might hear a sermon at least once in a while. Meeting a man in Illinois who said that he had been trying for ten years to buy a Bible, it was brought home to Mr. Mills' heart that this man was one thousand miles from any place where a Bible could be printed, and that many of the people in that wilderness must remain destitute to the end of their lives.

This second expedition brought Mr. Mills to New Orleans in the middle of February, 1815, a month after General Jackson's victory over General Pakenham and the English Army. He went about among the hospitals, distributing Scriptures to sick and wounded of both armies. He visited the prisons, comforting and cheering the British prisoners. He distributed in the city three thousand French Testaments which the Philadelphia Bible Society had sent to New Orleans; Roman Catholics receiving them gladly, and rarely objecting. It was to Mills a happy experience.

Mr. Mills returned directly to Massachusetts on fire with the tremendous needs of the West and South. His soul was burdened by the problem of awakening the people of the Eastern States to an understanding, in the first place, of the enormous possibilities of the Western country; and in the second place, of the religious destitution of the settlers throughout these new territories. In times when prompt and radical action in behalf of the kingdom of Jesus Christ is necessary, God commonly thrusts forward a man to show the people what should be done. For that critical moment the man thus thrust into the work by our divine Master was Samuel J. Mills.

CHAPTER III

OCCUPIED with strenuous labours for their daily bread and with efforts to lay the foundations of their future welfare, settlers in the West and South had no time to consider ideals. These sturdy well-meaning people, left without wise advisers, were carelessly preparing for themselves catastrophe, and for the nation humiliation. Many were inclined to say to God, like some of the ancients, "Depart from us for we desire not the knowledge of thy ways." Their fair lands were in danger of becoming strongholds of ungodliness.

The reports of Mr. Samuel J. Mills and his companions aroused Christians everywhere to the danger of such a situation. Mills' passionate words were not the ravings of an alarmist. But he wrote, "There are districts containing from twenty to fifty thousand people entirely destitute of the Scriptures and of religious privileges. How shall they hear without a preacher? Never will the impression be erased from our hearts that has been made by beholding those scenes of wide-spread desolation. The whole country from Lake Erie to the Gulf of Mexico is as the valley of the shadow of death. Only here and there a few rays of gospel light pierce through the awful gloom. This vast expanse of our country contains more than one million inhabitants. The number of Bibles sent them by all the Societies in the United States is by no means as great as the yearly increase of the population. The original number of people still remains unsupplied.

"When we entered on this mission we applied in person to the oldest and wealthiest of the Bible institutions, but we could only obtain a single small donation. The existing Societies have not yet been able to supply the demand in their own immediate vicinity. Some mightier effort must be made. Their scattered and feeble exertions are by no means adequate to the accomplishment of the object. It is thought by judicious people that half a million of Bibles are necessary for the supply of the destitute in the United States. It is a foul blot on the national character. Christian America must arise and wipe it away.

"The existing Societies are not able to do this work. They want union; they want co-operation; they want resources. If a National Institution cannot be formed, application ought to be made immediately to the British and Foreign Bible Society for aid." [1]

All seem to have agreed that Bibles were essential in this emergency. Missionaries could do little without them, and even where there was no missionary the Bible could awaken the conscience. In 1814 many persons thought that since there were nearly a hundred Bible Societies in the land, with patience, the danger of irreligion becoming rooted in the new settlements would be dissipated. This opinion sprang from blind ignorance. Referring to the inadequacy of the existing system, Mr. Mills said that in order to get five thousand copies of the Scriptures in French as a partial supply for forty or fifty thousand French Catholics who are destitute, "we have to go or send to the several Bible Societies from Maine to Georgia, and to wait until we receive information from the Directing Committees. Four, five, or six months must elapse, and perhaps a year before we are able to make a report. And by this time the most favourable opportunity for distributing the Bible may have passed by. And although it may be found that we are possessed of ability to effect the desired object, yet if we are obliged to conduct in this way, we shall be very liable to be defeated, and we may have to send to the directors of the British and Foreign Bible Society requesting that they would make a donation of Bibles for the supply of the destitute within the limits of the United States." [2]

Aspirations for some unity of action between the Bible

[1] Life of S. J. Mills by Gardiner Spring, p. 83–86.
[2] *Panoplist,* October 1813, p. 357.

Societies appeared occasionally in the religious periodicals, but nothing practical resulted. At last, in the autumn of 1814 the Honorable Elias Boudinot, LL.D., President of the New Jersey Bible Society, sent to all the Bible Societies in the United States a statement that on the 30th of August, 1814, the Board of Managers of the New Jersey Bible Society adopted the following resolution:

" Whereas it is the duty of the New Jersey Bible Society to use all the means which a kind providence has put into their power to promote the great objects of their association; and whereas the greatest union of Christians, of every profession, in so desirable a cause, promises most success to the undertaking — On motion it was resolved that a committee of three be appointed to take into consideration, and report their opinion of the most probable means in the power of the society for uniting the people of God, of all denominations, in the United States, in carrying on the great work of disseminating the gospel of Jesus Christ throughout the habitable world, making report to the present session of the Board of Managers."

Dr. Boudinot, and the Rev. Drs. Wharton and Woodhull were appointed a committee to consider and report on the foregoing, who, after duly considering the same, reported these resolutions, which, having been laid before the society, were approved and included in the circular to the Bible Societies. The substance of these resolutions was: First, that it would greatly promote the accomplishment of the important purposes for which the Bible Societies in the United States have associated, if a union of them all could be obtained, by an annual or biennial meeting of delegates, to be appointed by the societies in each state, at some central place to be agreed on, to conduct the common interests of the whole respecting the distribution of the Sacred Scriptures beyond the limits of particular states, or where a society in a state cannot furnish so many copies as are wanted. Second, that each Bible Society be requested to appoint at least two delegates to meet at Philadelphia on the Monday preceding the third Wednesday in the following May with full power to form a plan for a well organised and constituted body or society, to be called the " General Association of the Bible Societies in the United States," or such other name or title as may then be agreed on, for the purpose of disseminating the Scriptures of the Old and New Testament, according to the present approved version, without note or comment. Third, that the president of the New Jersey Bible Society, whenever he shall receive notice of the appointment of delegates from twenty societies, is empowered to give public notice thereof in the newspapers, and that the meeting of the said delegates will be had accordingly.

In the fall of 1814 Mr. Mills had explained in a leading religious periodical his idea of a General Bible Society which would meet the need of the country. Possibly this proposal of Mr. Mills had won favour. However this may be, as the months went by and answers to the suggestion of the New Jersey Bible Society for a General Association of Bible Societies were received, not even twenty of them approved the plan. A year had passed since the report of Schermerhorn and Mills had first called attention to the dangers threatening the nation, but nothing had been done!

The objections to the plan of the New Jersey Society were stated positively by the New York, and in most detail by the Philadelphia Bible Society. They were that the proposal was unseasonable; that it was without precedent; that such an association would be useless; that it might prove injurious and that the plan in any case was impracticable. In short a rooted antipathy was felt in some quarters for such an association of the independent Bible Societies.

Dr. Boudinot inherited Huguenot devotion from his father and Welsh tenacity from his mother. He was the sort of man that does not easily perceive defeat. He afterwards stated that he had determined in case of failure in another attempt " to commence the great business, at all events, with the aid of a few laymen who had testified their willingness to go all lengths with me." [1] For the moment he answered the Philadelphia Society by a " thick pamphlet." Thereby he won the support of the Connecticut Bible Society at its annual meeting of May, 1815. Correspondence with other

---

[1] First Annual Report of the American Bible Society, p. 46.

Bible Societies followed, and although difficulties of communication made it hard to know when the last word had been said, the New Jersey Bible Society made a new proposal, which was favourably received. On the 31st of January, 1816, Dr. Boudinot was at last able to call a convention of representatives of the Bible Societies to meet in New York. This first act in the formation of the American Bible Society was as follows:

" To the members of the several Bible Societies in the United States:

" Brethren:

" It is with peculiar pleasure that I once more address you on the interesting subject of extending the Redeemer's kingdom by an unlimited and gratuitous circulation of the Holy Scriptures.

" From the most correct information that has lately been received, it has become evident that the demand for Bibles in the remote and frontier settlements of our country, is far beyond the resources of the several Bible Societies now existing in the United States.

" An institution, founded on a more extensive plan, that will concentrate and direct the efforts of our numerous and increasing Bible Associations seems at present to be the general wish of the friends of revealed Truth. Such an institution has a powerful claim to the liberal support of the Christian public. This plan, which originated with the New Jersey Bible Society, has, within the last year, engaged the attention of the Board of Managers of the New York Bible Society.

" Their resolutions, inserted below, contain the result of their deliberations on this important subject. A brighter day appears now to have dawned on our Western Hemisphere.

" That the present effort may be rendered an efficient means of salvation to many thousands of destitute poor in our own, and more distant lands, should be the wish and prayer of every sincere Christian.

" And may the blessing of Him who is ' able to do for us abundantly more than we can either ask or think ' give it complete success —" unto whom be glory in the church of Jesus Christ, throughout all ages — world without end.

" These are the resolutions of the Board of Managers of the New York Bible Society:

" 'ıst, Resolved, that it is highly desirable to obtain upon as large a scale as possible, a co-operation of the efforts of the Christian community throughout the United States, for the efficient distribution of the Holy Scriptures.

" ' 2nd, That, as a mean for the attainment of this end, it will be expedient to have a convention of delegates from such Bible Societies, as shall be disposed to concur in this measure, to meet —— on the —— day of —— next, for the purpose of considering whether such a co-operation may be effected in a better manner than by the correspondence of the different societies as now established; and if so, that they prepare the draft of a plan for such co-operation to be submitted to the different societies for their decision.

" ' 3d, That the Secretary transmit the above resolutions to the President of the New Jersey Bible Society, as expressive of the opinion of this Board on the measures therein contained, at the same time signifying the wish of this Board, that he would exercise his own discretion in bringing the subject before the public.'

" In pursuance of the foregoing resolutions requesting me to designate the time and place at which the proposed meeting of delegates from the different Bible Societies of the United States shall take place; after mature deliberation, and consulting with judicious friends on this important subject, I am decidedly of opinion that the most suitable *place* for the proposed meeting is the city of New York — and the most convenient time the second Wednesday of May next — and I do appoint and recommend the said meeting to be held at that time and place.

" Should it please a merciful God to raise me from the bed of sickness to which I am now confined, it will afford me the highest satisfaction to attend at that time, and contribute all in my power towards the establishment and organisation of a Society which, with blessing of God, I have not the least doubt will, in time, in point of usefulness, be second only to the parent institution (the British and

Foreign Bible Society), will shed an unfading lustre on our Christian community, and will prove a blessing to our country and the world.

(signed)   " ELIAS BOUDINOT,
" President of the New Jersey Bible Society."
" Burlington, January 31, 1816."

Dr. Boudinot had rendered distinguished services to his country during the Revolutionary War; as President of the National Congress, at the close of that war he had signed the treaty of peace with Great Britain; and now it was his high privilege to sign a document which, in his hope, would stand for much in the history of his country saved to permanent loyalty to the Lord Jesus Christ. That the call for a convention of Bible Societies was signed on his sick bed detracted but little from his satisfaction.

FIRST PERIOD 1816–1821

CHAPTER IV

THE ORGANISATION OF THE SOCIETY

THE Garden Street Dutch Reformed Church, of which Rev. Dr. Matthews was pastor, in 1816 was a plain, unpretentious building of old New York. Long ago it gave place, with all of the residences about it, to the demands for space made by the money-getters. The very street on which it fronted is now hidden under the name of Exchange Place.

On the 8th of May, 1816, the Consistory Room of this church was opened to a meeting of clergy and laymen interested in the question whether the new West could be led to learn God's ways in nation-building. The struggle between good and evil was in the thoughts of all the delegates. In one sense that struggle was transferred from the frontiers in the valley of the great river to this city Meeting House. Here, God willing, the great question was to touch decision.

For this was the gathering which the president of the New Jersey Bible Society had called to choose some practicable method of carrying God's word westward to the thousands fast settling into content with irreligion. Dr. Boudinot was not able to be present at this memorable gathering; but behind the visitors, far back in the room, sat Samuel J. Mills the ardent believer in Bible Societies as missionary agencies. He had come there full of hope; but his heart was weighed down with fear when he realised that the gathering would be composed of representatives of different sects. Many of the most polemical theologians of the different denominations had been brought together there with the notion that they could agree on common ground of action.

21

Mr. Joshua M. Wallace, of Burlington, New Jersey, an Episcopalian and a leading member of the New Jersey Bible Society, was chosen chairman of the Convention. Rev. Dr. John B. Romeyn, delegate from the New York Bible Society, pastor of the Cedar Street Reformed Church; and Rev. Dr. Lyman Beecher, the father of " all the Beechers," a young man who as pastor of the Congregational Church at Litchfield, Connecticut, had already fought well as a champion of temperance among the clergy, were appointed secretaries of the Convention.

The Convention was composed of men who were all distinguished in some direction. There was John Griscom of the Society of Friends, organiser of the common school system of New Jersey; a philosopher, as well as a professor of Chemistry. Another man of note was Rev. Dr. Nathaniel W. Taylor, pastor of the First Congregational Church at New Haven, delegate of the Connecticut Bible Society. He was a very eloquent preacher, but was regarded by some of his contemporaries as a heretic. Another member was Rev. Gardiner Spring, pastor of the Brick Presbyterian Church in New York, then located in Beekman Street. His ministry was remarkable for its length and its power. He was pastor of the Brick Church for sixty-three years. Mr. Spring had often crossed swords with Dr. Taylor of New Haven, in a sharp controversy upon freedom of the will. Another battle-scarred controversialist was Rev. Dr. Jedidiah Morse, pastor of the First Congregational Church at Charlestown, Massachusetts. It was only a few years after this Convention that Dr. Morse, broken in health by brooding over the violence of his theological opponents, had to resign his pastorate. Next to him we may note Rev. Mr. Henshaw, a rising young Episcopal minister, who afterwards became Bishop of Rhode Island. Another man of distinction was Mr. Joseph C. Hornblower of Newark, who later became Chief Justice of New Jersey. Then there was Valentine Mott, the distinguished surgeon, of whom Sir Astley Cooper said later on, " He has performed more great operations than any man living or who ever did live." He, too, represented the Society of Friends. James Fenimore Cooper, the novelist, was there as one of the delegates from Otsego County Bible Society. He was notable on account of his participation in the work of that day, even if he had not afterwards gained admiration as a teller of entrancing American stories. Another delegate was a printer and publisher of Utica, New York — Mr. William Williams, whose son, S. Wells Williams, gained renown as a missionary, as a master of Chinese, as a statesman, and later as President of the American Bible Society. The originator of Sunday schools in the state of New Jersey was there — Rev. Dr. John Mac-Dowell, then pastor at Elizabethtown, New Jersey. The delegate of the Westchester County Bible Society was William Jay, Esq., son of the great statesman, John Jay, a schoolmate and warm friend of James Fenimore Cooper, and an eminent conchologist as well as statesman, who was moved by his benevolent spirit to elaborate the first detailed scheme for the arbitration of difficulties between nations. Several of the Virginia Societies united in sending as their delegate to the Convention the Rev. John H. Rice, a fervent and powerful preacher, who three years later became moderator of the Presbyterian General Assembly, and afterwards President of the Union Theological Seminary at Hampden-Sidney. Another eminent educator in the great Convention was the President of Union College, New York, Rev. Dr. Eliphalet Nott, distinguished as pulpit orator, and a most genial disciplinarian whose students always delighted to tell of their encounters with his keen wit. But this list must serve as a sample of the material making up this Convention. The names of all the members of the Convention are given in another place, for, as Bishop Eastburn of Massachusetts said, some years later, " Let us not lose from memory the instruments chosen by the Almighty for blessing in this work the land and the world."

Rev. Dr. Eliphalet Nott, President of Union College, was called upon to offer prayer. In that earnest petition for the guidance of the Holy Spirit were expressed the solemnity of the moment and the yearnings of every heart in that room. The solemn silence in the Convention was hardly disturbed by the quiet questions and answers as the list of delegates was made, and letters from other Bible Societies not represented by delegates were read, expressing approval of the general design of the meeting.

When the roll of delegates had been made up, the object of the meeting was presented and freely discussed, not without divergences of view. Dr. Lyman Beecher wrote of the Convention many years later: " There was one moment in our proceedings when things seemed to tangle and some feeling began to rise. At that moment Dr. Mason rose hastily and said: ' Mr. President, the Lord Jesus never built a church but what the devil built a chapel close to it; and he is here now, this moment, in this room, with his finger in the ink-horn not to write your constitution but to blot it out.' " The laughter caused by this sally dispelled the storm, and the clear sun appeared again. To the amazement of all present, these champions of denominational competition stood at one point of view. In the afternoon when a resolution was presented that " it is expedient to establish without delay a general Bible institution for the circulation of the Holy Scriptures without note or comment," it was adopted without a dissenting vote.

The chairman of the Convention, Joshua M. Wallace of New Jersey, could not control his emotion. His eyes filled with tears, and he said, " Thank God! Thank God! "[1] Almost hidden behind the crowd in the rear of the room sat Samuel J. Mills, the man who had concentrated upon securing the organisation of a National Bible Society his great executive power in exciting and combining minds for benevolent work. When he saw that the day was won, a look of heavenly delight spread over his countenance.[2]

The smiles exchanged between the members of the Convention showed that this unanimous action had drawn them all closer together, like the members of an exploring party when from some Pisgah they have gained their first view of a Promised Land. One thought was in every mind: " It is the work of God! "

These sixty men for the Master's sake set aside strong personal preferences. Under divine guidance at a crisis in

[1] Rev. Dr. Blythe of Kentucky at the 10th Anniversary of the American Bible Society.
[2] Life of S. J. Mills by Rev. Gardiner Spring.

the national growth they had called into being an institution suited to the emergency, which would provide the nation with Scriptures and make many souls glad forever.

Having appointed a committee to prepare a draft of a constitution, and also an address to the public, the Convention adjourned to Friday, May 10, at 11 A. M.; and its members joyfully congratulated each other, giving glory to God like the man who received his sight at the word of Jesus.

When the Convention met on the 10th, according to adjournment, the Committee, composed of Rev. Dr. Eliphalet Nott of Union College, Samuel Bayard of Princeton, New Jersey, Rev. Dr. John M. Mason of New York, Rev. Simon Wilmer of New Jersey, Rev. David Jones of Pennsylvania, Rev. Lyman Beecher of Connecticut, Charles Wright, Esq., of Long Island, Rev. John H. Rice of Virginia, Rev. Dr. Jedidiah Morse of Massachusetts, William Jay, Esq., of Westchester County, New York, and Rev. Dr. James Blythe of Kentucky, presented its draft of a constitution. This was read, discussed, considered paragraph by paragraph, and unanimously adopted. It was a well-considered document which has served its purpose (with some amendment, see Appendix) as the years have gone by. It is here given in its original form:

" 1. This Society shall be known by the name of The American Bible Society, of which the sole object shall be to encourage a wider circulation of the Holy Scriptures without note or comment. The only copies in the English language to be circulated by the Society shall be of the version now in common use.

" 2. This Society shall add its endeavours to those employed by other Societies, for circulating the Scriptures throughout the United States and their territories; and shall furnish them with stereotype plates, or such other assistance as circumstances may require. This Society shall, also, according to its ability, extend its influence to other countries, whether Christian, Mohammedan, or Pagan.

" 3. All Bible Societies shall be allowed to purchase at cost from this Society, Bibles for distribution within their own districts. The members of all such Bible Societies as shall agree to place their surplus revenue, after supplying their own districts with Bibles, at the disposal of this Society, shall be entitled to vote in all meetings of the Society; and the officers of such Societies shall be *ex officio* directors of this.

" 4. Each subscriber of three dollars annually shall be a member.

" 5. Each subscriber of thirty dollars at one time shall be a member for life.

" 6. Each subscriber of fifteen dollars annually shall be a Director.[1]

" 7. Each subscriber of one hundred and fifty dollars at one time, or who shall, by one additional payment, increase his original subscription to one hundred and fifty dollars shall be a Director for life.

" 8. Directors shall be entitled to attend and vote at all meetings of the Board of Managers.

" 9. A Board of Managers shall be appointed to conduct the business of the Society, consisting of thirty-six laymen, of whom twenty-four shall reside in the city of New York or its vicinity. One-fourth part of the whole number shall go out of office at the expiration of each year, but shall be re eligible.

" Every Minister of the Gospel, who is a member of the Society, shall be entitled to meet and vote with the Board of Managers, and be possessed of the same powers as a Manager himself.

" The Managers shall appoint all officers and call special meetings, and fill such vacancies as may occur by death or otherwise, in their own Board.

" 10. Each member of the Society shall be entitled, under the direction of the Board of Managers, to purchase Bibles and Testaments, at the Society's prices, which shall be as low as possible.

" 11. The Annual Meetings of the Society shall be held at New York or Philadelphia, at the option of the Society, on the second Thursday of May in each year, when the

---

[1] This article was rescinded in 1827, and the numbers of the remaining Articles changed accordingly.

Managers shall be chosen, the accounts presented, and the proceedings of the foregoing year reported.

" 12. The President, Vice-Presidents, Treasurer and Secretaries for the time being, shall be considered, *ex officio*, members of the Board of Managers.

" 13. At the general meetings of the Society and the meetings of the Managers, the President, or in his absence the Vice-President first on the list then present; and in the absence of all the Vice-Presidents, such members as shall be appointed for that purpose shall preside at the meeting.

" 14. The Managers shall meet on the first Wednesday in each month, or oftener, if necessary, at such place in the city of New York as they shall from time to time adjourn to.

" 15. The Managers shall have the power of appointing such persons as have rendered essential services to the Society, either Members for life, or Directors for life.

" 16. The whole minutes of every meeting shall be signed by the Chairman.

" 17. No alteration shall be made to this Constitution, except by the Society at an annual meeting, on the recommendation of the Board of Managers."

The Committee also reported an address to the people of the United States, which was approved by the Convention. This was written by Rev. Dr. John Mitchell Mason, minister of the Associate Reformed Church, and at the time of this Convention provost of Columbia College; an eminent leader in all that related to education of the ministry, a notable preacher, and an able orator on national occasions. In this address Dr. Mason spoke of the extraordinary reaction against a false philosophy widely taught in the eighteenth century, and pointed out the wide-spread feeling of desire on the part of American Christians to aid all that is holy against all that is profane; the purest interest of the community and the individual, against a conspiracy of darkness and disaster; and the eagerness felt in many quarters to claim a place in an age of Bibles to help the work of Christian charity.

" Under such impressions," he said, " and with such views,

fathers, brothers, fellow-citizens, the American Bible Society has been formed.   Local feelings, party prejudices, sectarian jealousies are excluded by its very nature.   It is leagued in that, and in that alone, which calls up every hallowed and puts down every unhallowed principle: the dissemination of the Scriptures in the received versions where they exist, and in the most faithful where they may be required.   In such a work whatever is dignified, kind, venerable, true, has ample scope; while sectarian littleness and rivalries can find no avenue of admission."

After pointing out the great possibilities both at home and abroad of a National Bible Society, the address urged the people of the United States to take part in an enterprise of such grandeur and glory, since it is not becoming that Americans should hang back while the rest of Christendom was awake and alert.   He closed with the following stirring appeal:

" Be it impressed on your souls that a contribution, saved from even a cheap indulgence, may send a Bible to a desolate family; may become a radiating point of ' grace and truth ' to a neighbourhood of error and vice; and that a number of such contributions, made at really no expense, may illumine a large tract of country, and successive generations of immortals, in that celestial knowledge which shall secure their present and their future felicity.

" But whatever be the proportion between expectation and experience, thus much is certain: We shall satisfy our conviction of duty — we shall have the praise of high endeavours — we shall minister to the blessedness of thousands, and tens of thousands, of whom we may never see the faces, nor hear the names.   We shall set forward a system of happiness which will go on with accelerated motion and augmented vigour, after we shall have finished our career; and confer upon our children, and our children's children, the delight of seeing the wilderness turned into a fruitful field, by the blessing of God upon that seed which their fathers sowed, and themselves watered.   In fine, we shall do our part toward that expansion and intensity of light divine which shall visit, in its progress, the palaces of the great and the hamlets of the small until the whole ' earth be full of the knowledge of Jehovah, as the waters cover the sea!'"

After having adopted the Constitution the Convention chose thirty-six managers in conformity with its Ninth Article. It then adjourned to meet May 11th, sending notice to the newly elected members of the Board that they had been chosen to be Managers of the American Bible Society.[1]

The managers met in the City Hall on May 11th and proceeded to choose officers of the Society, as follows:

PRESIDENT:

Hon. Elias Boudinot of New Jersey

VICE-PRESIDENTS

Hon. John Jay of New York
Matthew Clarkson, Esq., of New York
Hon. Smith Thompson of New York
Hon. John Langdon of New Hampshire
Hon. Caleb Strong of Massachusetts
Hon. William Gray of Massachusetts
Hon. John C. Smith of Connecticut
Hon. Jonas Galusha of Vermont
Hon. William Jones of Rhode Island
Hon. Isaac Shelby of Kentucky
George Madison, Esq., of Kentucky
Hon. William Tilghman of Pennsylvania
Hon. Bushrod Washington of Virginia

[1] The names of those chosen for the first Board of Managers are as follows:

Henry Rutgers	John R. B. Rodgers	Rufus King
John Bingham	Dr. Peter Wilson	Thomas Stokes
Richard Varick	Jeremiah Evarts	Joshua Sands
Thomas Farmer	John Watts, M.D.	George Warner
Stephen Van Rensselaer	Thomas Eddy	De Witt Clinton
Samuel Boyd	William Johnson	John Warder
George Suckley	Ebenezer Burrill	Samuel Bayard
Divie Bethune	Andrew Gifford	Duncan P. Campbell
William Bayard	George Gosman	John Aspinwall
Peter McCarty	Thomas Carpenter	Charles Wright
Thomas Shields	John Cauldwell	Cornelius Heyer
Robert Ralston	Leonard Bleecker	John Murray, Jr.

Hon. Charles C. Pinckney of South Carolina
Hon. William Gaston of North Carolina
Hon. Thomas Worthington of Ohio
Hon. Thomas Posey of Indiana
Hon. James Brown of Louisiana
John Bolton, Esq., of Georgia
Hon. Felix Grundy of Tennessee
Robert Oliver, Esq., of Maryland
Joseph Nourse,, Esq., of the District of Columbia

SECRETARY FOR FOREIGN CORRESPONDENCE:
Rev. Dr. John M. Mason

SECRETARY FOR DOMESTIC CORRESPONDENCE:
Rev. J. B. Romeyn, D.D.,

TREASURER
Richard Varick, Esq.

A committee of the managers communicated information of this choice to the Convention.

The Convention, having received notification that the organisation of the new Society was now complete, adopted a resolution by which the city of New York was fixed as the place in which the first annual meeting of the American Bible Society should be held. The business being now accomplished, the meeting was closed with prayer by Rev. Mr. Wilmer, and the Convention was dissolved.

On Monday, the 13th of May, a ratification meeting was held in the City Hall, the Mayor of the city of New York presiding. After addresses by George Griffin, Esq., William Jay, Esq., and Rev. Dr. Nott of Union College, a large and enthusiastic audience adopted resolutions pledging support to the Bible Society thus auspiciously set on its way.

CHAPTER V

WHEN the Lord distinctly calls a man to His work, an impression of unfitness and inability is the first response to the call. Moses in Midian said unto the Lord, " Who am I that I should go unto Pharaoh, and that I should bring forth the children of Israel out of Egypt?" Gideon, when told to save Israel from the Midianites, said, " O Lord, wherewith shall I save Israel? Behold my family is poor in Manasseh, and I am the least in my father's house." Yet, when convinced that the call was really from God Himself, each of these men went in the might of faith in God, and accomplished the work assigned to him.

Something of the same experience fell to the lot of the officers and managers of the American Bible Society when the Convention had dissolved and left them to do their best. They had no doubt that the work assigned to them was appointed by God Himself. The Convention had defined the work, and chosen them to put it into execution. There was no question at all of the greatness of the undertaking committed to them. They must plan to supply the destitute in a broad land with the written Word, and they must do it without delay. The plan before the Convention contemplated results alone; methods and instruments of action had to be found or invented. The Managers of the new Society must furnish Bibles to clamorous ministers, needy Sunday Schools, and destitute families in the distant wilderness; but they had neither printing press, money nor men to carry books to the West. They were to offer the Bible to French and Spanish among our own people; but the gift of tongues was not theirs.

When we look at the quality of the men upon whom these heavy burdens were cast, we must acknowledge that they were well chosen for the work. The two secretaries, Mason and Romeyn, were both pastors of great influence in the city of New York, and both of them had served — one as President, the other as Secretary — in the New York Bible Society. Of the Board of Managers, ten had been Managers of the New York Bible Society. It almost looked as if the older Society had become merged in the new. The Board of Managers of the American Bible Society included Mr. Robert Ralston, one of the founders and later President of the Philadelphia Bible Society, and Mr. Jeremiah Evarts, Treasurer and afterwards Secretary of the American Board of Missions. Richard Varick, chosen member of the Board of Managers, but elected Treasurer of the Society by the Managers at their first meeting, was one of the Staff Officers and private secretary of General Washington, acquainted with the hardships of the battle-field; a man of great business ability, warm heart, and earnest devotion to the advancement of piety. De Witt Clinton, a leader in many great works in New York, was chosen Governor of New York State while still a Manager of the Bible Society. Divie Bethune, a life-long philanthropist, might be said to be the first tract society of New York, since he had printed and circulated at his own expense many thousands of tracts. Henry Rutgers was another of the men of the Revolutionary War, notable as a man of wealth ready to help every charitable object. General Stephen Van Rensselaer commanded the attack on Queenstown in 1812, was a member of the New York Legislature in 1816, later was Chancellor of New York University, and founder of the Rensselaer Polytechnic Institute at Troy. These names are enough to show the kind of men deemed necessary for the management of a Society so high and so broad in aim as the American Bible Society.

Nevertheless these men felt almost like the apostles to whom Jesus Christ left the work of teaching all nations. They were like a forlorn hope chosen for the last desperate assault upon the stronghold of a mighty enemy. Difficulty was almost the only known feature of the duty which was laid upon them. Their circumstances as they took up the work could hardly be more hopeless. Yet these men were men of living piety; they had one assurance of power: He who directed that all people should be taught to observe the things which He had commanded had said, " Lo, I am with you alway." That promise was eternally valid.

The many expressions of enthusiastic good-will which welcomed the new organisation were an encouragement. The mere fact that an American Bible Society had been organised was a surprise and a joy to the churches; a surprise, because federation of denominations for religious work was unheard of save in some obscure corners of the land; and a joy because such a federation seemed equal to solving the problem of combatting irreligion in the newly settled areas. It promised concentration of forces, systematic and effective, for the salvation of America. The correspondence of the idea of such an enterprise with the eternal purpose of God for the race makes the story of the Bible Society hardly more than a study of the form by which the divine will and purpose here expressed itself.

Everywhere the American Bible Society was hailed as marking the commencement of a glorious era in the history of the United States. The General Assembly of the Presbyterian Church made immediate note of its appreciation and good-will.[1] The General Convention of the Baptist Church before the year had passed away voted its approval of the plan. During that first year also forty-three of the local Bible Societies which were in existence before the National Society was organised, connected themselves with it as Auxiliaries. More than forty Bible Societies were organised as Auxiliaries of the American Bible Society during the same year. The New York Bible Society and the Auxiliary New York Bible Society immediately became Auxiliaries of the national Society, and emphasised that relationship by presenting the American Bible Society with stereotype plates of the English Bible which they jointly owned, and with a thousand sets of sheets of the Bible in French. Bible Societies in a number of different states had

[1] Report on the state of religion approved by the Presbyterian General Assembly, May, 1816.

contributed to the cost of the plates and of the French Bibles, so that there was a sort of propriety in these materials being handed over to the National Society at once. The Mayor of the city of New York, the Governors of the New York Hospital, and later the New York Historical Society became the hosts of the Board of Managers when they sought a place in which to hold their meetings. Even printers in the city offered to print free of charge any circulars which the American Bible Society might wish to send out in collecting money.

Inspiriting as was the welcome in the United States to the new Bible Society, from Russia and from Germany came similar expressions of good-will which thrilled like miraculous messages from the unknown. Prince Galitzin, President of the Russian Bible Society, wrote to Judge Wallace of New Jersey as President of the organising Convention: " Notwithstanding the distance which separates us, being approximated by the same spirit of unity and action, we unanimously engage to exert ourselves for the same cause of benevolence." The Secretaries of the Hamburg and Altona Bible Society wrote to Bishop White of Pennsylvania, President of the Philadelphia Bible Society (probably supposing that the Philadelphia Society was merged in the National Society): " We have learned with great satisfaction from the publications which have reached us, that the loud voice of the friends of the Bible in America has demanded and produced a union of the interests of all the provincial Societies by the establishment of a national Bible Society. However great the distance at which we live from each other, we feel ourselves associated with you in the blessed vocation of presenting those revered documents upon which the faith of all Christians rests to such of the children of men as do not possess them."

The British and Foreign Bible Society, the recognised model and exemplar of the American Bible Society, outdid these friends from the continent of Europe. It sent not only a letter full of fraternal sentiments, but the promise of a gift of twenty-two hundred dollars (five hundred pounds), which was doubly acceptable at this juncture; especially when it was arranged by correspondence that a part of this donation should take the form of Bibles in French.

The letter which brought tidings of this generous gift was an ideal exhibit of Christian brotherhood. Let it not be forgotten that the correspondence was between men recently opposed to each other in a national wrangle of exceptionally bitter partisanship. Commending the founders of the American Bible Society for taking up a charitable scheme the moment that peace had been signed, the Briton hails the American as a true yokefellow, among the instruments effectively to be used by our Lord Jesus Christ. The letter was addressed to Dr. Boudinot, because the fulness of joy had led him to write of the organisation of the American Bible Society before the Secretary had time to prepare the official notification. To Dr. Boudinot Mr. Owen wrote as follows:

" *My dear Sir:*

" The Committee of the British and Foreign Bible Society have instructed me to offer you their warmest congratulations on the event of the formation of the American Bible Society; an event which they consider as truly auspicious, and pregnant with consequences most advantageous to the promotion of that great work in which the American Brethren and themselves are mutually engaged.

" To these congratulations, our Committee have added a grant of five hundred pounds; and they trust that both will be acceptable as indications and pledges of that friendly disposition which it is their desire to cultivate and manifest towards every class and description of their transatlantic fellow-labourers.

" The crisis at which the American Bible Society has been formed, and the cordial unanimity which has reigned throughout all the proceedings which led to its establishment, encourage the most sanguine hopes of its proving, in the hand of God, a powerful auxiliary in the confederate warfare which is now carrying on against ignorance and sin. May those hopes be realised, and many new trophies be added, through its instrumentality, to those triumphs which have already been reaped by the arms of our common Redeemer.

"I am, my dear Sir,
"Very faithfully yours,
"John Owen,
"Secretary of the British and
Foreign Bible Society.
"Dr. Boudinot,
"President of the American Bible Society."

Pleasing expressions of admiration in this world of ours are not rarely offset by unpleasing expressions of disapproval. Great plans like those of the American Bible Society could hardly be viewed from all points with equal satisfaction. During the first five years Watchmen of Liberty sprang up to denounce such a Society. "An institution," said they, "having hundreds of auxiliaries to extend its grasp over the whole land must become a menace to free government." The Conservator of Sects turned up with a shrill outcry because, for holy uses like the publishing of Scriptures, tainted money was being accepted from those whom he could not regard as Christians. And then the Supervisor of Public Morals added his protest against shortsightedness which proposes to give to uneducated people a book like the Holy Bible, without note or comment. Good Bishop Hobart of Albany had already drawn the keen weapons of controversy more than once against Secretary John Mitchell Mason, upon the question of the Episcopacy. It was hardly a surprise, therefore, when upon the publication of Dr. Mason's address to the people, he took opportunity by a letter to the New York *Herald* (May 13, 1816), in a dignified though voluble manner to announce his disapproval of a partnership of Episcopalians with other denominations in religious work, and especially in dissemination of the Bible, which he regarded as a prerogative of his church and clergy. He used arguments which in England had already been turned against the British and Foreign Bible Society: There was no necessity for the Society; the idea of maintaining a National Society was visionary; there was no perfect accord among the existing Bible

Societies in favour of the new one, etc., etc. It so happened that Bishop White of Pennsylvania, President of the Philadelphia Bible Society, was committed to the very interdenominational principle attacked by Bishop Hobart. Indeed, in an address at Philadelphia, he had praised what Bishop Hobart condemned. "It has been thought," he said, "an incidental advantage arising from Bible Societies that by combining persons of different religious denominations, they have the effect of promoting unity of affection under irreconcilable differences of opinion. The British and Foreign Bible Society set off on the fundamental principle of avoiding whatever could bring such diversity into view. They professed to deliver the book of God without note or comment. The Societies instituted in America have trodden in their steps. While this plan shall be pursued, there can be no dissatisfaction on account of interfering opinions or modes of worship. Is it possible that such a course can be persevered in without contributing to all the charities of life?"

Other men of his own church connected with the administration of the American Bible Society made answer to Bishop Hobart, but pamphlet succeeded pamphlet with no harm and some advantage to the new Society. William Jay said in 1817: "The Society must engage in no controversy. She must know no enemy; her sphere is one of love and harmony. She ought not even to ask her friends to defend her cause. Let her distribute her Constitution and the Report of her proceedings and let these be her only answers to the calumnies and falsehoods of her enemies. . . . To answer would begin a long controversy. No middle course can be taken." [1]

If any one would now read the documents of this discussion he must needs force himself through material enough to fill a volume of considerable size. More important matters have prior demands upon the space allotted to this story of the Society.

Strong men of affairs, like the Board of Managers — men whose abilities had weighed in the making of the Re-

[1] Letter of May 1, 1817, in archives of the American Bible Society.

public; men by vote of the people now connected with great enterprises of National development, whose business apti- tude was already building up a commerce between the con- tinents; men soberly resolved that the new Bible Society, without delay, should do effective work, were not disturbed by the criticisms of suspicion or ignorance. The well- known proverb of the Arabs, " The dog barks, but the cara- van goes on," makes the stately march of camels over the sands a type of any enterprise so great that it can be care- less of small obstacles. The desk of the Domestic Secre- tary was quickly clogged with proposals, advice, demands, and entreaties. A policy must be framed for securing and well utilising a steady supply of Bibles; for gaining the support of Auxiliaries wholly devoted like themselves; and for filling the empty treasure-chest. Managers and Execu- tive Officers must proceed almost like the blind man who feels with his staff before he plants his foot; yet they must proceed.

The bearing of these men during those years harmonised entirely with that of President Boudinot, as he formally accepted the office of President of the Bible Society. His acceptance addressed to Secretary Romeyn was a letter of which the spirit is revealed in the following extract:

" I am not ashamed to confess that I accept of the ap- pointment of President of the American Bible Society as the greatest honour that could have been conferred on me this side of the grave.

" I am so convinced that the whole of this business is the work of God Himself, by His Holy Spirit, that even hoping against hope, I am encouraged to press on through good report and evil report, to accomplish His will on earth as it is in Heaven.

" So apparent is the hand of God in thus disposing the hearts of so many men, so diversified in their sentiments as to religious matters of minor importance, and uniting them as a band of brothers in this grand object; that even Infi- dels are compelled to say, it is the work of the Lord, and it is wonderful in our eyes! — In vain is the opposition of man: as well might he attempt to arrest ' the arm of Om- nipotence, or fix a barrier around the throne of God.' Hav-

ing this confidence, let us go on and we shall prosper." [1]
This hearty assurance of a noble future for the Society Dr.
Boudinot emphasised by a splendid donation of $10,000.

[1] Letter of Boudinot, June 5, 1816, in the first report of the
American Bible Society, p. 38.

CHAPTER VI

THE American Bible Society when formed was given a free hand and thrown as fully upon its own initiative as is a missionary landing on a foreign and forbidding coast. On coming into practical touch with the details of the enterprise placed in their hands the Board of Managers hastily looked about for helpers. The undertaking was vast; the burden of responsibility for it was immeasurable. From Canada to the Gulf the eyes of the Board must see the needy. From the midst of nine million people those without Bibles must be sought out if these destitute ones were to be supplied with the Book which teaches discrimination between the bitter and the sweet plan of life. The leader of a military campaign of equal magnitude has but to command in order to mass his forces. The Managers of the Bible Society could do no more than plead for helpers.

The plan of the Board for finding and supplying the destitute in twenty States was to raise up Auxiliary Bible Societies in every part of the country. The foundation of the financial scheme of the Society, also, was the theory of Auxiliary Societies. These would collect contributions in pennies from those who deal in pennies, and in gold from those whose hoard is gold. Such Auxiliary Societies in every county with branches in every township could concentrate upon support of this noble, inspiring enterprise the attention of individuals everywhere with their interest, their prayers and their gifts.

The theory of Auxiliary Societies rooted among the people, having a near view of their needs, distributing Scriptures with deliberate judgment, and winning the support of rich and poor, came from the British and Foreign Bible Society. The system as developed in Great Britain did not

originate with the Bible Society.   In fact it had become a
success before the British Society took much notice of it.
The enterprise of supplying the poor with Scriptures was
so sensible and yet so novel that Christians in widely separated districts took up the work.   Bibles and Testaments
were gladly supplied to the poor of their immediate vicinity
by local groups or associations of Christians.   The members
of these associations contributed what they could and collected from others money with which to buy Bibles from
the British and Foreign Bible Society.   A notable feature
of the plan grew out of the wish to participate in the grand
work of the British Society in foreign lands.   One-half of
the money collected in various ways was sent to the British
and Foreign Bible Society as a donation for its general
work; the other half being used for the purchase of Scriptures and any local expenses of the association.   Scriptures
were given gratuitously to the very poor; but in order to
make the funds of the association go as far as possible, both
Bibles and Testaments were often sold on the instalment
plan.   For the Bibles which they wished to have even the
very poor were asked to pay each week, until the price was
paid up, a few pence.

This Auxiliary plan in Great Britain grew up of itself,
we might say, like any herb of the field.   Warm Christian
love was the sun which nourished it and its fruit was so attractive that the Committee of the British and Foreign
Bible Society took steps to encourage the formation of such
Auxiliary Societies.   The local Bible Associations counted
it a high honour to be recognised as Auxiliaries in so great
a work.   They naturally had no control over the affairs of
the great Bible Society, while that Society exercised an influence amounting to control over all the Auxiliaries.   In
a snug little territory like the British Islands it was easy to
sustain the interest of members of the local Societies by
printed notes from the wonderful story of the great Society
and by visits, meetings, and stirring appeals from delegations
sent out.   For years this Auxiliary system has been one
of the largest single sources of income for the British Society.

A very different basis had the Auxiliary system as transplanted to the United States. In the first place the point of view taken by the Auxiliaries toward the general Society was different. Since the local Bible Societies regarded the American Bible Society as their creation, in the management of the national Society, by vote of their officers in the Annual Meetings, all Auxiliaries had a certain measure of control while the national Society had no control whatever over the Auxiliaries. The Board of Managers recognised in the Auxiliary system a telling instrument for collecting money, but no plan of systematic collections had been worked out, and no fixed proportion of the money collected was insured to the national Society. Auxiliaries were to pay to it whatever was left from their revenues after supplying the needs of their own fields. The Auxiliary Societies would profit by the aid of the general Society in the work of distribution, and whatever they might or might not contribute as donations, they could always buy books at the mere cost of production. At the same time there were reasons which might deter the existing Bible Societies from becoming Auxiliaries to the American Bible Society. Their situation was somewhat like that of prominent social leaders who have been instrumental in the establishment of a college in a country town, but who find that the great institution of learning must sooner or later outrank in prominence and power the generous notables who encouraged its establishment.

The Board of Managers vigorously urged the formation of Auxiliary Bible Societies in all parts of the country. Not only did it show that an Auxiliary was necessary in every county; it asked that branches might be formed in all the townships. Women were reminded that the British Society received considerable sums from Women's Associations which collected a penny or two here, and sixpence there. They could do the same effective work if they would only organise Bible Associations.

One point of difficulty very soon came to light. The mails brought to the Secretaries of the Society letters from different local Bible Societies in rapid succession announcing their purpose to be Auxiliaries of the American Bible Society; some sending donations and some asking grants to supply pressing needs. It was quite evident that many good people confused the idea of co-operating with the National Society by sympathy and good will, with that of systematically labouring as helpers to extend its great work. They supposed that a vote of the local Society was all that was required to establish the Auxiliary relation. The point of view of the Board of Managers, however, was far from this. It became necessary in October, 1818, to issue a note explaining that no Bible Society can become Auxiliary to the American Bible Society without a special vote of recognition on the part of the Board of Managers. In this connection the Board gave its interpretation of the third article of the Constitution; the essential part of the statement being that no Society can be recognised as an Auxiliary to the American Bible Society until it shall have officially communicated to the Board that its sole object is to promote the circulation of the Holy Scriptures without note or comment, and that it will place its surplus revenue, after supplying its own district with Scriptures, at the disposal of the American Bible Society as long as it shall remain thus connected with it.

A lesser point of the duties of Auxiliaries had already been decided by the Board in 1817 when the Kentucky Bible Society made application for a set of stereotype plates, explaining that they wished to print Scriptures for all the Western States. The Board then notified Auxiliaries in a general statement that an Auxiliary Society cannot, at its own expense, distribute Bibles beyond the limits of its own district. Otherwise the local Society will lose its character as a helper of the national Society, since it will never have any surplus funds to transmit to the general treasury; transmission of such surplus funds being an essential part of the duties of an Auxiliary. Lest the constitutional limitations of the Auxiliary's activities should in this case limit the use made of the plates loaned to the Kentucky Bible Society, the Managers stated that the American Bible Society might, if necessary, have books for other States printed at its expense at the Kentucky press.

These conditions of the Auxiliary relationship had already been explained to many Societies in private correspondence; and to remove all doubts about the sympathies of the Board of Managers, in 1817 it announced to all Bible Societies that, of course, they were at liberty to withdraw from the Auxiliary relationship if they chose to do so. When the matter became thoroughly understood there was no longer question as to the intent of the Constitution. The line was clearly marked between Auxiliary Bible Societies who are recognised helpers of the national Society and other Bible Societies, which, like that in Philadelphia, voluntarily co-operated with the national Society although not organically connected with it.

An utterance of the Auxiliary New York Bible Society in its third Annual Report (1816) showed its hearty acceptance of this early interpretation of the Auxiliary relationship. " There are cases where it is more honourable as well as more dutiful to pay tribute than it is to claim the sceptre. . . . Feeling as we do upon this subject (the organisation of the American Bible Society) we cannot, at a time like the present, suppress the emotions of our joy and congratulations. . . . To that Society you have become tributary by profession. Let not your Auxiliary character be confined to the name. Subordinate duties are as certain and as urgent as those of a higher order which depend upon them." [1]

Another difficulty appeared when some of the Auxiliary Societies were unable to understand why, when they bought and paid for books, they were not helpers of the National Society. Why should they be asked to send other money for the general work? It had to be explained quite often and at some length that buying books from the general depository is merely replenishing a continually exhausted stock. The money received from sales simply restored the Treasury to the position in which it was before the books were sold. Only by gifts dedicated to the general work of the Society could an Auxiliary be a helper and not a mere dependent. A reservoir must be fed by streams larger than

[1] This Society was announcing its new condition as auxiliary to the A. B. S. See Third Annual Report of Auxiliary New York Bible Society quoted in the first Annual Report of the American Bible Society, p. 54.

those flowing from it, if it is to collect water for other districts.

In 1819 while the Board was urgently calling upon the people all over the country to form Auxiliary Bible Societies, it received an impression from a friendly letter that the Philadelphia Bible Society might at last consent to become Auxiliary to the national Society. Realising that the oldest society in the United States must naturally value highly its independent existence, the Society had adopted an addition to the Constitution (19th Article), permitting the Board to make special terms of recognition as Auxiliaries for any Society formed earlier which had commenced publishing Scriptures before the American Bible Society was organised.

A statement of the Board issued at this time shows its views: "The Managers are anxious to see an entire union of the Bible interest in this country; believing that such a union would do honour to the pious and the benevolent in our land; that it would prevent all injurious interference in the great work; that it would secure a larger amount of gifts in aid of that work; that the exertions, which all might make together, would be greater, more economical, and more vigorous, than can be made in a separate state; and that the consequence of combined efforts would be a measure of success, probably much larger, and certainly much more striking and impressive, than that which would attend disunited labours. With these views and opinions, measures have been adopted by the Managers. They wait patiently for the result. Should it be favourable, the Managers will be highly gratified, and will rejoice in the accomplishment of an object so desirable as a complete confederacy of the Bible cause in our country. Yet should the Societies to which the nineteenth article of the Constitution applies, and the other Societies in the United States which are not Auxiliaries, deem it expedient for them to remain unconnected with the national Society, the Managers will continue to regard them not with jealousy, but with love, and will always be anxious for their prosperity and their widespread usefulness." [1]

[1] Report of the A. B. S., 1820.

The hope of the Managers respecting the willingness of the Philadelphia Society to come into a closer relationship was dashed. The Philadelphia Bible Society expressed in the kindest terms its inability to consider it conducive to the general interests of the Bible cause to be at present so connected with the American Bible Society as to become an Auxiliary. At the same time its Board expressed its willingness to co-operate with their brethren of the American Bible Society in any plans which may be considered useful to the advance of the object for which both were labouring. These expressions of good will were not empty words. The Philadelphia Society rendered financial and other aid to the national Society repeatedly during the next twenty years. In 1840 it took the step of formally becoming Auxiliary to the American Bible Society.

The Auxiliary system which worked so well in Great Britain encountered many difficulties due to the wide expanses of the United States territory. These Societies must be left very much to their independent initiative since the interminable American distances and the hardships of travel would make frequent visits from Secretaries or other delegates of the national Society difficult, and in some cases impossible.

During the first five experimental years many Auxiliaries were a constant source of anxiety to the Board of Managers. Numbers of local Societies entered the ranks as formal helpers without a chance of maintaining work in their own fields. Their calls for help were unceasing and embarrassing. Money for the general work contributed by strong and active Auxiliaries was absorbed in keeping alive the anæmic ones. At times, it is true, sparseness of the population was a cause of these disappointing results. Sometimes it was the depression of the local currency, sometimes small calamities peculiar to a new country, or sometimes even the appearance of other schemes of missionary benevolence. Yet in those early days the Board had to admit many times that some Auxiliaries were constitutionally inactive and some deliberately chose to be dependent. It early became clear that the conditions of a truly helpful Auxiliary system are not easy to fulfil. If Auxiliaries established in the first heat of enthusiasm should maintain the passion to win souls, and if such Societies should never become physically too feeble for active life, the Auxiliary system would not be a drag upon the national Society, but would prove permanently as efficient as it was praiseworthy.

At the end of the fifth year of the Society, three hundred and one Auxiliaries were in existence. They had paid into the Treasury of the Society $39,360.90 as donations, besides what they paid for books.

Great sums have since been paid into the Treasury for the worldwide work by Auxiliary Societies. Many thousand volumes of Scripture have been taken by them to the destitute. Thousands of our people owe their religious awakening to their efforts. Some of the most important and fruitful measures adopted by the American Bible Society originated with a suggestion from one or another Auxiliary Society. Yet, as will be seen later on, a territory as vast and as sparsely inhabited as that of the United States in the first half of the nineteenth century was not quite suited to the success of the Auxiliary idea so hopefully imported from England.

SECOND PERIOD 1821–1832

CHAPTER VII

EARLY EXPERIMENTS

A LARGE movement of population marked for Americans the close of the second decade of the nineteenth century. Thousands of settlers moved into the country west of the Alleghanies. During the first five years of the existence of the American Bible Society immigrants from Europe arrived at the average rate of ten thousand each year. Indiana, Mississippi, Illinois, Maine, and Missouri were admitted to the Union as States. Florida was given up to the United States by Spain, and a quiet feeling of well-being prevailed throughout the land. In South America the establishment of independent republics which had commenced during the Napoleonic Wars, continued with more or less resistance from Spaniards and others interested in the monarchical system. Mexico was in continual unrest. In our land the war with the Seminole Indians blazed out and died away, only to flare up again; questions of tariff disturbed different sections of the country, and the debates concerning slavery foreshadowed their growth in bitterness; but on the whole there was throughout the country a feeling of steady prosperity.

Astonishment at the growth of the population was expressed on every hand. John C. Calhoun, writing in 1816, said: "We are great and rapidly, I had almost said fearfully, growing. Good roads and canals will do much to unite us." With this growth in the population throbbing like a pulse which all could feel, it might seem shocking that the Society formed to evangelise with Bibles the Western regions of the country, almost as its first act, told applicants that at present it would not supply any Bibles. The American Bible Society was hardly a week old when disconcerting orders for books began to come in, many of them ac-

companied by money in payment. The Board, which was
hardly organised for business, had to fix a policy. Its perplexity was like that of a man seeking a place to lodge who
has word that friends are coming to stay with him. It decided that the first use to which money contributions should
be applied was the acquirement of stereotype plates of the
Bible. Therefore it informed those who ordered Bibles
that money which came with orders for books would be sent
back to the donors, or handed over to one of the local Bible
Societies which had Bibles on hand.

A Bible Society without Bibles was as ineffective as a
railway without rolling stock; to purchase Bibles in the
market would merely delay ownership of stereotype plates.
Offers of plates or for the making of them were hurriedly
presented by various firms, and after close scrutiny of such
proposals the Board ordered a contract to be made at advantageous terms for six sets of stereotype plates of the
Bible; three in octavo, and three in duodecimo, to be cast
as soon as possible. The plates would not be ready before
the spring of 1817. Meantime the importunate local Bible
Societies must do without Scriptures.

It was at this fateful moment that the New York Bible
Society and its Auxiliary, loyally ready to serve their new
leader in the common cause, came forward with their timely
gift of a complete set of stereotype plates in minion type.
In November, 1816, by the generosity of these Societies,
the American Bible Society was able to put forth its first
issue of ten thousand copies of the English Bible. In the
minds of the founders of the Society the plan of distributing sets of stereotype plates among Auxiliary Societies
bulked largely. Probably it was suggested by the difficulty
of communication and transportation in 1816. In 1817 a
single set of plates was accordingly loaned to the Kentucky
Bible Society. An unexpected defect in the scheme startled the Board when Rev. Dr. Blythe of that Society in-
quired whether a printing press would be sent with the
plates. Perhaps, too, no one had remembered that the
books, after being printed, would have to be bound. At all
events, after many vexatious delays, the Kentucky Bible
Society early in 1819 printed at Lexington two thousand

Bibles. The edition was disappointing as to paper, printing, binding and cost. No one was to blame. That country was too young to undertake book publication. The
American Bible Society could supply Lexington well printed
and bound books from New York and pay the freight for
less than the cost of poor books printed there. After one
or two further trials the hope was given up of supplying the
West with Bibles by sending stereotype plates to Auxiliary
Societies.

Only by such an experience could all parties learn how
great a saving of cost is effected by printing very large editions. The motive underlying the plan of supplying Auxiliary Societies with stereotype plates was desire to relieve
them from the heavy cost of composition or of the purchase
of plates in cases where the local Society wished to print
Bibles for its own use. This benevolent purpose was not
lost to sight, although the earliest plan for accomplishing it
missed the mark. The Board of Managers, regarding the
cost of plates as an expense which the Constitution expects
the general Society to bear, left that element entirely out
of account in computing the price of books. It decided
that the cost of press work, paper and binding should make
up the selling price of Scriptures, adding, however, five per
cent to cover interest, insurance and the wear and tear of
plates. Bibles would be sold to Auxiliaries at cost, deduct-
ing the five per cent. added for interest and wear and tear.
Through this decision Auxiliary Societies have not only
profited by the reduction of cost gained by printing very
large editions, but they have received their books during a
hundred years at a price considerably less than the actual
cost of producing them.

By the end of the first five years the Board had decided
that the cheaper forms of binding only would be used for
free grants of Scriptures. This plan was received with
murmurs to the effect that the Holy Bible ought to be nobly
bound, since otherwise the common people would think it
of little value. The decision was like the poor man's choice
to build his house of wood since he cannot afford stone, and
the policy of making cheap books for the supply of those

unable to pay much commended itself to the judgment of the majority and later became the rule of the Society.

The most beneficent feature of Bible Societies was at first universally assumed to be their power to make the Word of God free to all. Under the then prevailing theory an enterprise that asks money from beneficiaries is not beneficent. But the human propensity to hold out the hand, whenever benevolent gifts are in sight, was another of the early discoveries of the Board. So one further step of cautious progress was the decision of the Board to discourage indiscriminate free distribution of Scriptures. Much argument was needed to convince contributors and beneficiaries of the necessity for asking pay for Bibles from those who could pay if they would. The rule, however, was maintained without at all diminishing free grants to the really needy, and resulted in profit, on the whole, to the self respect and the sincerity of those who received books from the Society.

The path of the Board of Managers would sometime open into a region where the relations of things could be clearly seen. As yet it was as full of mysteries as the route traced among the stars by a beginner in astronomy. It led to the unforeseen at every step. Only after actually finding strange tongues naturalised in several districts did it become clear that Bibles in foreign languages must be provided for the United States. The Board ordered from the British and Foreign Bible Society plates of the French Bible in 1816; and it ordered Scriptures in German and in Gaelic from London a year later, thereby causing an outburst of joy from homesick Scottish emigrants. As early as the end of 1817 it ordered a set of plates of the New Testament in Spanish.

The Board had not yet contemplated beginning labours in the foreign field when a Moravian missionary named Dencke sent to it a manuscript translation of the Epistles of St. John into the Delaware language. It was a perturbing as well as an awe-inspiring object. After laborious discovery of guarantees that the translation was accurate, the Board gladly undertook to print an edition of these

Epistles for the use of Indians speaking the Delaware. This formed the first of a series of benefits derived by the men of the forests from the organisation of a National Society.

The example of the British and Foreign Bible Society daily helped the new Society to stand upon its feet. The Board of Managers concluded its first report by observing that *" God has been pleased to make the people of Great Britain the instrument of forming, maturing, cherishing, and constantly and substantially aiding these (Bible) Societies not only within their own territories, but throughout the world.* Greater honour has never been conferred upon any people since the sceptre departed from Judah, and the law giver from between His feet." [1] Britain was the mother of most of the old Colonies. The British and Foreign Bible Society was a " Revered Parent " and it was also an " Exemplar." It had explored many rough places in the ways of Bible Society progress, and through this experience it had fixed upon many well chosen methods.

The Committee to whom the New York Convention gave the duty of drawing up a Constitution for the American Bible Society used that of the British and Foreign Bible Society as a guide, modifying it to suit American conditions. The form of administration chosen for the American Society closely followed the model in London. The British Society had found that Auxiliary Societies could canvass their fields, keep in close touch with the people, supply needs, and also collect money in amounts that were surprising. In fact such Societies already furnished a tangible part of the support of the British Society. The American Bible Society from its first active day counted as its " auxiliaries " all Societies which agreed to place their surplus funds at its disposal. The British model was followed again in the method adopted to furnish information to friends of the American Bible Society. It issued for its subscribers and the general public a little sheet called " Extracts from Correspondence." Its Secretaries suggested that the republication in America of these " Extracts "

[1] Report of A. B. S. for 1817, p. 24.

might be interesting to the people. Thereupon the Board decided to issue a sheet of information called "Quarterly Extracts." The idea and even the name of the Library which was shortly established for the benefit of the literary department of the Society was copied from that of the British Society, which had early founded a "Biblical Library" for the collection of versions of the Bible in various languages, and of books useful to translators or interpreters of the Bible. In debate an argument offered to the Board as conclusive was often "The British Society has" or "has not" done so and so.

There was no mere slavish imitation in this conformity to the usages of that great and experienced pioneer; the ways of wisdom are for universal use. Reasons for each decision were carefully considered by the Board. When the value of the various measures found practical by the British and Foreign Society was clearly seen, their wisdom was entitled to the homage of imitation by the new Society. The Board, however, took no step that might impair the independence of the American Bible Society. Within a year or two occasion arose which might have caused misunderstanding in this respect.

The donation of twenty-two hundred dollars with which the British and Foreign Bible Society emphasised its pleasure at the birth of the American Bible Society was in the form of a credit in London to be drawn upon from New York. Instead of drawing the money the Board ordered books and stereotype plates from the British Society which amounted altogether to thirty-five hundred and fifty dollars, and it finally remitted thirteen hundred and fifty dollars to London to close this account. In 1819 the British Society made a free grant of five hundred German Bibles to the American Bible Society and also sent out five hundred Spanish Testaments designated for free distribution in Latin America. At the same time its Directing Committee again authorised the American Bible Society to draw upon its Treasury for five hundred pounds as a donation. The Treasury of the American Bible Society was not as empty as the acceptance of the gift would imply. The Board felt refusal to be unavoidable, but softened it by its gratitude for the solicitude shown by the generous offer. The incident was closed by a second letter from London assuring the Board that notwithstanding its having declined the donation, friendly feeling in that quarter was unchanged.

The Managers of the American Bible Society believed with their whole heart that study of the Bible and obedience to it would mean the building up of the nation; while neglect of this privilege by America would certainly lead to its ruin. By the year 1821 the Board felt no longer hampered by scarcity of books. It granted for the use of sailors in the United States Navy thirty-five hundred Bibles in 1820, upon the request of the Secretary of the Navy. It was ready to entertain every request from indigent Bible Societies, or from destitute districts where no Bible Society had yet been formed, for grants of Scriptures. This was really a remarkable progress within five years for men who had to feel their way step by step. But the members of the Board did not dream that they had done any great thing. The crossing of Jordan had been accomplished through glad obedience to the command Go Forward. So much of success was an earnest and manifestation of the divine guidance that was to be theirs throughout the perplexities and struggles involved in the occupation of the Promised Land.

CHAPTER VIII

SEVERAL state societies were engaged in home missionary work before the formation of the American Bible Society, but these were of small resources and they worked with little systematic co-operation. In a general sense it may be said that until the Erie Canal was opened in 1825 there were no very efficient home missionary societies in the United States. Before the development of great Home Missionary Societies, the American Bible Society during several years had been engaged in its appointed task of winning men to Christ. It was putting the written word into the hands of the blind that they might see, of the deaf that they might hear and of the poor that they might know the gospel, East, West, North and South, throughout the United States. It, therefore, may be regarded as our first general home missionary society.

Home and foreign missions, however, are among the things which God has joined and man may not put asunder. The strictly home missionary vision of the Bible Society almost at the first moment revealed need of Scriptures in five or six foreign languages within the limits of the United States. The Society that was formed for the purpose of increasing the circulation of the Bible wherever its arms could reach, having obtained Scriptures in six languages could not limit its sphere of vision by the boundaries of the United States. French Scriptures, for instance, must be sent not only to Louisiana but to poor neglected Canada, and Spanish Scriptures not to the lower Mississippi alone but over the border to Texas, then a part of New Spain (Mexico), and even to the great South American Continent.

The reasons for undertaking Bible distribution in Latin America were very well put in a letter on the subject published in Boston in June, 1816.[1] In this letter occurs the following passage: " That it is the duty of Americans to supply their neighbours with the Bible no arguments are necessary to prove; and that New Spain (Mexico) and even a part of South America have claims on our bounty is equally clear." The writer then takes note of the fact that many people say all such wants should be supplied by the British and Foreign Bible Society, although that Society has already an enormous burden in the supply of Europe and Asia. He then continues: " Under these circumstances shall we look to England to furnish even the inhabitants of South America with the Bible, much less any part of North America? "

As early as August, 1816, the Board of Managers took under consideration the purchase of plates for printing the New Testament in Spanish; but it was not until a year later that a commencement of the work was made by ordering the stereotyped plates, which copied the best edition published by the British and Foreign Bible Society. It was about the same time that the Managers had before them a report of the Louisiana Auxiliary Bible Society calling attention to the situation: " The population of the Spanish provinces, commencing at the Isthmus of Darien and coming up to the United States, is not much short of ten millions. Yet among this great multitude of professed Christians a Spanish Bible could not probably be found after a search of years." Five hundred Spanish Testaments sent over by the British and Foreign Bible Society helped to begin the supply of this need.

A surprising variety of channels were found for sending Spanish Scriptures into South America. The different peoples in that continent had thrown off the Spanish yoke. In Europe these peoples were still regarded as " Spanish Colonies " but in America they were felt to be near kin because the form of government set up in each case was republican. The Board assigned to a committee the duty of discovering merchants or well-disposed sea captains going to South America who would take with them Spanish

[1] *Panoplist,* March, 1816, p. 123.

Scriptures.   One of the grants made in 1819 was five hundred Spanish Testaments with special designation for use in the public schools of Buenos Aires.   They were gladly received by the municipal officials who ordered them distributed among the primary schools of the city.

Letters began to come frequently to the Society asking for Spanish Scriptures.   One of these from a merchant in the Island of St. Croix spoke of the likelihood that the New Testament would find ready circulation in Porto Rico, and some Scriptures were sent to him in 1820.   Some of the books, at least, reached the Island and were gladly purchased.   This was the earliest venture of the American Bible Society in Porto Rico, where now the Bible is in the hands of thousands.

A touching letter came to the Managers in New York from a Spanish gentleman in one of the West Indies Islands. He wrote: "A few days ago, being on board of an American ship, I saw a Testament in the Spanish language.   My eagerness to obtain it led me to ask it of the supercargo. It was the only one at his disposal and he could not part with it.   The Bible Society had presented it to him.   I am not certain whether you are a member of the Society or not, but your general acquaintance may put you in possession of some of these books which I beg you will send me.   There are none at all to be obtained here, and I know many who would be proud to have one."   Books were sent to this gentleman, who wrote joyfully: "In three days all the books were disposed of without the least effort of publicity, and numerous applications have been made since by Spaniards and foreigners requesting the favour to send for more."

The Secretaries soon had correspondents in different parts of Latin America willing to undertake the distribution of Scriptures.   The American Consul in Valparaiso expressed his willingness to aid in circulating Bibles.   One of those who asked and received grants was Mr. James Thomson, Agent of the British and Foreign Bible Society.   The British and Foreign Bible Society wrote in 1821:   "We are glad to see you desirous of working with us in South America."   This was pleasant but lacked perception, perhaps, of the aim of the American Bible Society to supply the untouched fields in that continent. One of its early grants of money for Bible translation was five hundred dollars to help the translation of the Scriptures into Quechua, the language of the proud Incas of Peru.

In the course of the summer of 1816 a member of the Board of Managers, Mr. Jeremiah Evarts of Boston, who was also an officer of the American Board of Missions, wrote to beg aid for the Rev. Ferdinand Leo, a German residing in Paris, who was trying to bring out an edition of the whole Bible according to the version of De Sacy. A grant of five hundred dollars to Mr. Leo was the first expenditure for work in foreign lands. The money was sent to Mr. S. V. S. Wilder, the well-known New York merchant then living in Paris, and was received with great joy by Mr. Leo. Mr. Wilder, in acknowledging receipt of this donation, in the courtly phrases of the day wrote to Dr. Mason: " Never, Sir, perhaps, was the hand of God more conspicuous than in this act of the American Bible Society; and generations yet unborn will undoubtedly profit by their munificence."

Later some Americans residing in Paris called the attention of the Board to the newly formed Protestant Bible Society of Paris with which Mr. S. V. S. Wilder was connected. This Society was formed in 1818 for the supply of destitute Protestants. The Board gave it a cordial welcome, and fraternal correspondence continued during several years. After the revolution of 1830 had introduced some religious liberty into France, the French and Foreign Bible Society [1] was formed, in aid of which the Board granted $2,000 in 1833.

At this time American missionaries were taking up work abroad. A universal movement of enthusiasm followed the appointent of foreign missionaries, both because of the enlightenment which they would carry to pagan countries, and because of the notable heroism involved in their going forth, unable to imagine what was before them, to work for their Master among races inhabiting the ends of the earth. The

[1] Now called the Bible Society of France.

departure of a band of missionaries for the Sandwich Islands in 1819 may be noted as causing a principle to emerge
whose logic has always ruled the Society; namely, that
American missions everywhere have a right to claim help
from the American Bible Society.

In case of the missionaries for the Sandwich Islands the
Board of Managers sent to the American Board in Boston
" splendid " Bibles to be presented to the Kings of Owhyee
(Hawaii), and of one of the neighbouring Islands. Some
Sandwich Islanders who had been studying at a training
school in Connecticut were each furnished with a handsome
copy of the Bible and the American Board was presented
with two hundred Bibles and two hundred Testaments to be
distributed by the missionaries among Americans and Europeans drawn by commerce to the Islands. Ability to make
such gifts gladdened the hearts of the members of the
Board of Managers; for missionaries who would sail half
around the world would use these books to make known the ·
name of Jesus Christ to the Islanders now first receiving
worthy influences from Christian lands.

The American Board had a mission in the northern part
of the Island of Ceylon and, it having been represented
that the American missionaries could make good use of English Scriptures in their schools and otherwise, the Board
made a grant of two hundred Bibles and two hundred Testaments for distribution by American missionaries, in Ceylon.   The enterprise of the American Colonisation Society
which cost Samuel J. Mills his life in 1818, was carried forward by others.   The first body of American colonists
sailed for the coast of Africa in February, 1820.   They
received a grant of Bibles for presentation to various func-
tionaries in Sierra Leone who could use them, and two hun-
red and fifty volumes of Scripture, of which some were
Spanish and some French but the main portion English for
the use of the coloured colonists.

The Managers of the Society received letters of appeal
from Messrs. Carey, Marshman and Ward in Serampore,
begging for help in the great work of printing which the
press in that place had undertaken. The New York Bible
Society a year or two before had sent a donation to these

gentlemen in order to help them over the difficulties in which they found themselves after the burning of the Serampore press. The Board passed a vote expressing sympathy and interest in the work of these missionaries, and sent each of them a finely bound English Bible as a token of good will. Later a thousand dollars was sent to Mr. Carey and his associates to lighten their expenditures for translating and printing the Scriptures in the various languages of India.

These little incidents are notable because from them sprang most important results. They saved the Managers of the American Bible Society from any nearsightedness due to lack of exercise in long vision. When once the habit is formed of seeing in some detail features of this world of ours, their penetrating appeal, always in the minor key, is sure to move the hearts of Christians. Through glimpses of conditions abroad gained in its first five years the American Bible Society imperceptibly became committed to the principle that its work is American in origin but not in limit. By such short steps impelled by faith and trust in God many different denominations in different lands have become engrossed in world evangelisation so that the knowledge of God may cover the earth.

CHAPTER IX

GROWTH OF AN ADMINISTRATIVE SYSTEM

THE warmth of President Boudinot's interest in the Bible Society persisted notwithstanding physical weakness. But his residence was in Burlington, New Jersey. In 1816 the ordinary way for him to reach New York would be by private carriage or post-chaise. It was a ride of eight or nine hours, which for a feeble man of seventy-seven was a serious matter. So Dr. Boudinot presided at Annual Meetings of the Society in 1818 and the three following years only; his last public appearance being in 1821, the year of his death. He did not share in the discussions about practical difficulties in those early years. But his heart was with the Board in this work. In July, 1816, he wrote to Dr. Romeyn as follows: "We are extremely anxious to know how far the glorious work in which we are engaged progresses toward maturity. . . . The time is short — we have delayed until late in the eleventh hour — we have need of double diligence. . . . I hope you will not mistake my desires as if I wished to proceed in this arduous business *per saltem.* No; I hope we shall, like wise master-builders directed by the Spirit of God, go on steadily and firmly, laying a solid foundation for this glorious superstructure to the praise and glory of His Grace."

The Board of Managers needed all the counsel and sympathy which such a man could give. The members of the Board had seen their duty as simple though difficult. They had to raise money, to provide books, and to find helpers for both lines of effort. But from their very first meeting they began to perceive that these three simple duties dragged in their train unforeseen complications and new problems.

One of these problems sprang from the quality of the membership of the Board. Denominational sensitiveness had to be considered at every step. In the absence of President Boudinot the presiding officer at Board meetings was General Clarkson, a member of the Episcopal Church and a Vice-President of the Society. At the outset one of the Secretaries was a Presbyterian and the other a minister of the Reformed Dutch Church. Other denominations were also present. If prayer, whether liturgical or extemporaneous, were offered in a Board meeting some present could not say " Amen."

When a committee prepared by-laws in August, 1816, the first of these was as follows: " The business of the Board shall be commenced by reading such portion of the Scriptures as the presiding officer may direct." The delicacy of the question of having prayers or other religious exercises at Board meetings appeared in the report of the Westchester County Auxiliary Bible Society the next year. A remark on its own experience illumines the situation: " This union (of Protestants) so consonant with that spirit of brotherly love by which our Saviour declared his disciples should be distinguished from others, has probably been strengthened by the determination of the Society to discontinue the exercises of prayer and preaching at their meetings, and thereby to avoid all interference with the various opinions of its members respecting the forms of religious worship." Many members of the Board felt that in the Lord's own work prayer for guidance ought to be the first act in every meeting. The question came up in the Board again some years later, when the Board of Managers formally reasserted the principle of this first by-law; namely, that there should be no religious exercise besides the reading of a portion of Scripture at the opening of a meeting of the Board of Managers.

In the meantime the same question had been raised from a slightly different point of view in the Committee of the British and Foreign Bible Society, and so much heat had been generated that for a moment it seemed as if the principle of denominational federation were at stake. The question was settled in England in the same way that it was settled in America; that is to say by adopting the rule that no prayer should be offered at these meetings.

Another unexpected perplexity arose on hearing of people who cannot read. Friends of the Bible expected their difficulties to lie in the direction of providing Bibles. But in Michigan Territory three-fourths of the French population could not read, and they composed two-thirds of the whole population of the region of Detroit. The Vermont Bible Society pitied the French on the Canadian border and tried to help them with Bibles. They found that very few of the French Canadians of the border could read. Similar reports were sent in respecting the Spaniards of Louisiana. The priest would let them read the Scio version of the Bible, but few able to read could be found. What shall a Bible Society do in such a case?

Reports of destitution flowed in from all quarters to the Board of Managers. For instance, a man was troubled by destitution in Maryland and threw off his burden for the Managers to take up. Within five or six miles of a thriving town he found thirteen families without the Bible. In all the families there were one or more who could read. In one place a father said that he had eight children all living at home and no one of them could read. There was no school to which they could go; he himself could not read nor could his parents. The man's wife, however, could read. She said it would be her greatest comfort to read the Bible and she was sure that her husband and children would be glad to hear a chapter read every night and morning. This family was said to be typical of hundreds of families in that region. To supply one such family, the applicant said, would be worth the expense and trouble of his whole journey.

One reason for the failure of Auxiliaries to collect support, as well as a hint of the customs of the people, is seen in an appeal sent out in 1820 by an Auxiliary Bible Society. "No man should ever say," declared the appeal, "that he cannot contribute to Bible work who uses spirituous liquor. The price of even a pint a week, of the cheapest kind, would enable you to be a member of a Bible, Missionary and Education Society and to have something left for Sunday School." [1]

[1] Annual Report, A. B. S., 1821, p. 122.

Of course these discouraging reports formed but a small part of the many small matters brought to the attention of the Board. In Virginia an essembly in an open field was talking of forming a Bible Society. Six poorly dressed women from the mountains came to the group with fruit for sale. All of them said they would like to have Bibles, but they could not buy for lack of money. The need of these poor women thus brought actually before the eyes of those lovers of the Bible led to instant action. A subscription paper was passed around. Then and there they raised money to send thirty or forty Bibles into the mountains whence these women had come, so as to supply as many poor families as possible. From one place in New Jersey was reported interest among the women, who had formed a little association to provide the poor with Bibles. A widow with five children was advised not to subscribe to the Association since she needed every cent she could earn. " Indeed I shall," she answered, " I have got much comfort from the Bible the Society gave me and I am going to spend something to take it to others."

Other problems sprang like warriors fully armed from the office desks. When the Hamburg-Altona Bible Society wrote its congratulations upon the formation of the American Bible Society, its Secretary sent the letter, enclosing some printed matter, to Bishop White, President of the Philadelphia Bible Society. The Bishop had to pay for this letter from Hamburg $2.49 postage. Not long afterward the Board petitioned Congress to exempt the correspondence of the Society from payment of postage. The fate of the petition was to lie in a Congressional Committee's pigeonhole until at a convenient season some one might call it up.

Before many months of 1816 had passed the Board of Managers saw that whether the matters presented were grave or trivial they could not sit continuously to read the letters which poured in a stream into the hands of the Secretaries. It appointed a " Standing Committee " to act for the Board during the intervals between its sessions. This Committee settled a multitude of small matters quickly and so secured for the Board time to study the large affairs.

But in the growth of any great undertaking the record

of minute details which seems often drudgery is an essential part of its story. The Rev. William Goodell, D.D., a translator of the Bible into Turkish, once comforted a brother missionary burdened by a multitude of such small affairs by saying, " The disciples who went after that donkey at Bethphage have become a part of the world's history because the Lord had need of just that service."

Already the Secretary for Domestic Correspondence, Rev. Dr. J. B. Romeyn, was at the point of being smothered under an avalanche of letters. He was pastor of an important church whose interests might well occupy all his time. But the Board of Managers claimed his strength for its interests. A short experience revealed to members of the Board the load which was being laid upon the Domestic Secretary and at last a clerk was hired to do the more mechanical part of the work. The sum of four hundred dollars a year was given for this service. It was the first salary paid by the American Bible Society to any one.

As the multitude of details increased the Board found it necessary to help the Treasurer as well as the Secretary by appointing a Recording Secretary and Accountant. Mr. John Pintard was chosen for this office. A Huguenot in origin, during the Revolutionary War he had care of British prisoners under his kinsman, Dr. Boudinot. Later he had an important influence in the purchase of " Louisiana " from Napoleon. He was a man of considerable prominence in New York life, the first Sagamore of the Tammany Society, the " father of Historical Societies," the treasurer of the Sailors' Snug Harbour on Staten Island, and the author, it is said, of the plan of streets and avenues in upper New York City. Mr. Pintard was a man of earnest piety. He was a member of the French Episcopal Church, for the use of which he translated the Book of Common Prayer into French.

Dr. Romeyn manfully struggled with his two lines of duty which dragged at his heart and his nervous system. In the third year of his self-sacrifice he resigned his office as Secretary of Domestic Correspondence, explaining that he must give his time wholly to his people. The Rev. James Milnor, D.D., was then elected Secretary for Domestic Cor-

respondence. He had been educated for the law, had prac-
tised his profession in Pennsylvania for some years, and had
represented his district in Congress in 1810. Afterwards
he felt called to enter the ministry. At the time of his
election as Secretary he was rector of St. George's Protestant Episcopal Church in New York, continuing in that position until his death. During twenty years he was a Secretary of the Bible Society. His grasp of the essentials of
any problem and his resource in difficult situations made
his services of great value to the young Society.

Rev. Dr. J. M. Mason, the Secretary for Foreign Correspondence, in 1820 was ordered away by his physician.
He therefore resigned his office. The Board of Managers
were sorry to lose his wise counsels, for in the Committee
room as well as in the Secretary's office Dr. Mason's services had been greatly valued. Upon this Dr. Milnor was
given the foreign correspondence in Dr. Mason's room, and
the Rev. S. S. Woodhull, a well-known and influential minister of the Dutch Reformed Church in Brooklyn, succeeded
to the post of Secretary of Domestic Correspondence. He
administered his office to the satisfaction of the Board of
Managers until 1825, when he became Professor of Pastoral
Theology at the Reformed Dutch Seminary at New Brunswick, New Jersey. He died in 1826.

Colonel Richard Varick, the Treasurer of the Society, like
Elias Boudinot and John Jay, was one of General Washington's able men. His commanding presence and courtly
manners made him a striking figure in public gatherings.
He brought to his office great business ability. The choice
of Colonel Varick as Treasurer guaranteed the proper use
and the security of all the money placed in his care. His
tested efficiency and high character was a better protection
than bolts and bars for the cash of the American Bible Society. In 1820, after four years of most careful service,
he resigned. He was succeeded as Treasurer by Mr. W.
W. Woolsey, an active and influential member of the Board
of Managers. Colonel Varick was then elected a Vice-
President and later became President of the Society.

After the presses began to furnish Bibles the Board discovered that a General Agent was needed to care for the

books, supervise printers and binders, look to the provision of paper, and see to the safety of stereotype plates and other property of the American Bible Society. Mr. John E. Caldwell was chosen General Agent of the Society in February, 1818, and took a heavy burden from the Managers. Mr. Caldwell had been Corresponding Secretary of the New York Bible Society until he was chosen member of the Board of Managers of the American Bible Society. Since the General Agent would be required to give his whole time to the work of the Bible Society, it was natural that he should receive a salary and he was allowed twelve hundred dollars a year. Mr. Caldwell occupied this office for a short time only. He died in 1820 and was succeeded by Mr. John Nitchie.

The American Bible Society all this time had led a nomadic existence. It held its annual meetings commonly at the City Hotel on Broadway near Thames Street. Its Secretaries were housed wherever they could find place. The depository was a seven by nine room in Cedar Street; then a larger place on Cliff Street and later a room in Hanover Street. After careful consideration a site was bought, plans were made and it was agreed that none of the money contributed for Bible circulation should be used for building the Society's house. In the spring of 1822, with elation and with special gratitude to God, the friends of the Bible Society attended the ceremony of laying the cornerstone, and in the following year the Managers were able to hold their first meeting in their new quarters.

The Society's house was at number 115 Nassau Street, between Ann and Beekman Streets. It had a front of fifty feet on Nassau Street, and extended westward a little more than one hundred feet, narrowing to about thirty feet at the rear. The house was three stories high and had a commodious basement. The Managers' Room was forty-eight feet long and thirty wide. The depository contained space for about one hundred thousand Bibles. The printer with eleven hand presses, and the binder, both doing work by contract for the Society, were given rooms for their machinery. There was abundant storage room for paper and materials purchased by the Society, as well as for keeping the printed sheets; and with the offices and the rooms assigned to the committees, the American Bible Society was at last housed under one roof in a place easily accessible, to which public attention would be constantly drawn by the name on the sign.

The Managers felt that the new depository furnished facilities for a large business of manufacture of Scriptures. They made known the fact, and at the same time called upon friends of the Society to help by special contributions to pay the cost of the house. This amounted to twenty-two thousand, five hundred dollars, and the Board stated once more that not one cent would be diverted from the purpose for which it was given to the Society, so that money given for Bible distribution should be wholly devoted to that object. About ten thousand dollars had been received for the Building Fund before the house was occupied, and in 1826 the debt was paid off. The Society was thus left in possession of an establishment which in itself would be a means of forwarding the circulation of Bibles.

Possession of a house gives to a young man who is commencing a new order of life an entirely new bearing and outlook. He holds his head up. His thoughts become filled with hope; he almost feels that with such a point on which he can stand he can conquer the whole world. Perhaps something of this optimism took possession of the Managers of the Bible Society. At all events in humble trust that God had work for them to do, from this day in 1823 they foresaw extension for the Society far beyond their early visions.

CHAPTER X

SOME OF THE GREAT MEN

INFLUENCE is not a quality which one may pick up like a dropped gem in the highway. In its most worthy sense it is a result of noble character which comes to a man or woman unawares and unsought. God has so constituted his truth that when made concrete in any human life it becomes a seed which lodges in the consciousness of others; germinates, grows, yields fruit many fold.

None may call it accident that the American Bible Society has had the support and collaboration of great, famous and intellectual men — servants of God who seemed to be divinely thrust into this service. The first President of the Society, the Hon. Elias Boudinot, belonged to this class. On the twenty-first of October, 1821, Dr. Boudinot passed from this life. Mr. Samuel Bayard says that he was at the deathbed and was perhaps the last to converse with him. He reminded Dr. Boudinot of the amount and variety of good which he had been able to effect during his life. " The dying philanthropist at once turned from this view; his hopes rested on Jesus Christ alone. But when his agency in establishing the American Bible Society, and its probable benefit to the country and the world were brought to his recollection he was silent but afterwards admitted the consolation given him by this thought. It was soon after this that raising his eyes to heaven he exclaimed: ' Lord Jesus receive my spirit,' and passed away." [1]

He was notable for his services during the Revolutionary War in close intimacy with General Washington. He was great in Congress where he helped to knit together the separate elements of the young nation. He was honoured as President of Congress, and he was sincere as a child in

[1] Report of the 10th Anniversary of the A. B. S., 1826.

his devotion to Jesus Christ and his passionate desire to ensure the use of the Bible by all the people for their worthy development.

Dr. Boudinot was always thoughtful of need, and unostentatious in benevolences. In his will was a legacy of two hundred dollars left to the New Jersey Bible Society, the interest of which was to be devoted to supplying spectacles to the elderly poor, that they might not be deprived of the comfort of Bible reading in their latter days. His munificent gift of ten thousand dollars to the American Bible Society on its formation has already been mentioned. He gave one thousand dollars also to the special fund for building the Society's house, and in his will he left four thousand five hundred acres of land in Pennsylvania to be held by trustees until sold, the proceeds to go to the American Bible Society.

When Dr. Boudinot was requested by the Board of Managers to sit for his portrait, his natural shrinking from noisy publicity showed itself in his letter of acceptance. " It would be inconsistent," he wrote, " with that candour that should strongly mark all my conduct, and a mere affectation of humility not to confess the great pleasure afforded me from so lively and delicate a manifestation of their unmerited respect and attention to me by such an impressive testimony of their liberal and generous construction of my conduct. That I may not, therefore, appear callous to some of the finest feelings of the human mind, I know not how to refuse the request of your Board. To live in the memory of those with whom I stand associated in a godlike work must be a gratifying reflection, and ill would it become me to withhold my concurrence to this effect; although I must acknowledge that I feel some reluctance to a measure that may prevent the circulation of a single copy of the Scriptures."

During ninety-five years the portrait referred to, a fine work by Sully, has hung at the head of the Managers' room, during more than sixty years in the present Bible House.

The Board of Managers in mentioning the evidence from all parts of the country and even from other countries of the high estimate placed on the character of Dr. Boudinot, adds: "The monument in his honour more durable than brass is the American Bible Society; and instead of merely some friends and strangers reading his epitaph on his tombstone and thus learning or retaining the remembrance of his name and his worth, there will be thousands on thousands in successive ages blessing his memory and blessing God on his account while they witness the usefulness, or experience the benefits of the National institution."

In December, 1821, the Hon. John Jay, Vice-President, was elected President of the American Bible Society; a worthy successor of Dr. Boudinot. Like him, Mr. Jay was of Huguenot descent. His mother was a daughter of Jacobus Van Cortlandt, so that two choice strains of blood ran in his veins. He was an intimate friend of General Washington and may be called very properly one of the founders of the Republic. As a creator and moulder of public opinion during the Revolution, as a patriot and a statesman he is often classed as next to Washington. He was President of Congress, which sent him to Europe to take part in negotiating the treaty with Great Britain at the end of the Revolutionary War. Dr. Boudinot succeeded him as President of Congress and signed the treaty. By General Washington's appointment he became Chief Justice of the United States, and though he withdrew from that high office before long, during twenty-eight years he served his country in many notable emergencies, and his state as Chief Justice and Governor. The purity and elevation of his principles of conduct made him eminent among men. He had a very high sense of justice and of the rights of others, and his religious feelings were deep. The Bible he constantly studied. When informed in May, 1816, of his election as Vice-President of the American Bible Society he expressed great satisfaction and remarked in his letter of acceptance, "The events and circumstances under which such Societies have been established and multiplied, in my opinion indicate an origin which makes it the duty of all Christians to unite in giving them decided patronage and zealous support." At this time he had been for some years President of the Westchester County (New York) Bible Society, thus living up to his principles.

Six years later in the written address to the Annual Meeting of the Society after his election as President, Mr. Jay returns to the thought of the divine origin of the Bible Society movement. The following extract shows the warmth of his feeling:

" Whence has it come to pass that Christian nations, who for ages had regarded the welfare of heathens with indifference, and whose intercourse with them had uniformly been regulated by the results of political, military and commercial calculations, have recently felt such new and unprecedented concern for the salvation of their souls, and have simultaneously concurred in means and measures for that purpose? Whence has it come to pass that so many individuals of every profession and occupation, who in the ordinary course of human affairs, confine their speculations, resources and energies to the acquisition of temporal prosperity for themselves and families, have become so ready and solicitous to supply idolatrous strangers in remote regions, with the means of obtaining eternal felicity? Who has ' opened their hearts to attend ' to such things?

" It will be acknowledged that worldly wisdom is little conversant with the transcendent affairs of that kingdom which is not of *this* world; and has neither ability to comprehend, nor inclination to further them. To what adequate cause, therefore, can these extraordinary events be attributed, but the wisdom that cometh from *above?* "

Mr. Jay was a confirmed invalid and was not able to come from Bedford to preside at any meeting of the Society. Being opposed to any nominal office-holding, he resigned in 1827, after his physicians had told him that there was no hope of his being able to rise from his bed. He died in 1829.

Colonel Richard Varick was elected President of the Society upon the resignation of Mr. Jay. At the time of this election he was well past the proverbial three score years and ten. He was strong and healthy, warm in his service of the Bible Society of which during the four first critical years he had been Treasurer. On retiring from this rather arduous office he was elected a Vice-President of the Society and presided at its meetings and those of the Board of

Managers with grace and dignity.   Colonel Varick like his two predecessors in the Presidential office was an intimate friend of General Washington; in fact he was a member of Washington's military family.   His energy of mind and his military habit of punctuality made him a valuable officer. He loved the work and the Society and he contributed fifteen hundred dollars to the building of the Society's House. His donations to the Society at various times amounted to twice that sum.   In civil life and in religious circles of New York Colonel Varick held a high rank.   He served as President until his death in 1831.

At the meetings of the Standing Committee and other Committees of the Board Samuel J. Mills was often seen. He was a Life Member of the Society and took pleasure in its meetings.   When he thought that the Managers were not keen enough about providing Scriptures in Spanish, suppressing himself in his usual fashion, he persuaded a distinguished minister in the city to write urging an immediate provision of Spanish Scriptures.   In July, 1816, seeing the small success of the Board's strenuous efforts to collect money, Mr. Mills offered to take up that work for the Society, and in November he was appointed to collect funds and to organise Auxiliary Societies during six months in all the Southern States.   In 1817 Mr. Mills was interested with the author of " The Star Spangled Banner," Francis S. Key, who was a Vice-Presient of the American Bible Society, in organising the American Colonisation Society and the formation of a colony of freed slaves on the African coast.   They supposed as everybody did that blacks were all one people.   Mr. Mills was sent to Africa by that Society to select a suitable region for a colony.   After completing this mission he embarked for home in 1818 while ill with a fever contracted in the African jungles.   A few days later he died and his body was buried in the great ocean.   In this untimely fashion came to an end the ardent life of Mills which had promised so much.

Mills was on fire with love for Christ and the Kingdom, as though his lips had been touched with a live coal from the altar of God.   Dr. Boudinot, as a Christian, in his own person made concrete the abstract idea of the Christian duty

of combination to pass on the Bible to all who have it not.
Jay, renowned in the political world as one of the founders
of the Republic, gave weight to every statement or appeal
of the Society through his own love for the Bible and
eagerness to popularise its use.   Varick differed from his
two predecessors in the office of President.   He had not a
record of achievement to be compared with either.   But as
having been a member of General Washington's staff this
plain, bluff soldier had influence also.   In sheer amazement
at the combination of military renown and love for Jesus
Christ and His gospel many would stop and think and yield
to the Bible cause the homage of their support.

Either of these three Presidents, even had they not rendered precious services in the process of organising its work,
should be rated as of the highest value to the Bible Society
at this period because each commanded attention to whatever enterprise he might support with his esteem and his
subscriptions.   " Their sanction was a passport to public approval."

In the Managers' room at the Bible House in New York
over the President's chair hangs the fine portrait of Dr.
Boudinot of which we have already spoken.   On the right
of Dr. Boudinot as he sits at his table is another large oil
painting, an almost life size portrait of the intellectual giant
and master of expression, John Jay.   Opposite Mr. Jay's
portrait, on the left of that of Dr. Boudinot, is a very fine
painting of Colonel Varick, erect, commanding, noble.
Among all the paintings which in that room bring to mind
the great men who have served God in this Society, the first
three were friends who stood together in the day of small
things.   These seem to represent the time of special struggle
and the whole group of grand men who in the first quarter
of the ninteenth century, by the help of God, laid the foundations of the great work of the American Bible Society.

CHAPTER XI

In the steps by which the Bible became newly known in the great continent, which with its adjacent islands is sometimes called Latin America, eagerness of the people to read the Scriptures weighed with the Board, leading it from interest to experiment and from experiment to a fixed policy. In the first quarter of the nineteenth century Latin America from the point of view of our own nation was a vast region whose attractions were offset by many repulsive features. The mass of the people were illiterate; political disturbances were not uncommon; and, in any case, difficulties of travel repelled those who would fain visit the interior of any of the countries upon whose seaboard they had landed.

Counteracting somewhat this feeling of repulsion was a Christian sympathy with the Latin-American people expressed by Rev. Dr. James Blythe of Lexington, at the tenth Anniversary of the American Bible Society. He said: " The American Bible Society stands connected in a peculiar manner with South America. God has begun to do that immense country good of which the heart of every man in this commonwealth is glad. Liberty now sheds her blessings where despotism forged her chains. It is especially committed to this Society to be instrumental in giving that long oppressed people those sacred writings which shall enable them to perpetuate their new civil liberties and make them, too, the freemen of the Lord." [1]

The sympathy thus expressed was accompanied by no desire whatever to propagate a sect or interfere with religious beliefs; in the hearts of the members of the Bible

[1] " Extracts from the Correspondence of the American Bible Society," No. 47, August, 1826.

Society it stirred a simple, earnest purpose to give these people information through the Bible. In the words of William Maxwell of Norfolk, Virginia, " God has chosen this book to be the very wand of His power and wisdom; to work all His mightiest and most moving miracles withal. It is by this that He wakes the dead and brings them back from the gates of the prison house; and it is by this that He feeds the life which he has given, and cheers and strengthens and consoles saints and wafts them away in the spirit into paradise again." [1]

As we have seen, the Society very early began to send Scriptures in Spanish and later in Portuguese to different parts of Latin America. No American missionaries had yet undertaken to establish themselves in the southern continent. As commercial correspondence with South American countries increased, a number of persons were brought to light in various seaports who were willing to help circulate the Scriptures. In 1822 and 1823 letters from people living in Buenos Aires, Chile and Peru brought news to the Bible House of the readiness with which Scriptures could be sold in those places. In Lima, Peru, a Mr. Lynch having received from London five hundred Spanish Bibles and five hundred Testaments in two days sold the whole of the Bibles at three dollars apiece.

In Colombia and what is now Venezuela by 1827 the Colombia Bible Society had been organised at Bogota; the Caracas Bible Society had been organised; both had put themselves in communication with the British and Foreign Bible Society and the American Bible Society; eight hundred Spanish Bibles had been sent by the American Society to Colombia; Spanish Scriptures had been furnished merchants at Carthagena and Maracaibo which were readily sold.

In Peru Mr. James Thomson, who was exploring the country for the British and Foreign Bible Society, asked and received from the American Bible Society a grant of five hundred dollars to aid in translation work for the benefit of the Quechua Indians in Peru; and in 1825, when Rev.

[1] Report of the 10th Anniversary of the A. B. S. in " Extracts," No. 47, August, 1826.

John C. Brigham exploring the country on behalf of the American Board of Commissioners for Foreign Missions reached Lima, Peru, he found some boxes of Scriptures from the American Society which had been left unopened in that city by Mr. James Thomson. Mr. Brigham immediately put the books in circulation and sent the Society $195.75, proceeds of copies sold.

The correspondents of the Society at Valparaiso distributed Scriptures from that centre to Arica, Coquimbo, Concepcion, and other towns. In Mexico as early as 1824 the Board of Managers considered the wisdom of opening an agency; Mr. J. C. Brigham, however, wrote frequent letters and served the Society almost as a regular Agent. In 1826 Messrs. Parrot and Wilson were selling Spanish Bibles in Mexico City at two dollars and fifty cents and Testaments at fifty cents apiece. Mr. Pearse at Matamoras wrote to the Bible Society for a grant of Spanish Scriptures, saying that there was a serious demand; and the next year having received a grant he sold the whole consignment immediately for three hundred dollars. In 1827 Messrs. Parrot and Wilson of Mexico City remitted $396.87 as the proceeds of sales in Mexico City and the surrounding region. In 1827 the British and Foreign Bible Society sent an agent to reside in Mexico City, but this did not diminish the work of the American Society in other parts of that region.

In the West Indies Scriptures were sent as opportunity offered to many of the islands. In 1825 a shipment was sent to some of the Roman Catholic clergy connected with the Archbishop of Havana, Cuba. Shortly afterwards a secretary of the Archdiocese, Don Justo Valez, acknowledged with thanks this gift from the Society and sent to the Biblical Library in New York a gift of twenty-six volumes of the writings of the Church Fathers. Upon this Don Justo was made Life Director of the Society. In a courteous letter he responded that he could not accept the position of Life Director of the American Bible Society, but that he would be very glad indeed to accept another consignment of Scriptures for sale; and in 1827 he sent three hundred dollars, proceeds of sales, to the Treasurer of the Society.

These experiences seemed to justify a statement of Mr. Brigham that the people of the southern continent " are ready to receive the Scriptures not only by hundreds and by thousands, but by millions. I never yet met an individual, of any rank, in those countries who would not receive one of these books with gratitude and often was willing to pay even a high price for it." [1]   This statement was confirmed by the fact that Spanish Bibles purchased at the Depository in New York for a dollar fifty were sold by merchants in the City of Mexico for five dollars each at wholesale, or eight fifty at retail.

The whole number of books sent into Latin America in the year 1826 was only 3,967 volumes; but since they were scattered extensively throughout the continent and on the islands, the important possibilities of the work thus begun are easily realised.   The craving to lend a kindly hand to the people who had cast off the Spanish rule grew with knowledge of their wish to read the Bible.   Every possible channel of communication was used.   American Consuls, Naval officers, and merchants were appealed to for help in taking the Bible to the different countries.   Even Mr. J. H. Poinsett, the South Carolinian whose long sojourn in Mexico immortalised his name through the decorative poinsettia of our greenhouses, was appealed to concerning methods of Bible distribution in the country which he knew so well.

Before long, however, the Board began to perceive that this method of sending Bibles to Latin America by well-meaning merchants and others left much to be desired. The men volunteered service in Bible distribution in perfect good faith, but they found it hard to press their own business and the business of the American Bible Society at the same time.   Priests could not understand why any man should wish to distribute the Bible among the common people unless he had an ulterior purpose akin to proselyting. Merchants who found themselves looked upon with suspicion might easily reach the point of diminishing activity in Bible circulation.

[1] Report of the 10th Anniversary of the American Bible Society, " Extracts," No. 47, August, 1826.

It was at this time that the Board of Managers realised the wisdom, energy and devotion of the Rev. J. C. Brigham, already mentioned as having rendered services to the Bible Society in different parts of South America, where with Mr. Parvin he was making explorations for the A. B. C. F. M.   Mr. Brigham graduated from Andover Theological Seminary in 1822.   Both in college and in the seminary he had taken high honours.   He was classmate and intimate friend of Rev. Dr. Rufus Anderson of the American Board, and of Rev. Dr. Hallock of the American Tract Society. Almost as soon as Mr. Brigham graduated from the seminary he was sent to South America by the American Board on an exploring expedition.   The thoroughness of his procedure is shown by the fact that his first step was to sit down and learn the Spanish language.   This once acquired he pressed forward the purpose of his mission, journeying from Buenos Aires through the heart of the continent to the Pacific coast in Chile, and returning to the United States by way of Peru, Ecuador, Colombia, and Mexico.

Mr. Brigham's correspondence with the Secretaries of the Society had so revealed his acquirements that within a week after his return to Boston in 1826, he was asked to deliver an address at the Society's tenth Annual Meeting. In this address he pointed out the effects of the colonial servitude from which the people of South America had suffered.   " Of the means of information," he said, " they were in great measure deprived.   Some of the most valuable books, particularly those of mental philosophy and political science, were wholly kept from them.   The Sacred Scriptures were furnished in but small quantities and these in the Latin tongue and confined to the clergy.   Every means which could be was employed by their tyrannical masters to continue them in their state of vassalage. . . . And what do we behold calculated to interest this noble Society?   We behold fifteen millions of human beings, beings professedly Christians, believing in revelation, baptised in the name of the Trinity, and yet almost entirely without the Bible.   By the efforts of this Society and that of England they have, it is true, within a few years received seven or eight thousand copies of this Holy Book; but what are these among so great a multitude?

" Throughout the long road from Buenos Aires to Chile excepting a very few in Mendoza, not a solitary book of God was found and I more than once presented copies to aged priests tottering over the grave who told me they had never before seen it in their native tongue. Coming down the coast of Chile, Peru, Colombia, and Mexico a few copies were met with in the large towns on the Pacific and were useful; but the great mass of the people are yet destitute and generally in the interior they never saw, and in some instances told me they never before knew that the Scriptures existed in their own language. Even in the capital of Mexico, a city more populous and in some respects more magnificent than this great metropolis (New York), I have reason to believe there is not one Bible to two hundred families; and that the other great cities of that Republic are still more destitute."

Mr. Brigham's address made a profound impression upon his hearers. The Board of Managers at that time were seeking an Assistant Secretary for the Society. A few weeks before this an Assistant Secretary had been chosen, Rev. Mr. Crane, missionary to the Tuscarora Indians, who died a week after his appointment. To fill this vacancy Mr. Brigham seemed to be exactly suited, and in the month of July he received and accepted an appointment of Assistant Secretary of the Bible Society; only stipulating that he should not be required to take up his duties until September.

Mr. Brigham remained in service as Secretary of the Society thirty-six years, until his death in 1862. In 1828 the office of Assistant Secretary was abolished, and Mr. Brigham was elected Secretary for Domestic Correspondence. Five years later when the duties of the Secretary for Foreign Correspondence had greatly increased, the distinctive titles of the Secretaries were suppressed and the four Secretaries of the Society were thereafter styled Corresponding Secretaries.

When summoned to service in the Bible Society Mr. Brigham was its youngest officer, being in his thirty-third year.

At Andover Theological Seminary when he was studying there the fire of missionary devotion was at white heat. Perhaps the effects of this experience, and certainly a controlling feature of his character, showed itself in 1828 when he declared the salary of fifteen hundred dollars assigned to him to be too large for his needs and persuaded the Board of Managers to reduce it to twelve hundred. Energy and resolute persistence were traits natural to his character which had been developed by his experiences as an explorer in his thousand mile journey across South America from the Atlantic to the Pacific. Moreover, his four years' sojourn in the southern continent had given him mastery of the Spanish language, knowledge of the needs of the people, and personal acquaintance with many Americans and others friendly to the Bible cause. The object and the policy of the Bible Society toward Latin America would be advanced by a man with such qualifications. In fact his appearance on the scene at this moment seemed providential. His after history, too, made his appointment worthy to be listed among the occurrences which seemed to show that the very hand of God was leading the Society.

About this time two gentlemen of rank from Colombia visited New York and became interested in the Bible Society. Of these two men Don Joaquin Mosquera was an ex-president of Colombia, and General F. B. Santander an officer of distinction. In 1832 each of these gentlemen accepted office as Vice-Presidents of the Bible Society. The appearance of their names in the roster of officers of the Society foreshadowed the more cosmopolitan character which, in the good providence of God, that Society was to gain.

In those early days suspicion showed itself in the bearing of the Roman Catholic clergy toward distributors of the Bible in Latin America. When the Society in 1820 sent its first shipment of Scriptures to Buenos Aires the Secretary of the British and Foreign Bible Society, after gently hinting that steps had already been taken by its committee to do what was needed for that continent, gave a cordial approval to the fraternal purpose of the American Bible Society to assist. At the same time the Secretary remarked that no Scriptures could be circulated in Latin America except Roman Catholic versions such as that of Father Scio in Spanish. This suggestion was sufficient to lead the Board to order as early as 1822 a set of plates of the whole Bible in Spanish made from the Roman Catholic edition of Father Scio. The suspicions of the priests were generally dissipated when they found that the people were being offered a Roman Catholic version only. This Scio version was used by the Society until 1841, when by direction of the Board the plates were removed from the printing house, after some twenty thousand volumes had been printed. The cause of the tragic end of the Society's Scio version will appear later in this story.

CHAPTER XII

A NOTABLE ADVANCE

MEN called of God to work for Him are often driven to do what they shrink from doing, and deem contrary to sound reason. Jonah is an example often repeated in the history of the Church, where a good man hangs back because the call of duty seems a crazy impulse to court disaster. By way of some such experience as this the men of the Society were led to realise that God willed the great advance which they now had to make, although it seemed impossible of accomplishment. Before long they surrendered themselves to God's leading in a new sense, received new vision and a new energy, and did wonders.

At the end of five years the Society had secured about three hundred Auxiliary Societies to study destitutions and supply them, had received two hundred and sixteen thousand dollars for the work, and had issued about one hundred and forty thousand volumes of Scripture. This was progress unexpected; it was a wonderful growth from a small seed. But tales of destitution kept pouring in from the visible East and the invisible and immeasurable West. The theory as to the share of Auxiliary Societies in the work was that the initiative in cases of destitution belonged to them. They would raise the money, obtain the books and take them to the needy in their fields. The national Society would print the books, aid where necessary by gratuitous supplies of books, and do what it could for regions where Auxiliaries had not yet been organised. This theory did not justify itself in practice.

The Board of Managers sent out repeated appeals to the Auxiliary Societies asking them diligently to supply the people with whom they were in touch in their own fields. Some of the Societies bent to the work with vigour and sturdy perseverance. But discovery of the tremendous needs of the country was so startling that it led some of the Auxiliary Societies to fall helplessly on the ground, withdrawing from the sacred toil.

In the Western States six years after the Society's organisation the most careful estimates showed that at least one-third of the population was without either Bibles or Testaments. Within twenty years the population would be doubled. Where could means be found to supply such a population? The prospect seemed appalling. "Unless greater exertions are employed," said the Managers in their report, "to give these people the Bible, there must ere long exist in our country many millions of civilised human beings unenlightened by the oracles of God."

Reports of destitution came to the Board like voices warning them of the tremendous responsibility placed upon them. The population of the United States was increasing at the rate of four hundred thousand persons every year. Yet these facts led to more urgent appeals to the Auxiliaries, and an increase of the output of books, but to little other action. In 1827 the Society, with all its efforts, was unable to issue more than seventy-two thousand volumes of Scripture. The Board of Managers commanded a printing plant on Nassau Street consisting of eleven hand presses. With such an equipment what could be done for the evangelisation of the population grouped along the coast, or straggling out westward along a wide network of rivers and small streams?

The Board now allowed the work of the bindery to be carried on in their meeting room in the Society's house, and so space was made for nine hand presses to be added to the equipment. Finally in 1831 the Society's House on Nassau Street was enlarged to receive eight power presses worked by a steam engine in the basement. Twenty hand presses on the floors above completed the plant which was able to send out three hundred thousand volumes a year, two hundred persons being employed on the premises.

Meantime the hour had come for a revolution in the existing system. This system made direct action by the national Society in the field of an Auxiliary seem interference even for the relief of destitution which the Auxiliary was too torpid to deal with. The change came about naturally enough. It sprang from the vigorous initiative of really living local Bible Societies.

In 1824 the Bible Society in Monroe County, New York, adopted the Board's suggestion that Auxiliaries should determine the exact needs of their fields. It sent agents into every school district, who came back with accurate statistics. Then a public meeting was called in Rochester attended by Christians of all denominations. The story of local destitution was read to this audience and proved exceedingly moving. The meeting unanimously agreed that every destitute family in the county must be supplied. Money was raised; an order for twenty-three hundred Bibles and Testaments valued at eleven hundred dollars astonished the depository in New York; and the County Society supplied every destitute family that would buy or accept the Bible.

In 1827 the Philadelphia Bible Society carried the policy a step farther. It decided to supply within three years every destitute family in the state of Pennsylvania. This was a glorious advance upon former plans for the supply of the destitute. Nothing had been done with a specified time limit or on so large a scale as the supply undertaken by the Philadelphia Society. The supply of Pennsylvania was completed in 1830, about forty thousand volumes having been distributed among the destitute; three thousand of them being in the German language.

In February, 1829, the Bible Society of Washington County, N. Y., sent a formal memorial to New York requesting the American Bible Society to undertake " at its Thirteenth Anniversary to supply within two years " Scriptures to every destitute family within the limits of the United States. If the national Society would agree to do this the Washington County Auxiliary pledged five thousand dollars as a donation in aid of the undertaking.

The population of the United States at this time was about thirteen million. The number of destitute families throughout the country could not very well be estimated; how the destitute could be supplied could not readily be seen, but the Board of Managers concurred in the opinion of Rev. Dr. Proudfit, President of the Washington County Auxiliary, who wrote: " The question now agitated, for giving the Bible to all the destitute of our great and growing nation is, in my opinion, equal in the importance of its results to any that ever has involved or can involve the deliberations and decisions of the American Bible Society." [1]

Because of three pertinent, persistent and unanswered questions the Board of Managers hesitated about assenting to this proposal. First, was it possible to provide the necessary number of Scriptures? Second, could money to meet the expense of this great undertaking be found? Third, could agents be set to work in sufficient number to canvass the country? A farmer contentedly living on ten acres of land might possibly dare to undertake the cultivation of a quarter section. But the proposal of the Washington County Society implied a far greater increase of activities. Men take up great enterprises for God only when they believe that if God wishes them to do it He will teach them how to find the means.

Accordingly at the Thirteenth Annual Meeting of the American Bible Society on the 14th day of May, 1829, Secretary Milnor on behalf of the Board of Managers presented resolutions which were seconded by Rev. Dr. Lyman Beecher and adopted, as follows:

" I, Resolved, that this Society feel deeply thankful to Almighty God, that He has excited in the hearts of so many of the conductors of its Auxiliaries the generous determination to explore the wants of the destitute within their several regions of operation, and to supply them.

" II, Resolved, That this Society, with humble reliance on Divine aid, will endeavour to supply all the destitute families in the United States with the Holy Scriptures, that may be willing to purchase or receive them, within the space of two years, provided sufficient means be furnished by its Auxiliaries and benevolent individuals in season to enable its Board of Managers to carry this resolution into effect.

[1] Letters from the Washington County Bible Society, A. B. S. Report, 1829, p. 77–78.

SUPPLYING WORKINGMEN IN NORTH CAROLINA

" III, Resolved, That with the full purpose of accomplishing, by the blessing of God, this most necessary and important work, it be earnestly recommended to ministers of the gospel and laymen of every denomination, in places where no Auxiliary Societies have yet been formed, or where they have relaxed their efforts, to take immediate measures for carrying into effect the general distribution of the Scriptures in their respective neighbourhoods." [1]

This action took the American Bible Society out of its original position as a sort of clearing house for co-ordinating the surplus energies of a body of local Bible Societies. If any Auxiliary became inactive the national Society would now be answerable for the souls so left to starve. Henceforth the supply of the destitute in the United States, whether within or without the fields of Auxiliary Societies, was a responsibility resting upon the Bible Society. The Board immediately shouldered the responsibility. Through a committee specially appointed, it appealed to churches, individuals and local Bible Societies for help in the great undertaking. At this time there were five hundred and sixty-eight Bible Societies, of which three hundred and seventy-eight were within and one hundred and ninety without the original thirteen states. All of these Auxiliaries were urged to use the thoroughness shown by the Societies in Pennsylvania and in counties where a complete supply of the destitute had already been completed. The appeal was heard with good will; many answered as to a divine call, " Here am I; send me!"

In North Carolina a Bible Convention was called to meet in the Legislative Hall at Raleigh. The Governor of the state was in the chair. Many important men addressed the meeting with the result that the convention pledged itself to supply every destitute family in the state with a copy of the Scriptures. Upon hearing of this the Board of Managers voted a grant for the state of North Carolina of eight thousand Bibles valued at five thousand dollars. Great enthusiasm was shown in other states. The purchases of Scriptures by Auxiliaries amounted to one hundred and

[1] See Report of A. B. S., 1829, p. vi.

forty-seven thousand, five hundred dollars in three years. Some of the Bible Societies which had recently supplied the destitute in their own fields sent, generally at great self-sacrifice, considerable donations of money to the national Society. For instance the Philadelphia Bible Society, still feeling the stress of its labours in supply of its own state, sent to the American Society a donation of $1,000 in 1829 and $500 in 1830 in aid of the general supply. Other Societies besides the one in Washington County already mentioned made large pledges of aid. The New Hampshire Bible Society pledged $12,000, the Vermont Bible Society $10,000, the Connecticut Bible Society $10,000, and so forth. During the next three years (for the work was not finished in two), churches and individuals sent special gifts designated for the General Supply amounting to $119,000. This tangible and hearty support of the undertaking was to the Board and its staff like a direct word of approval from the Most High.

During 1830 twenty thousand New Testaments were committed to the American Sunday School Union with special reference to the supply of Sunday School children. These Testaments cost twelve cents apiece and the Board authorised a discount of twenty per cent. where the books were paid for as a part of the equipment of a Sunday School room.

The activity of the Auxiliary Societies led the Board of Managers to take a very optimistic view of the effect of the effort to supply every destitute family in the United States. It hoped that the effect would be a permanent strengthening of all the Auxiliary Societies.

During the two stated years of this general supply the books issued by the Society amounted to 480,766 volumes. The work was not completely finished within the two years and at the end of the third year further issues amounted to 115,802 volumes. The people at the Society's house in New York were kept very busy printing, binding and sending out Scriptures; and the volumes which they furnished in these years formed a very much greater number than they had expected the Society's plant ever to produce.

One curious result of this effort to supply every destitute

family in the land was the discovery that in a growing population a general supply must be renewed again and again. This means, of course, that there is no such thing as a permanent supply of all willing to use the Bible in such a country as the United States.   Immigrants arrive from abroad; children grow up and form new households; and settlers move into newly opened regions with more or less loss of books in the process.   Like an army on an enemy's soil the Bible Society's duty is perpetual vigilance, and its work is never done.

It is always an interesting question whether simple Bible distribution produces results among the people justifying the labour and the expense.   The country gains by such efforts because, as in this case, a great number of persons are brought under the influence of the Word of God who had not paid attention to it before.   This general supply added to the number of copies of the Scriptures in existence several hundreds of thousands.   By the distribution of these precious volumes among the people in different parts of the country the lamp of life was lighted in innumerable huts and houses along our northern and western and southern frontiers— houses which before this time had been without a wax taper to show the way out from moral darkness.   Numbers who wished the Bible but knew not where to get one were discovered; in this case the General Supply brought cheer to many a weary pilgrim in his journey through the world.   These results for the benefit of the country at large were not limited to regions near the centres of American civilisation.   Great numbers of Bibles were sent to parts of the country where no Auxiliary had ever been formed and to settlements of which the Society had never before heard.

It is sometimes said by those who are asked to contribute to Bible dissemination that " all who wish for the Bible can readily obtain one without the officious mediation of Bible Societies."   One of the great facts of Bible distribution is that multitudes of people who have never read the Bible and who have no wish for it are every year persuaded by the colporteurs of Bible Societies to read the Book and so are led little by little to yield to its influence for good.

This fact disposes of that objection which commonly arises from lack of knowledge and from the wish to excuse refusal of contributions. An incident of this General Supply in the state of Kentucky is a further illustration. The Bible Agent called at a house where the head of a family said that during the larger part of the last fourteen years he had been a member of the church, but he had never had a Bible in his house. His wife and even his children had often begged him when he went to town to bring back a Bible, but whenever he reached the town he found other uses for his money. He said that during all of this time had a Bible been offered to him at his house he would have bought it gladly, but that he would not ever have possessed a Bible had it not been brought to his house by an agent of the Bible Society.

Numbers of incidents coming to light during the two years of this supply show how this wonderful book changes the atmosphere of a home and a village where it is read. One old man in Maryland was apparently past hope of reform even though his allotted years had nearly come to an end. He was a bad man and a hard drinker. A Bible Agent offered him the Bible and urged him to take it and read it. Passing that way the next year he found this same man sober and leading an orderly life, happy because he had taken up the reading of the Bible. The influence of the work spreads slowly from neighbour to neighbour and from house to house. One of the local Bible Societies tells joyfully of a case where their agent had persuaded a woman that she needed to read the Bible. She read it and saw that she ought to lead a higher and nobler life. She cast in her lot with the church, and little by little through her influence her husband, a dissipated and worthless man, had his eyes opened and he also came into connection with the church. Because the Bible makes a silent but powerful appeal to conscience, men and women in many a town and village who have been corrupters of society have been changed into supporters of all good; their influence becoming an uplift in the whole neighbourhood. Such facts brought to light during this first general supply are not surprising, for Bible lovers know that such improvement of the race is what the Bible is for. But they confirm faith, and so prepare the servants of God for doing " greater things than these."

CHAPTER XIII

THE AUXILIARY SOCIETIES AT WORK

UNDERLYING all the activities of Bible Societies one sincere desire is the force which controls. This is the earnest wish to awaken men through the Bible to realisation of their utter dependence upon God. As we look back over the sixteen years of the Society's story, from 1816 to 1832, it becomes clear that this controlling wish gave life to the Auxiliaries, called out money for support of the work, took away from losses or changes among members of the staff any irreparable quality, and gave to the whole organisation a clearer view of its responsibilities both toward the supply of the people and toward the Book which was being sent forth.

At the end of the period of which the story has occupied us thus far, the band of eighty-four Auxiliary Societies in 1816 had become in 1832 a host of over seven hundred. In the general supply of the destitute in the United States, and in the decision to take up work abroad these Auxiliaries took an immense interest. Without their aid the American Bible Society could not have found its feet, could not have hopefully begun its great work, and could not have aroused the country to the need of a General Supply. The reports and other publications of Auxiliary Societies instructed as well as informed the people, even in so obvious and simple a truth as that subscribing to a Bible Society is virtually a new undertaking; an undertaking to labour in our Lord's vineyard.[1]

In New York City there were in 1832 three Auxiliary Bible Societies: the New York Female Bible Society formed

[1] See Seventh Report of the Virginia Bible Society, quoted in American Bible Society's Report, 1820, p. 105.

in 1816, the New York Marine Bible Society formed in
1817, and the Young Men's New York Bible Society formed
in 1823. The New York Female Bible Society has, at the
time of this writing, been active in its chosen field for almost 100 years. During its first sixteen years and within
the period over which we may now look back it made donations in money to the American Bible Society amounting to
about six thousand dollars. The New York Marine Bible
Society was active in providing with Scriptures the sailors
on ships in the harbour. During this early part of its service one tour of its Secretary along the coast eastward from
New York to Maine resulted in the formation of twenty-
three Marine Bible Societies at the various centres of shipping, in order that a friendly hand might be extended to
the sailors frequenting these ports.

As we have already mentioned, the New York Bible
Society founded in 1809 was practically merged in the
American Bible Society in 1816. Four of its officers and
ten of its Managers were called to the direction of the new
Society. The New York Bible Society continued a formal
existence as an Auxiliary until November, 1819. Then it
coalesced with the Auxiliary New York Bible Society
founded in 1813 and formed a new Society which asked
and received from the American Bible Society in 1820
recognition as an Auxiliary under the name New York
Bible Society. In September, 1823, this (second) New
York Bible Society recognised as Auxiliary to itself a new
Society formed of ardent young men under thirty years of
age and called the Young Men's New York Bible Society.
In 1827 the various ward Bible Societies which had been
planted by the second New York Bible Society were all
that remained of that institution, and in the spring of 1828
the Young Men's New York Bible Society having stated
to the American Bible Society that it wished to become
Auxiliary to it because of the dissolution of its parent Society, the Managers of the American Bible Society granted
the privileges of an Auxiliary to the Young Men's Society
(together with an outfit of two hundred Bibles and five
hundred Testaments) until it could formally change its
relations. In March, 1829, the constitution of the Young

Men's Society was formally modified to meet the Auxiliary requirements and this new member was received into the family of Auxiliaries of the American Bible Society. The Young Men's Bible Society was keenly interested in all city work. In 1831 the New York Marine Bible Society was absorbed by the Young Men's Society, which divided with the American Bible Society the considerable liabilities of the Marine Society.

The Young Men's Society now entered enthusiastically upon work in the city and harbour, with liberal aid in the form of grants of books from the American Bible Society. In 1839, having modified its constitution to remove the age limit of its members, it struck the words " Young Men's " from its name and so became the New York Bible Society, being the third Society of that name. It is still active in work for its old field in the Borough of Manhattan and what is now the Bronx; it has a worthy history; and many of its members have rendered invaluable services as Managers and officers to the American Bible Society. The only other Auxiliary now (1915) labouring in that field is the New York Female Bible Society, one of that small group of strong and active Societies whose Auxiliary connection dates from the very first year of the American Bible Society.

The total of the donations from Auxiliary Bible Societies to the Treasury of the American Bible Society during sixteen years, up to 1832, was $226,192. There were seven hundred and ten Bible Societies on the list of Auxiliaries at this time but three hundred and sixty-eight Societies only were givers; three hundred and thirty-two Societies not yet having acquired that grace. These contributions from Auxiliaries constituted about twenty-two per cent. of the whole receipts of the American Bible Society during the sixteen years. The total receipts, of course, included the proceeds of sales of books and amounted to $1,031,261. It is a matter of curious interest that only nine Societies in the whole Auxiliary list each contributed, during the sixteen years an aggregate of five thousand dollars or more in donations for the work of the national Society. Eight of these were organised before the American Bible Society, and the ninth was the New York Female Bible Society which came into existence in 1816.

Much anxiety was felt by the Board of Managers because many Auxiliary Societies did not immediately answer the expectations formed in the minds of the Managers. From the first implicit confidence was felt in their honour, and whenever an accident or a shipwreck was reported by one of them as having caused the loss of books, the national Society like a kind parent made good their loss. The Board of Managers in their report of 1828 testified that while credit for books purchased had been given on request to Auxiliary Societies in every part of the Union without further security than that which springs from religious principle, scarcely a dollar had ever been lost to the Treasury. The Societies paid their debts sooner or later without legal obligation. This fact is a commentary on the principles of the Book which the Societies circulate.

It is right to make sure that the obstacles encountered by these local Bible Societies are recognised. The Auxiliary Bible Societies in some of the Western states had a path to travel which was strewn with rocks and thorns compared with that of workers in the older parts of the country. An agent in Missouri, explaining in December, 1832, the long delays in finishing the General Supply of the destitute, pointed out that Missouri was divided into thirty-three counties; some of which were equal in area to the whole state of Connecticut, the most of the counties being larger than Rhode Island. For an agent to visit every county would require of him about two thousand miles of travel; but to watch over the men visiting single houses in all this area of sixty-three thousand square miles, the agent must face a task beyond the ability of any human being.

Besides these natural difficulties besetting many of the Auxiliary Societies there were other causes of weakness among them. Some finding it difficult to remit funds to New York, hoarded them instead of sending in their surplus; some invested such funds with the idea of increasing their donation, but through errors of judgment or the unsettled state of the finances of the country, they lost the whole amount.

The financial condition of some of the states is illustrated by the circumstance that Auxiliaries from one district west of the Mississippi wrote to the Board inquiring whether it would receive shipments of corn and wheat in lieu of money; it being difficult to get drafts on New York.

Travelling Agents rendered effective aid to Auxiliaries during the special effort to supply the destitute in the United States; and later, in view of the growing Bible work abroad, did good service in focussing the enthusiasm of the people upon the duty of giving money for the Bible Cause. The members of the Board were cheered by receiving contributions like that from a minister in New York State, the Rev. L. H. Halsey, who sent a little more than seventeen dollars as a collection taken among the people on the Fourth of July; he thinking that such a contribution to the American Bible Society would be the most sure application of patriotism. The Agents reported many similar illustrations of a widespread popular feeling. A little girl in Virginia proposed to eat no butter for a month so that she might get the twenty-five cents necessary to make her an annual member of a Female Bible Society. One of the Agents was speaking on the needs of the world in one of the upper counties in Virginia when a poor woman in the audience whispered to her husband: "I have fifty cents saved to buy coffee with; it is hid in the blue pitcher on the shelf in the cupboard. Go home and get it, and make haste back lest the good man be gone. I will do without coffee a little while longer until these people get the Gospel among them." Rev. Dr. Plummer of Virginia in telling this story, pointed out a great truth. "The treasury of the Lord," he said, "is the hearts of his people. Get them rightly affected and to a good object they will give all, if necessary." With such a spirit abroad in many parts of the country it is not surprising that the receipts of the Bible Society during the years 1829 to 1832 when the General Supply was in progress, amounted to more than three hundred and sixty thousand dollars; the average of the annual receipts being more than double those in any year previous to 1827.

It was during these years that the Society was gradually increasing its somewhat haphazard shipments of Scriptures abroad. Besides grants of Bibles for South America and the Islands of the West Indies including Porto Rico, something was done for Indians in Canada and in Surinam; and one package of Spanish Scriptures was sent to the Philippine Islands by a gentleman engaged in the South American trade who was going to that almost unknown part of the world. The languages of the books which the Society printed or otherwise provided for labourers among aliens at home or abroad in the first sixteen years of its effort numbered twenty.

When the Emperor of Russia dies the sad event is no sooner certain than the crowds in the streets may be heard shouting "Long Live the Emperor!" with every manifestation of joy. The feeling of the populace is not necessarily careless as to the death of the Emperor. It is merely signifying in its own way the fact that the empire is not dead, but is strong and capable as ever. Something of the same conditions obtain in a Society that outlives the generation in which it is formed. President Boudinot, President John Jay had passed away, and now in July, 1831, President Richard Varick reached the end of his allotted years. His career had been useful as well as picturesque. In the early years of his life he had thrown his soul into his duties as a soldier. After serving with credit throughout the Revolutionary War, he became a most energetic Attorney General of New York State and in 1787 he was elected Mayor of New York City. Later he became prominent in a number of works of benevolence. During the time of his connection with the American Bible Society he was one of the parishioners of Rev. Dr. J. B. Romeyn, and he served the Society as Treasurer, Vice-President, and then for four years as President.

In December of the same year the Hon. John Cotton Smith of Sharon, Connecticut, a Vice-President of the

Society, was elected President. Mr. Smith's father during fifty years was pastor of the Congregational Church at Sharon; and he himself had served his state as member of the Legislature, Judge of the Supreme Court, Lieutenant Governor, and Governor. He was the first President of the Connecticut Bible Society, and was President of the A. B. C. F. M. for several years while serving the American Bible Society in the same capacity.

In looking over the list of changes in the staff of the Society during its first sixteen years one is surprised at their number. In 1825 the Hon. John Quincy Adams, a Vice-President of the Society, became President of the United States. This did not diminish his interest in the Society which was shown in the letter accepting office as Vice-President in 1817, when he was Secretary of State. He then wrote: " In accepting the appointment I am duly sensible to the honour conferred upon me by this invitation to join the assembly of those whose voices in unison with the heavenly host at the birth of the Saviour, proclaim good tidings of great joy to all people." While President of the United States his duties in Washington prevented his attending the Annual Meetings of the Society, but he was careful to write his regrets with his own hand, and a number of these interesting autographs are among the archives of the Society to-day.

In 1827 Vice-Presidents Thomas Worthington of Ohio, William Tilghman, Chief Justice of the state of Pennsylvania, William Phillips, a well-known educational philanthropist and a warm friend and supporter of the American Bible Society from the very first day of its existence, passed away. In 1828 Governor De Witt Clinton died. Governor Clinton as Vice-President of the Society was a familiar figure in the Board room and in the Annual Meetings, as while Governor of the State he frequently came to New York to preside at these meetings. On the front of the Chamber of Commerce in New York one may see Governor Clinton's statue, with Alexander Hamilton on his right, and on his left John Jay, the second President of the Bible Society, whose love for the Bible was the key to his successful public life. In 1829 Vice-President Bushrod

Washington of Virginia, a nephew of General George Washington, a soldier of the Revolution, and a Justice of the Supreme Court of the United States, came to the end of his life. The same year General Matthew Clarkson passed away, profoundly respected for good works wherever he was known, and most faithful to his duties as Vice-President of the Bible Society by presiding at almost all of the Board meetings up to the time of his death. In 1830 Vice-President Andrew Kirkpatrick of New Jersey died, and in 1832 Colonel Robert Troup of New York finished his long and useful life. The vacancies caused by death among the Vice-Presidents were filled by the choice of W. W. Woolsey, for eight years Treasurer of the Society; of John Pintard, the sturdy Huguenot who was the Society's first Recording Secretary; and worthily to fill the place of Bushrod Washington, the Honourable John Marshall, Chief Justice of the United States, who was removed by death in 1835.

Two of the Managers passed away during this period. Mr. Divie Bethune died in 1824 full of good works and remembered by all charitable institutions in the city; and Dr. John Watts, who died in 1830. The Recording Secretary, John Pintard, resigned in 1832 and was succeeded by Mr. R. F. Winslow. In 1825 the Rev. S. S. Woodhull resigned his office as Secretary for Domestic Correspondence on the 7th of April. On the same day he was re-elected with two others, the Rev. Thomas McAuley, D.D., LL.D., Professor of Mathematics in Union College, a man of varied scholarship and an eloquent preacher, together with Rev. Chas. Sommers, preacher of the South Baptist Church in New York City; the understanding being that they might work collectively or separately in different departments of the work. It is well enough, perhaps, to repeat the circumstance that the Secretaries were men occupied by their own professional duties who received no remuneration from the American Bible Society. The Treasurer of the Society, W. W. Woolsey, after eight years of faithful service for which he received no remuneration, resigned in 1827. Mr. Woolsey was elected a Vice-President of the Society. Mr. John Adams, a member of the Board of

Managers, was elected Treasurer, but resigned on finding the work too heavy. Mr. Garrat N. Bleecker, also a member of the Board of Managers, was then chosen to be Treasurer with a salary of one thousand dollars a year; but he too found the work too engrossing and resigned after three months, being followed in this office by Mr. Hubert Van Wagenen, also a member of the Board of Managers.

In the latter half of this period the Board of Managers had to meet the question of issuing Bibles containing the Apocrypha. Quite early in the history of the British and Foreign Bible Society the Societies which it had promoted in various parts of Europe and aided by grants in money, printed Bibles in various languages which contained the books of the Apocrypha either grouped together at the end of the canonical books, or scattered among those books as in the Septuagint. When Scriptures printed in England were sent to the Societies on the continent, they met strong objections because they did not contain the books of the Apocrypha. As early as 1812 these objections were made in louder tones because the British and Foreign Bible Society asked the European Societies to omit the Apocrypha in printing Scriptures with the money of the British Society. Protests arose and finally the British Society decided that it would not object to the use of the Apocrypha provided the expense of printing it was not paid by the grants from England. This satisfied the Continental Societies since they could get the Scriptures from England in sheets and bind them with the Apocrypha printed elsewhere. Upon this a storm arose among the people at home which was not easily quieted. In 1827 the British and Foreign Bible Society decided not to grant Scriptures in sheets and unbound, and later, in accordance with the wish of the majority in Great Britain, it made drastic rules to the effect that its money must never be used in any way to circulate Scriptures with the Apocrypha. The Scottish Auxiliary Societies considered this action as proof that the Committee of the British and Foreign Bible Society up to this time had not acted sincerely and demanded that all members of the Committee be removed from office to make way for more trustworthy men. Very naturally, this demand was not granted and

nearly all the Scottish Auxiliaries withdrew from the support of the British and Foreign Bible Society and later
formed the Scottish National Bible Society.

It was impossible that so much heat could be generated
by this discussion in England without warming feelings in
America. To make a long story short, in 1827 the Board
of Managers voted that thereafter no books containing the
Apocrypha might be sent out from the depository of the
Society. It was the presence of the Apocrypha in the
Bibles circulated in South America (in the version of
Father Scio) that gave those Bibles free circulation among
the very suspicious Roman Catholic clergy. Under the
vote of the Board respecting the Apocrypha the plates containing the Apocrypha were removed from the Society's
set and all editions of the Scio version printed after this
edict were without the Apocrypha. This caused, for some
little time, an interruption of sales in Latin America; but
since the books contained the canonical books according to
the Scio version, the Bibles of the Society were not entirely
proscribed, while the Testaments were circulated as usual.

CHAPTER XIV

GO IN THIS THY MIGHT

An incident of the year 1823 was the arrival at the Bible House in New York of a copy of the Holy Bible in Chinese translated by Rev. Dr. Morrison of the London Missionary Society, assisted by Rev. Dr. Milne. This book, a donation to the Biblical Library, was a sort of revelation to the warm-hearted lovers of the Bible who directed the affairs of the American Bible Society. The Holy Bible actually translated and printed in the language of the vast, hostile, self-complacent Chinese Empire seemed a modern miracle and a concrete illustration of the gift of tongues. Looking at that book one would call to mind its character as a missionary's enterprise; the tremendous labour involved; the long, intense study; the struggles to overcome prejudice on the part of helpers; the great learning which enabled the translator to use the Hebrew and Greek originals for a text; the utter forgetfulness of self; the sturdy determination and faith which persisted through all those years of the translation work. This was indeed an illustration of devotion to the Saviour, wherein the servant gives himself up hoping that something of his work may help to complete that which his Master began upon earth. The sight of this book representing for the Chinese a new era, and for the Christian church an evidence that the martyr spirit yet exists, must have had influence in impelling the men of the Bible House to meditate upon what great things for God they could undertake.

Even while the great effort to supply all the destitute in the United States was in progress, the Bible Society looked abroad. Missionaries of the American Board in Ceylon and in the Sandwich Islands had asked and received grants in aid of printing and distributing the Scriptures, in the one case in Tamil, and in the other in Hawaiian. Because Americans residing in Paris asked support for the Protestant Bible Society of Paris, through them the Board had made grants for France.

In 1827 the various influences inclining the Board to extend its effort to foreign lands as suggested by the Second Article of the Constitution acquired force. From India came a little suggestion which penetrated even careless minds and bore fruit. It was the simple question, ought not the American Bible Society to supply Bibles needed by American Missions? The question answered itself. The need of Bibles in American Missions abroad, other things being equal, can best be supplied with Scriptures from the home source. In the case of translations, rules of interpretation should control which are usual with the missionaries who are to distribute the books. In so small things as printing and binding, questions of taste can best be decided by canons common to all educated Americans.

The Bible is as essential to the missionary as education or as clothing. Parents do not let their children beg for food or clothes even from respected and beloved neighbours. When rightly viewed the missionary's need of the Bible is the need of the churches who support him. American enterprises in the service of God should be sustained in all of their departments by American benevolence. Culture in giving for God's sake comes to naught if other nations are called upon to pay any serious part of the cost of the missions which our churches claim as their own. It became quite clear, in an instant as it were, that American churches have as their privilege and their birthright the supply of their missions by the American Bible Society; not for its sake, but for their own.

This little suggestion from India was put into the minds of the Secretaries in New York by learning that American missionaries among the Mahrattas near Bombay had applied to the British and Foreign Bible Society for aid in printing the Scriptures which they had translated for their own mission work. About the same time the Greeks were attracting attention by their determined struggle for independence. In 1827 their independence had been secured by the coalition of European Powers which annihilated the Turkish fleet at Navarino. Rev. Jonas King, a missionary of the American Board in Syria, immediately went to Greece to see what could be done in the way of Christian comfort for the Grecian warriors. It was not long before he was appealing for modern Greek Testaments to distribute, for the common people cannot understand the ancient tongue. The Board granted him $500, and in 1828 $1,000 more to buy Testaments in Modern Greek from the British and Foreign Bible Society; and thus the Board advanced in the direction of adopting the rule to supply American Missions with the Scriptures which they needed. In 1830 the Rev. Dr. Rufus Anderson of the American Board, writing on the need of a better version of the New Testament in Modern Greek which he wished that the American Bible Society would prepare, said to Secretary Brigham: " My dear brother, this is a work worthy of your Society and I feel extremely anxious that your Society should do it. It will bring blessings upon us from many ready to perish in that country. Let us have a memorial in Greece! " [1]

About the same time one of the American missionaries in Ceylon speaking about the need of more Tamil Scriptures than they could get, wrote to the Secretaries in New York: " The people are within the limits of the grant made by the King of Zion and as a channel of communication between them and you is widely open they are become your neighbours. Living waters from your Society may flow in a direct course to this distant land and here by the missionaries upon the spot those waters will, permit me to assure you, be guided to the very plants which we believe are destined to become trees of righteousness." [2]

We have already spoken of the decision of the Board to send an Agent to South America. This action did not commit the Society to a definite commencement of work in foreign lands. Latin America was barely beyond the home limits; a field for which responsibility could not be denied. Moreover, the habit of adopting policies approved by the British and Foreign Bible Society doubtless weighed for

[1] Report of the American Bible Society, 1830, p. 73.
[2] Report of the American Bible Society, 1828, p. 55.

something in the decision to send a man to South America just as that Society had done. But the decision was another step in the direction of a recognised policy of foreign work for the Society. The new path diverged only a little from the one already trodden, although when followed it led far afield.

Another force which influenced the American Bible Society at this time, curiously enough, sprang from the enthusiasm aroused by the General Supply at home. There was in the hearts of Christians a deep yearning to see the influence of the Bible widely felt to the glory of God. When the plan to supply all the destitute in the United States was successfully carried through, it was a revelation of possibilities to all warm-hearted Christians. Like any discovery in physical science, once made known it led many persons to make new applications of the principle. People now thought of Bible work abroad as something which might be undertaken; therefore it must be done.

In July, 1831, the Rev. Josiah Brewer, missionary of the American Board at Smyrna, Turkey (father of the late Justice D. J. Brewer of the United States Supreme Court, a Vice-President of the Society), wrote a letter from the island of Patmos in which he said: that here where St. John saw the visions of the Apocalypse the thought had come into his mind, since the work of supplying every family in the United States was so nearly accomplished " foreign parts may justly claim a larger share of the attention of the Society. Why should you not then, as the next great work, undertake to furnish with a copy of the word of God every family dwelling where were the churches mentioned in the New Testament and those especially to whom its holy Epistles were addressed ? "

Mr. Brewer saw the difficulties in the way of such a scheme but leaving out of account the Muslims, the Jews, the bigoted and the illiterate, there would still remain some tens of thousands who have succeeded to the soil, the sky, and the oppressions which belonged to the first Christians, while they have a very imperfect knowledge of the divine guidance which the early Christians enjoyed.

Great interest was always aroused among the people in

the United States by reference to missionary work in pagan lands. One agent wrote: " The topic of sending Bibles to the heathen almost invariably arrests the attention of the audience and creates a deathlike silence in the building." Something of this effect was the result of the publication of Mr. Brewer's suggestion. Like a cry from those ancient churches it stirred the hearts and touched the consciences of the people. In planning for benevolent work Christians throughout the land would find a sacred joy in reaching out their arms afar to embrace destitute nations.

A little later the missionaries of the American Board in the Sandwich Islands needed for printing on their own press an edition of twenty thousand Hawaiian New Testaments about five thousand dollars. The mission in Ceylon needed about five thousand dollars to bring out a new edition of the Tamil Bible. The missionaries among the Mahrattas in the region of Bombay, India, needed a new edition of the Marathi Bible that would cost about five thousand dollars; the first edition having been printed at the expense of the British and Foreign Bible Society. About the same time the Rev. E. C. Bridgman, missionary of the American Board at Canton, China, wrote to Dr. Milnor urging help from the American Bible Society for printing the Bible for China, whose enormous population comprises about one-third part of the human race. " Probably," he said, " no one enterprise of equal extent and importance can ever engage the attention of the American or any other Bible Society." [1] Then a letter from Russia showed that Bible circulation in the great empire promised great results. At the same time missionaries among the American Indians (then still classed as foreign nations), begged for the publication of Scriptures in the Ojibwa and Mohawk languages.

These appeals placed the Board of Managers in a somewhat serious dilemma. The Society was in debt and that debt must be extinguished by economy and, if possible, by an increase of income. General Supply of the destitute families in the United States was not yet finished. In Alabama and Missouri, and the territories of Arkansas and

[1] Report of the American Bible Society, 1832, p. 58.

Florida less than half of the destitute had yet been reached. Moreover the promise must be fulfilled to supply Sunday School children with Bibles or Testaments; in itself no small undertaking.

The first of the items just named seemed to bar progress. That is to say, the Society being in debt could not spend money upon new enterprises until the debt was paid off. These calls for help from the ends of the earth would move hearts of stone, but the common sense of business men protested against appropriation of money while people had deliberately left the Treasury empty. There were those whose missionary zeal thought that to refuse these appeals showed lack of faith. If some urged the danger of beginning a new enterprise without visible means of completing it, others insisted on the danger of weak faith. The situation of the Board of Managers so far as means were concerned was something like that of the officers of a steamer whose coal bunkers have been emptied and swept out when five hundred miles from the shore.

The Board was, in fact, beginning to feel the burden which continually hampers Managers of every missionary enterprise. Mr. Brigham, the youngest of the Secretaries, had been a missionary of the American Board. Naturally his sympathies were closely connected with the needs of that Society. Moreover, having travelled among people abroad who knew nothing of the Bible, he knew both the grievous quality of their needs and the precious fruits of Bible distribution among them. Nevertheless, with all his faith and his enthusiasm he, too, felt restricted by inability to see the way out of a maze. Yet, in the words of Rev. G. W. Bethune of Albany at this time, " The bread of the soul ought to be as common as the bread of the body."

To the Bible Society, in short, its sixteenth year was a year of crisis. It had already distributed Scriptures in foreign lands; in 1831, however, duty to aliens presented itself to the Board and to the friends of the Bible in America with an appeal to conscience as irresistible as that which the vision on the Jaffa housetop left with St. Peter. The Managers in their report say, " The voice of Providence is now speaking on this subject in a manner so striking and distinct that few can but hear and regard it. The Society seems to have reached an interesting crisis; a point from which its charities must take a wider range and flow in a deeper and broader stream." [1]

The difficulties of the Managers did not arise from any attempt to carry on a work too large for the country to bear. They were like men among flinty rocks containing nuggets of gold, who have no hammer that can break the rocks. There is a certain advantage in such experiences. By means of such difficulties Christian workers are held back from the folly of self-confidence. Enthusiastic missionaries may often feel that self-sacrificing energy is the principal thing; but our Lord places prayer before this when He exhorts men to pray and not to faint. It is true that Christian workers must take risks, and perhaps their Master expects them to encounter the risk of failure in order that they may be led more constantly to remember their dependence upon Him. However this may be, through such experiences of inability on account of lack of means to do what ought to be done men learn the axiom that in work ordained of God no check can be a permanent check.

Little by little light came to the perplexed Board of Managers. In the very beginning of 1831 the Massachusetts Auxiliary sent a donation of five hundred dollars to the Treasury, signified its approval of any efforts which the Society might take to raise money within the field of the Massachusetts Society; and more than this, deposited $5,000 in the Treasury as a loan, the interest on which should be five per cent., payable in books. After Mr. Brewer's proposal from the island of Patmos had time to become known and be thoroughly grasped, the New Jersey Bible Society, by an entirely undesigned coincidence which fitted in very happily with the wishes of the Board, wrote to say that it had decided to raise in New Jersey during the year $5,000 for printing the New Testament in Hawaii. Toward the end of the year the Philadelphia Bible Society (not Auxiliary) announced a decision to raise $10,000 for printing Bibles in foreign lands; either in the Sandwich Islands

[1] Annual Report, 1832, p. 34.

or in any other needy region which its Board of Managers might select. A little later the Washington County, N. Y., Bible Society pledged to the American Bible Society $1,000 for foreign work. These good people, without consultation, all seemed to be moved by the sentiment expressed by Robert Denniston of the Orange County, N. Y., Auxiliary, when he said: "Because of the silent but incalculable control of the Bible over public opinion, all American citizens should support the American Bible Society." [1]

And so it came to pass that when a committee of which Dr. Milnor was chairman reported upon the general situation, it called attention to these facts: that the supply of Scriptures for foreign lands was no new thing — the Society had expended during fifteen years $23,133 for this purpose; that the General Supply at home would probably make no further great demands upon the Treasury; while the interest in foreign missions was sufficient to ensure liberal contributions for work abroad. The Board thereupon adopted resolutions to the effect that, relying upon Divine favour and upon the good-will of Auxiliaries and friends of the Society to furnish adequate means, it would endeavour during the next year to send $15,000 to the Missions of the American Board in Bombay, Ceylon and Sandwich Islands; that it would print as soon as possible for use in Greece twenty thousand Testaments in Modern Greek; and that, within the year, it would appropriate and pay to the Baptist Missionary Convention $5,000 toward printing Dr. Judson's version of the Bible in Burmese.

Following this brave utterance the Society, at its sixteenth Anniversary, May 10th, 1832, formally declared that "it is the imperious duty of those connected with this Society and its Auxiliaries to furnish liberal contributions for the purpose of promoting Bible distribution abroad as Divine Providence opens the way."

This momentous decision would not bear fruit which many of those who united in it could live to see, but their faith was sound that through this action deliverance would

[1] Monthly Extracts, July, 1832.

gladden thousands now hopelessly enslaved by the powers of evil. Like Gideon when trusting God he led his little band against the hosts of Midian, the Society had heard the voice of God saying, as it waited on Him, " Go in this thy might."

THIRD PERIOD 1832-1841

CHAPTER XV

A MOST CHRISTIAN ENTHUSIASM

DURING the year 1832 the Board was surprised and delighted to find that the debt of $22,000 with which it commenced the year was gradually being paid off. It received $4,190 from legacies, and $41,800 in donations for the general work or for special enterprises abroad.

One of the donations is worthy of special notice. It was a contribution of four hundred and fifty dollars from a Protestant Episcopal clergyman of Yonkers, New York, who during four years had given to the American Bible Society one thousand and twenty dollars. These generous gifts were taken from a benevolent fund for which the donor had set apart one-tenth of his salary and portions of any fees which he received for various services; the incident illustrating a fact which our people sometimes forget, namely, that by setting apart a fixed proportion of their income at the time when it is received, they offer their Lord regularly the worship which they owe. Then the decision as to apportioning their gifts of benevolence, having relation to a fund that is already the Lord's is made without pain or anxiety. The Board of Managers, as a token of unfeigned respect for this generous donor, constituted him a Director for Life of the American Bible Society.

The home usages of the people of the United States were still very simple at this time in matters of dress, food and amusements; in fact, the home life of professing Christians very largely centred about the Church and its interests. The decision to take up work abroad in a serious manner appealed directly to the eagerness of the Christian people for the advance of the Kingdom.

Lands ruled by paganism and Mohammedanism were known as blighted by systematic oppression of the poor.

111

Religious superstition seemed to have united with selfish greed to grind the faces of the poor, whom ignorance made helpless.   The missionary impulse to aid people in such straits now resembled the great surges of a reformation. Wherever the appeal was heard the people were deeply stirred and they were in haste to see the whole world profiting by the gospel of Christ.

Meantime manifold activities at the Bible House continued.   The Bible Society laid its hand upon the shores of the Pacific by sending a grant of books to a colony at the mouth of the Columbia River in Oregon.   It engaged in " foreign " work among the Cherokee Indians.   It sent Scriptures to Java to be used by the American Board's missionaries, Lyman and Munson, who, however, had been killed by the natives before the books reached their destination.   It sent a small grant of Scriptures to Labrador where good Archdeacon Wix was looking after the spiritual welfare of the fishermen dear to Dr. Grenfell's heart to-day. In Texas an Auxiliary Bible Society had been formed and received recognition and grants.   Correspondence with foreign missionaries brought many calls for large, if not lavish, grants of money.   Dr. Gutzlaff writing from China about this time, gave this warning: " You may rest assured that we will drain your funds, for we have a large nation before us and if only the hundredth Chinaman was to get a Bible from you, a ten years' income of your Society would not be sufficient to defray expenses."   Such a sentence must have brought a cold chill to the veins of many who looked for a quick triumphal march of the Kingdom through the world.

Many persons felt that the decision of the Society to aid American Missions abroad while a real advance, was not adequate.   It was a cautious step rather than a swinging stride toward a fixed goal.   Thousands in pagan lands trembled on the edge of the grave from which the Bible could show them a way of escape.   The Society had supplied every family in the United States within two years' time; why should it not be an instrument for the prompt delivery of the ignorant and terror-stricken everywhere?   Mr. Brewer's proposal to accomplish in a definite time the supply of all families in the Seven Churches of Asia seemed reasonable enough, and the adoption of that proposal would be a wise beginning. The Rev. Dr. William S. Plummer of Virginia voiced a general opinion by suggesting that it would be possible to supply all destitute families in the world in twenty years, if a Christian enthusiasm in all Western lands could be aroused to move all Bible Societies in the world in pursuit of the one noble object.

The Board of Managers saw difficulties in the way of an undertaking to supply all the world in twenty years; but on the other hand it was not willing to do anything that might diminish the enthusiasm of Auxiliary Societies like that of Petersburg with which Dr. Plummer was connected or that of Virginia which heartily supported his proposal. An Auxiliary without an object to call out its energy is sure to lose efficiency. So it set about preparing resolutions which would engage the Society in world-wide Bible distribution. It invited Dr. Plummer to visit New York for conference respecting the resolutions to be offered to the Society in May, 1833. Dr. Plummer brought to the Board a draft of a resolution which definitely committed the American Bible Society to an effort to supply all the destitute in the world within twenty years. Letters from distinguished men like Dr. Cauldwell, President of the University of North Carolina, Dr. Baxter, President of Union Theological Seminary of Virginia, Bishop Moore, President of the Virginia Bible Society, and from distinguished clergymen in Philadelphia, Baltimore and Princeton, New Jersey, urged the adoption of the twenty years' limit for the supply of the whole world.

As a result of somewhat long discussions in a Special Committee and in the Board, Dr. Plummer's definite limitation to twenty years of the supply of the world was, with his consent, taken out of the resolution to be proposed to the Society. At the Annual Meeting, May 9, 1833, after addresses which insisted on the enlargement of the foreign operations of the Society, Secretary McAuley presented a series of resolutions in which was concentrated the essence of the feeling so generally prevalent; namely, that just as is done when any much needed public work is to be con-

structed, a time limit ought to be fixed within which all
the destitute in the world shall be supplied with the Bible.
To this end the resolutions instructed the Board of Managers to confer with other Bible Societies and friends of the
Bible cause, engaging them to co-operate in an attempt to
supply the Bible to all destitute inhabitants of the globe
within a definite period.

The emotion caused by these resolutions as adopted can
hardly be imagined. Few of the leaders in the discussion
had deeply considered the difficulties in the way of such a
supply of the whole world. But these resolutions took the
Bible Society far beyond the position of helper to American
Missions abroad, pledging it to independent responsibility
for the distribution of Scriptures wherever destitution existed.

The Board now sent out a pamphlet containing the resolutions adopted by the Society with the letters and addresses which supported them. The pamphlet was hardly
so concrete as the appeal sent to Israel by Saul in behalf of
Jabesh, but it had a similar effect. It was given the widest
distribution through the religious press, the educational institutions, the Life Directors and Life Members of the
Bible Society, and the Auxiliary Societies all over the country. The Virginia Bible Society issued once more a moving appeal telling its supporters that " all these things stir
men to action. The deputation of Flathead Indians fifteen
hundred miles to St. Louis to ask for the Book of Life is
a command as truly as the cry of the man from Macedonia." The Methodist Episcopal Conferences in several
places responded with confidence and enthusiasm. Many
denominations were thrilled as in a great revival. Replies
came to the Board of Managers from fifteen ecclesiastical
bodies and thirty-five Auxiliary Societies insisting upon the
supply of the whole world within twenty years. The one
feeling in every quarter seemed to be readiness to face any
sacrifice, because when God calls for service great sacrifice
alone can satisfy the demands of conscience.

The missionary idea was rooted in the hearts of the people; its execution seemed to them to demand haste. This
was the meaning of the persistent cry for finishing the work

in twenty years, which cynics of our day might class with a baby's cry with outstretched hands for the moon. Rev. Dr. Plummer wrote in December, 1833, to the Board of Managers a new appeal for the claim that every family in the world can certainly be supplied with Bibles in twenty years. The greatest difficulty, if not the only difficulty, seemed to be that of providing the necessary money; but his enthusiasm was at a high tide and carried him over even this difficulty. " Shall such noble causes as your own," he asked, " be forever compelled to add up a few scores of thousands per annum and no more, while one single horse race in the United States gets three hundred thousand dollars?" Dr. Plummer estimated the population of the world at eight hundred million, and the total of families to be supplied at one hundred and thirty million. This would mean a cost of one hundred and thirty million dollars in twenty years, or six and a half cents apiece each year to raise six and a half million dollars per year. But, he stated, the cost would be less than this. Many Bibles would be paid for by those who received them. Moreover, some families would entirely refuse the Bible, so they should be left out of account. Furthermore, commercial publishers sell a great many Bibles at such a time, for experience shows that every Bible distribution increases the sales of those who print the Bible for profit. There could be no difficulty in raising the money save cupidity, selfishness and sloth so glaring as to make the Christian world blush with shame.

This appeal seemed to many Christians in America to spring from facts quite incontrovertible. Just as every family in the United States was supplied in two or three years by the American Bible Society alone, so every family in the world might be supplied in twenty years by all the Bible Societies in concerted effort. The weakness of the people swayed by such a proposal was their inability to see beyond the limits of their own country. To the masses English was the only intelligible language of the world. The people knew very little indeed of the vast expanses to be travelled; of the strange sounds encountered in the speech of every country reached; of the illiteracy which prevents the masses in pagan lands from reading their own languages.

It was quite impossible for people in the United States to realise that a Christian Bible Agent entering a purely Mohammedan country at that time, might easily suffer death merely because of a religious animosity. Nor could they imagine that a stranger going into some countries without knowledge of the local language would be killed as being, of course, an enemy. Moreover, no one outside of the highest institutions of learning could challenge Dr. Plummer's figures. When his vigorous imagination interpreted his declaration that " the estimates of faith are the only basis on which we are justified in acting in the affairs of our royal Master, Jesus Christ," there was no more to be said.

The Board could not disregard the almost unanimous feeling of its impatient supporters; yet under the restraint of its own calm judgment it quietly waited for the opinion of the other Bible Societies. Meanwhile various influences acting upon the business world suggested delay and deliberation. The nullification trouble in South Carolina took place in 1832. The Compromise Tariff was already causing some disturbance among commercial houses, and President Jackson's removal of government deposits from the banks in different parts of the country threw a warning shadow over financial circles.

The answers from the British and Foreign Bible Society and the French and Foreign Bible Society were decisive. The last named Society warmly approved the spirit of the proposal sent out by the American Society and heartily favoured a general appeal for funds to press on the work; but its cautious conclusion was that it should not commit itself to complete the work in a fixed time. The Committee of the British and Foreign Bible Society was also fraternally kind in its treatment of a proposal which it must have regarded almost as due to the zeal of youth and inexperience. It pointed out several points which should be considered. People now accessible may become otherwise at any moment. Calculation as to the number of versions of Scripture which will be necessary, or of the time that will be required for making them was, as yet, quite impossible. To supply every family throughout the world would involve a gratuitous distribution exceeding the ability of all the Bible Societies; and this opinion was based upon years of experience among the half-clad natives of the Far East. For these reasons the Committee of the British Society decided that the multiplication of agents to distribute the Bible is not a duty so long as the prospects of their work are entirely undefined.

The plan to supply Bibles to all the destitute families in the world within twenty years had disappeared like a fog before a gale. Dr. Plummer was invited to come to New York, and under the circumstances readily agreed that the time limit for the supply of the world must be given up. The matter necessarily came before the Annual Meeting. There one of the Secretaries, Rev. Dr. S. H. Cone, moved, Rev. Dr. Plummer seconded, and Rev. Mr. Winslow of the American Board's Mission in India supported a resolution to the effect that the Society ought to aim to supply the destitute in all the world *in the shortest possible time,* and that all other Bible Societies should be invited to strive for the same object.

More than a year after this decision contributions were received from different parts of the country for Bible distribution abroad, conditioned upon the union of all Bible Societies to supply the whole world in twenty years. The hearts of the people had been moved. They saw the duty of giving to others the Book which they found precious themselves. Even the self-seeking, hearing the discussion of motives for doing this work without delay, had some appreciation of the value of noble self-sacrifice in such a cause and joined their contributions with those of their neighbours. The principle that America is bound to do its share in supplying Bibles to the world had pervaded the churches as the sweet perfume of lilies pervades a house. It was with much difficulty that the Board of Managers could make people believe that the work could not be finished in twenty years, and it is to the credit of those who sent donations limited by that condition that in general they did not recall their gifts on being told that the condition could not be fulfilled.

This Christian enthusiasm persisted although directed into more practical channels, for it was rooted in love for Christ and devotion to His work.   The sending out of the Book in different languages could proceed with more certainty when freed from limitations of haste and hurry.   The great object of the Society and of its warm-hearted supporters was to increase the circulation of the Bible.   What that means David Abeel, the American missionary, had explained at the Anniversary of the British and Foreign Bible Society.   He said, in effect, " There is a missionary who can go where I cannot; who can do what I cannot.   He is not a Churchman; he is not a Dissenter.   He is not a Calvinist; he is not an Armenian.   He is not an American, nor an Englishman, nor a Scotchman, nor a Hollander.   He seems to hate sects and many of the most prominent sects he never even mentions.   That great missionary is the Bible!"

CHAPTER XVI

RESPONSIBILITIES FOLLOWING A GREAT DECISION

DEVOTION to God's service is an essential to progress, as simple and as sweeping in its demands as loyalty to military service. In history, as commonly written, the sword and more complicated instruments of slaughter outrank many other forces. The arrest of attention and the control of men by the still, small voice of God when the overturnings of the warrior have come to an end receive scant attention. We must bear in mind, however, that in the period of which we write that voice was heard. It was a period teeming with events, mysteriously related, whose importance becomes more clear as the world grows older.

In England the year 1832 brought the Reform Bill with its vindication of the right of franchise, and 1833 saw the abolition of slavery in the colonies; an event which later became a solid ground for moral pressure upon the United States during the long struggle over the slavery question. In 1837 Queen Victoria, that true and noble woman, came to the throne. In Spain, 1833 saw the beginning of the Carlist War, and thus in 1834 was brought about the abolition of the Spanish Inquisition, a revolution whose effect upon liberty of conscience was felt throughout the world. In 1840 there was war between Great Britain and China. It was a war of which the motives cannot, perhaps, bear much investigation, but which began to rend the rock of Chinese ignorance and prejudice; so giving opportunity for Christianity to find a foothold in the vast empire.

In the United States in 1832 New England echoed the appeals of Wilberforce and his associates by establishing the first anti-slavery society; and during this same period, when churches throughout the country were giving freely to religious enterprises, friends of science outside of the churches were also moved to give, and in 1833 Girard College was endowed, and in 1835 the Smithsonian Institution. In 1836 Mexico, the heir of great Spanish lands, had to yield a part when Texas gained independence, and vainly begged admission to the Union. It was in this same period that one of the greatest steps toward a closer relation between nations was gained by the invention of Morse's electric telegraph in 1837.

With the decision for extension abroad which the American Bible Society adopted in this same period, are associated not only improvements, advantages and progress, but unexpected troubles. The Society had become a power for good in the home land. It was noted as a successful maker of books. It was known as energetic in seeking to supply the destitute, and it won a liberal degree of support which attracted attention and even led some to declare that charitable institutions were sucking the blood of the nation. To the Society success gave a wider vision, and the fruit of such success is normally new impulses toward helpfulness of others. The successful benevolent society naturally tends to attract congenial minds so that many become occupied in fixing in permanent form those principles upon which it is based. The plan of the cathedral is the work of one man, but the erection of the noble structure represents the labour and the sweat and skill of hundreds.

The period from 1832 to 1841 with the Bible Society was a time for consolidation of its organization. There were a number of changes in the home office. In 1832 the Rev. S. H. Cone, D.D., Pastor of the First Baptist Church in New York, became one of the Corresponding Secretaries. He was a very able man, a successful and eloquent preacher, and rendered good service to the Society during the three years of his connection with it. He was an active member of the Committee on Distribution and served with honour on several special committees. In intellectual power he was, perhaps, second only to Dr. Milnor, the Senior Secretary of the Society.

Mr. Hubert Van Wagenen, the Treasurer, resigned his office in 1835; and the General Agent, Mr. John Nitchie, who had admirably conducted the work of his department since 1819, was elected Treasurer in place of Mr. Van

Wagenen, retaining the care of orders for books on the general depository. Mr. Robert Winslow, after four years of service as Recording Secretary and Accountant, resigned his position; and the duties of the Accountant were passed over to the Treasurer, while those connected with the printing and shipping of Scriptures, care of plates, etc., were brought together again under charge of Mr. Joseph Hyde, chosen to be General Agent.

A little later (1840) the Rev. E. S. Janes, D.D., an eminent Methodist Episcopal minister, was appointed Financial Secretary; this new office involving extensive travels among the churches to present the Bible cause and its needs more thoroughly than had been done by Auxiliary Bible Societies. Dr. Janes proved very efficient in this work, which he continued until his election as a bishop of the Methodist Episcopal Church.

Several occurrences outside of the usual sphere of action of the Bible Society tended greatly to strengthen its power of forceful action. Denominational questions had not, up to this time, threatened much difficulty to the Board, but in 1834 one of the Auxiliary Societies felt difficulty in making a free grant for Methodist Sunday Schools, that denomination possessing a Bible Society of its own. The grant was made but out of this incident sprang a discussion respecting a possible union of the two Bible Societies. A year later, in 1836, the General Conference of the Methodist Episcopal Church recommended that the Methodist Bible and Tract Society be dissolved. It was an act of noble self-abnegation for the benefit of the American Bible Society and its Auxiliaries, like that of a physician who gives over his patients to a skilful specialist.

Another element of strength was added to the National Society by the decision of the Pennsylvania Bible Society in 1840 to adopt the Auxiliary relationship. The Pennsylvania Society, formerly the Philadelphia Society, was organised in 1808 and had done a noble work in the state of Pennsylvania. It had also made liberal donations to the American Bible Society, not feeling, however, that the Auxiliary relationship would add anything to its power for effective service. Under such circumstances this strong and active Society received a warm welcome when formally declared a helper of the national Society.

Incorporation of the Society had been suggested by Dr. Boudinot years before, but the suggestion had not been adopted. Now, the Society was the owner of real estate in New York City and elsewhere. To this it held title through trustees whose names appeared in the title deeds as the owners. Changes in the laws of New York state made such tenure of real property quite uncertain; and after some difficulty the legislature of the state of New York finally passed an act in 1841 incorporating the American Bible Society.

A good deal of enthusiasm was aroused in the Board, after the decision to take up foreign work, by expressions of satisfaction with which the decision was received. Rev. Mr. Patton, travelling for the Society in the Southern States, wrote from Alabama in 1832: "So far as I have gone I have found friends everywhere prepared to see the American Bible Society stretch her arms all around the earth." And Rev. Mr. Winslow, of the American Board's Mission in South India, wrote: "It is a noble thought, we might almost say a divine thought, to give the Bible to every family under heaven."

Yet the Board of Managers very soon found that expansion multiplies anxieties; that is to say, the larger the field the more demands are made upon sympathy, intelligence and activity. As soon as it became noised abroad that the Society was prepared to aid the American missions, the most moving appeals came from India, China, the Sandwich Islands, as well as from South America. It soon appeared that the destitute to be supplied were increased immeasurably by this decision. In China it was known that at least one-fourth of the population of the globe had no Bibles; that in India there were nearly or quite three hundred million pagans destitute of the Scriptures; that the vast continent of Africa, utterly unknown at that time, contained another mass of destitution fearful to contemplate.

In such circumstances there was little satisfaction in laying plans. They must be tentative; difficulties, unexpected objections would multiply; the world's inheritance from the tower of Babel barred access to multitudes of people. In short the Society found itself in the position of a man who has inherited a vast estate which must be cultivated and kept up because he is responsible for it.

One of the greatest anxieties was the condition of some of the helper Societies. If the helper does not help, it becomes a millstone about the neck of the one who has encouraged it to live. Of course a considerable number of these Societies were models in the matter of efficient and untiring labour; but one-half or more were in a state demanding constant attention. Many of them came into existence during the period of the General Supply of the destitute, after 1829. When this effort was commenced almost every Auxiliary Society received a new and powerful impulse. Many individuals in different communities waked up to a sense of the value of the effort to distribute the Bible. One man attracted by the work done by Auxiliary Societies in his vicinity, calculated in dollars and cents how much the Bible had been to him throughout his life; and he immediately contributed five thousand dollars to the fund for supplying all the destitute, as being arrears of his dues on account of gains.

On the other hand one of the evil results of this great effort was that the lavish distribution of Scriptures among the destitute, and the abundant aid given to weak Auxiliary Societies for this work cultivated a love for the luxury of dependence. Errors of judgment on the part of those who would engage in Bible work caused great annoyance, and the blame of such mistakes reacted upon the Board. Sometimes an Auxiliary announced in its field that it would supply all the destitute, and began the work without making sure of a supply of books large enough to complete it. Or a society ordered books for the supply and after they arrived discovered that it had no one who could possibly attend to the work of distribution. Such occurrences led to repetitions of the common sense suggestion that Auxiliary Societies have a care to appoint efficient officers for their work. Later a Committee on Agencies was appointed by the Board of Managers especially to see to the efficient operation of the Auxiliary Bible Societies.

It should not be understood that what has been said diminishes in any sense the value of the work of active Auxiliary Bible Societies in the United States. Instances of most valuable work even by small Auxiliaries abound. In 1833 the use of the Erie Canal was proving it a main artery for commerce and travel. The Oneida County, New York, Bible Society, finding some fifteen hundred canal boats passing and repassing Utica, and conveying during one year from one hundred and fifty thousand to one hundred and seventy-five thousand passengers, chiefly immigrants going to the West, turned its energies upon supplying New Testaments or Bibles to the people on the canal boats, including the eight thousand or more men regularly employed in this traffic. Another little Auxiliary Society at Strafford, New Hampshire, in five years spent nearly three thousand dollars in distributing Scriptures among more than two thousand families in the county and supplying some six thousand children with the New Testament.

The Young Men's New York Bible Society, as soon as the decision was made to take up work abroad, sent word to the Board of Managers that it would undertake to raise ten thousand dollars in New York City to be used for supplying Chinese Scriptures to Dr. Charles Gutzlaff. The Board, in thanking the Society for this offer, suggested that the special designation to Dr. Gutzlaff might prove to be a hampering limitation. It informed the Young Men's Society, however, that if the limitation was removed so that the money could be used where most needed, in China or elsewhere, the Board of Managers would certainly use in China from the money thus contributed the amount necessary to fill up the appropriation for Chinese Scriptures just decided upon; and that it would relinquish its intention of making a special appeal in New York for the support of foreign distribution in that year; and furthermore would use its endeavours to aid the Young Men's Society in raising the ten thousand dollars proposed.

The Young Men's Society then requested the Board of Managers to pass a formal resolution covering this statement. The Board therefore adopted the following resolution: " Resolved: that, confiding in the exertions of the

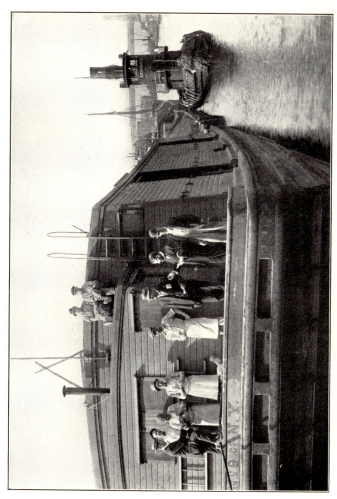

AMONG THE CANAL BOATS IN NEW YORK HARBOR

Young Men's New York Bible Society, this Board will relinquish the city of New York to them for the purpose of
raising funds during the current year for the distribution of
the Bible in foreign fields; and do hereby commend the
Young Men's Society in their undertaking in this behalf to
the friends of the Bible in that city." [1]

Nevertheless the Society deemed it necessary at its Annual Meeting, May 14, 1835, to censure careless Auxiliaries,
saying that while some of them had done good work during
the year in Bible distribution, it was evident that other Societies had "greatly neglected this important duty," and it
earnestly requested such Societies to procure Scriptures
without delay and see that every dwelling in their fields was
furnished with a copy.

One of the measures adopted for the purpose of animating inactive Societies was the appointment of Travelling
Agents assigned to the work of encouraging and stirring up
the Auxiliaries in different districts. In 1840 there had
been for ten years from ten to fifteen agents engaged in the
specific work of keeping Auxiliary Societies alert and efficient. The Board of Managers had many times considered
the question whether this large expense was justified.
There was a distinct tendency to diminish the number of
agents in the hope that the enthusiasm of the new undertakings in Bible distribution at home and abroad would furnish
all the necessary incitement to the Auxiliaries.

The question was frequently asked, however, in the midst
of these perplexities, why should the Society not dispense
with the Auxiliaries entirely? It was felt by the members
of the Board, however, that, as Dr. Brigham expressed it in
the Annual Report for 1836, this idea is a great mistake.
The national Society has no funds for its undertaking; nor
has it the agents, if the wants of the country are to be met,
to perform a thousandth part of the labour requisite for the
collection of funds and the distribution of books. This
work must be done by local Societies, and mostly by the unpaid exertions of their devoted members. The Managers
in the midst of forebodings that the Auxiliary system was

---

[1] Managers Minutes, Volume 5, p. 116.

more or less of a failure, had to admit that no other system had yet been devised so well calculated as that of Auxiliary Societies for the supply of Scriptures to the needy.

Anxieties concerning the Bible distribution at home became more pressing as the number of immigrants increased from year to year. The Society took pains to supply Auxiliary Societies at the points of landing of the immigrants, and also at several points along the lines of travel to the westward, as in the case of Utica just mentioned, and at Pittsburg in Pennsylvania, and Wheeling in Virginia, and Natchez and New Orleans on the Mississippi. In 1835 grants made to sixteen different Auxiliaries at points where foreigners first touch the United States amounted to two thousand, three hundred and seventy-five Bibles and four thousand Testaments. Five hundred dollars was sent to the French and Foreign Bible Society to enable it to supply emigrants sailing from Havre.

The question of languages for the immigrants soon became a serious one. Scriptures in the European languages were commonly purchased from the British and Foreign Bible Society; German and Spanish Scriptures being printed, however, in New York. In 1836, Scriptures for immigrants were ordered from Europe in Italian, Portuguese, Swedish, Danish, Dutch and Welsh. In 1837 the Society, at its Annual Meeting, passed a resolution stating the great importance to the country of supplying immigrants with the Scriptures since " the rapid influx of these foreigners, mostly without the Bible, will make them a danger to the country while in this condition." From this point began a systematic work for the immigrants on the part of the Society which has taken on enormous proportions, and has placed the Society in the position of carrying on foreign mission work in the home land as well as abroad.

More and more urgent appeals for aid in supplying the destitute throughout the United States poured in as the years passed. At the twenty-third Annual Meeting of the Society in May, 1839, on motion of Rev. Sylvester Holmes of New Bedford, Massachusetts, seconded by the Hon. William H. Seward, it was resolved to recommend to the Auxiliaries to commence a second General Supply and prosecute

it with vigour.   Governor Seward, in supporting this motion, made the pertinent remark that he knew not how long
a republican government could flourish among the people
who had not the Bible.   The experiment had never been
tried, but this he did know; that the existing government of
the United States could never have had existence but for
the Bible, and further, he did in his conscience believe that
" if at every decade of years a copy of the Bible should be
found in every family of the land, its republican institutions
would be perpetuated."

The choice of the Bible Society to extend its field indefi-
nitely abroad, while weighed down by the burdens of the
great field of the United States, set before it a future most
strenuous in its demands for determination, perseverance,
and uninterrupted prayer-life.   By undertaking to serve all
American evangelistic efforts, by aiming to circulate the
Bible in all languages abroad as well as at home as soon as
need or opportunity appears, the Society had been following the path trodden by the Master.   Like Him the Society would meet opposition, fatigue, demands upon its
strength, physical, mental and spiritual; but like Him it
would be fed as well as feed others through doing the
will of God for the benefit of thousands and tens of thousands.

CHAPTER XVII

VENTURES IN LANGUAGES

It is said that the people in some of the islands of the New Hebrides are divided into separate and often hostile groups by different languages, so that the villagers on one side of a mountain are not able to understand the people in villages on the other side of the mountain. The result is that the two mountain sides are often at war with each other. Among uncivilised tribes in different parts of the world difference in languages fosters suspicion and encourages enmity. The Germans and the Slavs are commonly spoken of as opposed to one another. In looking back over their history it seems probable that difference of language has had much to do with this opposition. The name applied of old by Slavs to Germans is " Niemtzi," which is equivalent to calling them " dummies " because they could not speak Slavic. Since men look askance at those who speak an unknown language, Babel is a bar to Missions.

On the other hand missionaries can make Babel serve God. Knowledge of the language of the people to whom they are sent is in some degree a key to the gates which Babel guards. How far this is true appears in a little incident reported a few years ago by a Bible Agent in California. He saw a Hindu working in a field by the roadside and shouted a salutation to him in Hindustani. The Hindu immediately dropped his hoe and ran towards the stranger who could speak his home language. His employer called to him to come back and go on with his work. The Hindu called back: " I can't work, my brother has come." He had never seen the missionary before, whose use of Hindustani made him seem like a brother. The mastery of an alien language by a missionary attracts attention, opens doors, levels false distinctions and cultivates friendship. If the

Master has sent the missionary as His ambassador the chief duty of the messenger is to speak, and when he speaks in the language of the country it is only a step further to make him a voice crying in the wilderness, " Prepare ye the way of the Lord ! " So that if Babel is a bar to missions, the languages of Babel clear a way by which the truth of Christianity finds its target. The Zulus in South Africa are often known to buy the Bible in Zulu for the sole reason that it is a book, and in their own language. A great truth is hidden in that sentence of Lloyd: " Speech was made to open man to man."

One great principle guided and compelled the action of the Bible Society in the matter of its ventures in foreign languages. This principle was that it is impossible to train any community in virtue without the Bible. Had the Board wished to hold back from extensive work in different languages abroad, the pressure at home would have compelled it to reconsider the situation. Immigrants speaking many diverse tongues were flowing into the country, and by 1835 the Society found itself obliged to supply for immigrants alone Scriptures in almost a dozen different languages. As has already been noted the existence of people speaking Spanish and French in the United States was one of the influences which led the Society to work abroad.

But as soon as the Society began to print in French and in Spanish it found the people asking for a Roman Catholic Version of the Bible, thus raising a serious difficulty. The Roman Catholic Versions not only contain the Apocrypha, which can be separated from the Canonical books, but they are all based upon the Vulgate Version and not upon the originals. The translation of St. Jerome contains no intentional divergencies from the Hebrew and the Greek. For this reason the Board of Managers saw little objection to its use, while the fact that Roman Catholics would use the Vulgate versions was a strong argument in favour of their publication by the Bible Society. The Board had to choose between two roads ; one blocked, or at least obstructed and the other leading smoothly straight to the objective of Bible circulation in Latin America. In the first quarter of the nineteenth century, so far as Roman Catholic nations were concerned, it would be necessary to give them the Vulgate Bible or to leave them entirely without the Bible.

The story of the issue of the Scio Spanish Version by the Society has appeared in an earlier chapter. As late as the year 1839 a question of the propriety of using Vulgate versions having been brought before the Board of Managers, a decision was reached that these versions could be tolerated. When it was proposed, however, to publish the Douay Version in English for the use of English speaking Roman Catholics in the United States, the question took an entirely different form. The constitution of the Society says definitely that its publications in the English language shall conform to the version in common use; that is, the Authorised Version. And when it was decided that the Douay Version in English could not be printed by the Society, the propriety was questioned of printing any version that could not be classed among the most accurate. The Society was attacked in the press and on the platform for violating its constitution. It was shown that the circulation of the Bible among Roman Catholics had not been by any means limited to the circulation of editions that follow the Vulgate. Finally in 1841 the Board of Managers retraced its steps and decided that no versions from the Vulgate may be printed by the Society. The existing plates of the Scio Spanish Version were finally melted down and sold as type metal. The place of the Scio version was taken by the Valera version, a Spanish translation made in 1602 from the original tongues; and it is this version, with various revisions of style, which has been the principal version circulated in Spanish-speaking countries by the Society. After 1885 an alternative version known as the " Version Moderna " was issued, being prepared by Rev. H. B. Pratt, D.D.

In 1835, after the decision had proved wise to aid American Missions abroad, the Board sent a circular to foreign mission stations informing American missionaries of the different denominations that whenever the Old Testament or the New Testament or any entire Gospel or other book of the Bible is correctly translated into any foreign language and ready to be printed, missionaries, on giving intelligence of this to the Bible Society, may expect to receive the aid

requisite for its publication; and any information communicated by the missionaries concerning Bible translation or the best mode of receiving Scriptures in their vicinity, or any suggestion whatsoever in the interests of the
Bible cause would be carefully considered by the Board.

Later the Board announced the class of expenditures
connected with the preparation and distribution of the Scriptures in foreign languages which the Society could consistently defray. These expenditures included first, the cost
of printing approved versions of the Scriptures, comprising
the cost of paper, of superintendence and correction, and of
binding; second, the cost of purchasing Scriptures for distribution, where versions have already been published; third,
the cost of newly translating and revising the Scriptures in
cases where these undertakings seem to be expedient; and
fourth, the cost of transporting and distributing the Scriptures under the direction of missionaries or Bible Society
Agents. It need not be said that the agents would, of
course, be supported entirely by the Bible Society.

These decisions of the Board, simple and natural though
they were, committed the Society to a great and important
work in many different languages.

Up to this time the Bible had been translated into about
one hundred and eighty languages. Out of these the American Bible Society had printed or circulated about twenty.
And now there came, as if in answer to an announcement by
a benevolent millionaire, urgent appeals from over the seas
for help in printing or in translating the Scriptures. From
the Sandwich Islands, Dr. Green wrote: "The isles wait
for His law!" From India Mr. Scudder wrote that in the
region immediately about him were five hundred thousand
families whose language he could speak, but who had no
Bibles. "Will not the American Bible Society supply these
five hundred thousand families," he asked, "with the New
Testament or at least with one Gospel each in the space of
the next two or three years?" Mr. Winslow, writing from
an adjacent field in South India, let his thoughts carry him
back to the days of the wandering Israelites when a pesti-
lence was abroad in the camp punishing the people for their
sins, and Aaron ran in to stay the plague. "The Mission-

aries," he said, " have been placed under the responsibility of standing between dying men and Him with whom they have to do. So we feel constrained to call upon you to fill the censers which are in our hands with the fire and incense that we may run quickly unto the people and stay the plague which is abroad among them!" Mr. Bridgman, writing from China, repeatedly and vigorously urged the Bible Society to take up the supply of Scriptures for the Chinese, because no other one question of equal gravity could possibly come before the Board. Then, as if to hasten the decision of the Society, careful estimates were sent on, comparing the different methods of printing in Chinese; whether by wood cut blocks or by lithography, or by metal type. In either case the cost at that time would be enormous, because the Chinese Government would not allow the printing by foreigners in China of anything in the Chinese language, and all apparatus, together with the skilled workmen required, would have to be transferred to Singapore, out of the reach of the old Chinese conservatives.

One call from abroad which particularly moved the American public was that already mentioned for a New Testament in Modern Greek to be used in the newly established kingdom of Greece. This was urged by the Secretaries of the A. B. C. F. M. who pointed out that the British and Foreign Bible Society was printing the Old Testament in Modern Greek; that the version then existing of the New Testament was not satisfactory; that the American Bible Society might safely take in hand the making of a new version in this language, printing a tentative edition, and after the test had been made and corrections attended to, the stereotype plates could be quickly prepared. This Greek Testament was finished in 1833. During the next fifteen years it was sent out in large numbers to Dr. King of the A. B. C. F. M., and Dr. Robertson of the Protestant Episcopal Mission in Greece, and to Mr. Brewer of the A. B. C. F. M. at Smyrna in Turkey. The use of these plates was then discontinued.

Up to the end of its fifteenth year the Society had granted to American Missions abroad for printing and circulation of Scriptures in foreign languages eighteen hundred dollars.

At the end of its twentieth year one hundred and four thousand, four hundred dollars had been added to this amount. The grants to American Missions abroad for printing and distributing Scriptures in ten languages at the end of the twenty-fifth year had reached a total of one hundred and eighty-eight thousand, nine hundred and fifty dollars.

The provision of Scriptures in foreign languages is of greatest importance in the eyes of a Bible Society. Skilled translators have to be found, and arrangements made for properly printing and binding the Scriptures when they are translated. It is always necessary to remember when looking at Bible work in foreign lands that nothing whatever can be done until the Bible is translated into the tongue of the people. This implies very slow progress but the delay, like that in building a temple, must not dampen ardour since time is needed for laying foundations for the future.

This work in foreign languages is not only of great importance but of the most solemn responsibility. Typographical errors may corrupt the text while in the hands of the printers. It is conceivable that conflicting opinions of translators might colour the version; or that a too sensitive criticism might mutilate a translation which is to be sent forth in a foreign language. In all questions of the accuracy and propriety of versions the Bible Society must satisfy itself, for it will be held responsible for whatever goes forth published in its name. For this reason all who receive aid from the Bible Society in the work of translation are warned against following individual preference as to expression lest this add to or take from the originals. The responsibility of the Bible Society for the English version is everywhere understood. As President J. Cotton Smith remarked in his address at the Annual Meeting of the Society in 1836: " The Society is charged with the preservation, not only of the truths of the English Bible but of its precise language." An interdenominational Society only can properly secure the text against alteration; it being a body trusted by all denominations, it watches over the inviolability of the text. A copy bearing the imprint of such a Society is of guaranteed authenticity.

The text of the English Version is now, therefore, safer

than for centuries before the organisation of the British and Foreign Bible Society. The first English Bible, that of Coverdale printed in Zurich in 1536, had no protection excepting the good intention of those who printed its different editions, against error or purposeful change. The King James Version, issued in 1611, was printed and reprinted during two hundred years before any general and thoroughly effective system protected it from mistakes and variations. Only after Bible Societies became established could one feel that an authoritative control guaranteed the new editions as they came from the press.

The Bible Society has, besides the function of watching over the accuracy of the text of the Bible, the opportunity of improving and ennobling the languages in which it publishes the Bible. Language is the dress of thought, Dr. Johnson used to say. One of the great services to the world performed by Bible translators and Bible distributors is their taking a language which is the dress of miserable, impoverished and perhaps vile thought, and putting into it the noble, pure and inspiring thought that fills the Bible. The work of the translator is necessarily slow. He finds difficulties in himself, in his own scholarship which has to be carried to a very high point in order justly to carry through the work which he undertakes. He finds the work a heavy responsibility for he is dealing not with his own words, but with words whose truths, relations and suggestions must be accurately carried over into the language into which he translates them. This part of the process is that suggested by Horace when he describes a skilful writer " whose dexterous setting makes an old word new." The work of the translator frequently becomes a work of purifying a language by filling words with new meaning and unwonted beauty, just as the slow drudgery of the diamond cutter brings out the full splendour of a gem which was hardly more than a pebble.

Aiding the missions along the lines marked out at the beginning, now making a new version possible by money support to a translator, now paying for new editions issued by a mission printing press, by the end of its twenty-fifth year the Society had fostered Bible versions not only in the

Mohawk, the Ojibwa, the Cherokee, Seneca, Delaware and Choctaw for the American Indians, but it had authorised printing at its expense in Turkish, Armenian, Hebrew-Spanish, Siamese, Chinese, Hindustani, Tamil, Telugu, Uriye, Grebo (West Africa) and Hawaiian.   The Society had thus rounded out the sphere of its activities as seen afar in the vision of its founders.   For a Bible Society by printing the Scriptures in many different tongues wields a God-given power, and brings nearer the time when every considerable race of men will rejoice to read in their own tongue wherein they were born, the wonderful works of God.

CHAPTER XVIII

INDIVIDUALISM IN DEMOCRACY

THE general expectation of Europe respecting the Republic of the United States in its early days was that individual convictions too strongly rooted to be subordinated to the good of the nation would some day set aside the principle of decision by majority vote. This would rend the Union so that all semblance of cohesion between its parts must disappear.

Curiously enough by the time the Society had reached its twentieth year a similar test of cohesion had been applied, in a small way, to its management. Had not the purpose of the Society been grand enough to hold control over the personal views of its members, keeping them loyal to the federation; had not some members for the sake of this loyalty, sacrificed personal convictions, it is quite possible that this story would not have been written, and the views of European monarchists about democracy would have been justified so far as permanence of the federation in the Bible Society was concerned.

During this period the question of slavery more and more occupied the minds of men. It was gradually becoming a test of the ability of good men patiently to set aside their personal views for the sake of the future of the nation. Little by little the question became a question of conscience. In the Northern States the influence of the suppression of slavery in the colonies of Great Britain, and the arguments of Wilberforce which led up to this result had great influence in awakening the consciences of the people. Of course the same literature was in the hands of the people of the Southern States, but their whole system of agriculture and thus their general interests depended upon the continuance of slavery.

With the Missouri Compromise a divergence between the North and the South was acknowledged and a system adopted for preserving between the two sections a balance of power. Possibly the issue might have been different had there been intercourse between the Northern and Southern States, but the means of travel were few. People of the masses discussed this matter at a distance, as if each had been seated on the top of a high mountain shouting across the interval instead of getting together in the valley good-humouredly to arrange their differences.

The man of one idea on both sides now came to the front of the crowd — the man who knows that the fragment of truth which he has grasped is of supreme importance to the world; who resents every proffer of direction or advice, but claims the right to advise and direct authoritatively all of his opponents. He is the man whom the European monarchists had in mind when they prophesied the failure of American democracy. It was his influence in either of the two hotly disputing parties which finally led to the announcement of the doctrine that men who are disappointed by the result of the ballot may bodily withdraw from the National union and execute by themselves the plans defeated at the polls.

With the terrible Civil War which years later washed out in blood this doctrine we have nothing here to do. What concerns us is the strain upon the principle of democracy in the management of the American Bible Society which reached the danger point in this period of our present narrative. In 1834, just in the warmest part of the excitement in New York concerning abolitionists and their suppression, a delegation from the American Anti-Slavery Society appeared before the Board of Managers with a proposal to raise five thousand dollars if the Bible Society would set apart twenty thousand dollars for putting a Bible into every coloured family in the United States in two years' time from July 4th, 1834.

A natural desire existed among members of the Board and Christians everywhere to have the Bible opened before the slaves. The Book has a message of manliness for all who read it. But on the other hand the members of this delegation must have known that an attempt by the Bible Society to send agents to every negro hut in the South would be violently opposed; and even if the Bible agents reached the slave's quarters, hardly two per cent. of the coloured people could read the book set before them.

The Board of Managers were in a dilemma. The proposal, like a handful of sand thrown into the lubricating oil of a steam engine, might cause a wreck. The Society has no right to interfere with any man's politics or religious belief, but any refusal on this ground to send Scriptures to the slaves when money was offered for the purpose would be called proof by some that the Board was without feeling. If, however, the offer of the Anti-Slavery Society should be accepted, the two hundred or more Auxiliaries of the Society in the Southern States, deeply offended at such an interference, might resist the action of the Board.

It was perfectly clear, moreover, that there was no escape from dissension within the Board, if this specific proposal were to call for ayes and nays. Mr. Arthur Tappan, the president of the Anti-Slavery Society, had been a member of the Board, and was highly respected by his old associates there. The welfare of the whole enterprise of the Bible Society at this point depended upon the discovery of a general principle upon which all could unite and which would, by itself, settle the question proposed by the Anti-Slavery Society.

The case before the Board was like the question of building a new schoolhouse before a town meeting. The project winning the majority of votes must be a final decision, whether all liked it or not. It is a misfortune, of course, for the man of one idea not to convince his associates; but whoever imagines that he has a monopoly of truth finds himself in a lonely path. The rule of such a compact as that of this interdenominational Society must include self-abnegation for the sake of achieving the one object of the compact.

After considerable discussion the Board of Managers found the principle governing this case. It adopted the two following resolutions:

" RESOLVED that the Managers of this Society, pursuing

the great Catholic object which they have ever had in view, viz., the circulation of the Holy Scriptures without note or comment among their destitute fellow men of every name and nation wherever they can be reached, will thankfully receive the contributions of all societies and individuals who may be disposed to co-operate with them in their benevolent undertaking.

" Resolved that while Bibles and Testaments will always be furnished at the lowest prices to Auxiliary Societies for distribution and even furnished gratuitously when necessary for the supply of the needy, yet the direct labour of the distribution of these books as well as the responsibility of selecting the proper families and individuals within their respective limits who are to receive them, must, heretofore, be left wholly to the wisdom and piety of those who compose these local associations in the different States and Territories."

This action was unimpeachable and peace remained with the Board, which, being composed of diverse elements united in a great common purpose, did not enter into controversy concerning details governed by the rule. A year later the Anti-Slavery Society made an offer again of five thousand dollars which it would give to the American Bible Society in order to foster distribution of Scriptures among the slaves in the South. The Board of Managers, however, had no different answer to make than the one previously given; but in the most friendly manner they showed the reports of the Auxiliaries in the South pointing out what they had done and were steadily attempting to do.

From what has been said it will be obvious that the Board of Managers has had to decide questions of magnitude beyond the competence of any individual member. In the discussion of delicate and divisive questions its only safety is in following the rule just illustrated.

Another question, which proved controversial and occupied the Board during more than six months, came up the next year (1835). It grew out of a very simple and innocent proposal. The Rev. Mr. Pearse, a missionary in Calcutta, asked aid from the Society for printing the Scriptures in the Bengali language. In order to ensure favourable action by the Board, Mr. Pearse added that the British and Foreign Bible Society had advised him to apply to the American Society which would probably grant his request.   Mr. Pearse stated, however, that the British Society would not grant his request for aid because in translating the New Testament he had rendered the Greek word *baptizo* by a Bengali word meaning " immerse."   The Board of Managers followed its usual method in referring the application to the Committee on Distribution, and passed on to other matters.

The Committee on Distribution reported in due time, advising that aid could not be granted since the translation did not seem to agree with the usual practice of the Society. Some objection was made to the views of the Distribution Committee, and the Board, with due respect for those who raised the objection, referred the report to a special committee composed of one member from each of the seven denominations then represented in the Board of Managers. This Committee considered the question with prudent deliberation, and finally brought in a report confirming the decision of the Committee on Distribution that aid should not be granted for the publication of the Bengali Testament translated by Mr. Pearse.   This decision had the support of six of the seven members of the Special Committee ; Secretary S. H. Cone, the Baptist member, offering a written expression of entire dissent from the action.

In ordinary cases a report presenting the view of so large a majority of a committee would be adopted by the Board without much discussion ; but this report was laid on the table for consideration at the next meeting.   Meanwhile a number of letters came to the Board, some warmly favouring and others equally warmly protesting against the adoption of the Committee's report.   Among others Rev. Dr. Francis Wayland of Brown University, a Life Member and one of the warm friends of the American Bible Society, wrote to Secretary Brigham urging that a principle be laid down which would apply not to an application from one denomination only, but to all applications for aid.   With such a principle established a detail like Mr. Pearse's application would settle itself.

This wise suggestion was timely.   Secretary Milnor, who was eminently capable of analysing and clearly setting forth principles, wrote and offered to the Board, Nov. 19, 1835, such a resolution, as follows:

" RESOLVED, that in appropriating money for the translating, printing or distributing of the Sacred Scriptures in foreign languages the Managers feel at liberty to encourage only such versions as in the principle of their translation conform to the common English version, at least so far that all the religious denominations represented in this Society can consistently use and circulate said versions in their several schools and communities."

This resolution, having the cordial approval of distinguished Baptist friends of the Society, was considered by the Board and brought to a vote on the 17th of February, 1836. A number of ministers who as Life Members were entitled to vote in the Board were present and the resolution was adopted by a vote of thirty yeas and fourteen nays.   This principle has been followed ever since by the American Bible Society in making its appropriations for Bible translation.

The Board of Managers now sent the resolution adopted on the 17th of February to all of the missionary societies accustomed to look for aid to the American Bible Society, accompanying it by an official notice that applications for aid for translating or printing Scriptures should carry with them a statement that the principle of this resolution will be observed.   The resolution was agreed to by all of the societies addressed excepting the Baptist Missionary Society; and money which had been granted by the Board for the use of Baptist missions in Burma was declined as not acceptable on the condition which had been laid down by the Board.   The Board very naturally regretted extremely the feeling which had been called up in connection with its decision; but clearly the question really was: can the American Bible Society publish Bibles varying from the standard, according to the peculiar views of Methodists, or Presbyterians, or Episcopalians, or Baptists?   It is clear that decision by the Board to print a Bible which one denomination alone could use must ultimately overthrow this interdenominational Society.

The Baptist Board of Missions at the same time (April,

1836) adopted the following resolution setting forth the
principles that should guide its translation of Scripture into
foreign languages: " RESOLVED, that the missionaries of the
Board who are or who shall be engaged in translating the
Scriptures be instructed to endeavour by earnest prayer and
diligent study to ascertain the exact meaning of the original
text; to express that meaning as exactly as the nature of
the language into which they shall translate the Bible will
permit and to transfer no words which are capable of being
literally translated."

This resolution might be said to agree in principle with
the views of the American Bible Society.   The only point
of difference concerns the question as to whether a word
is or is not capable of literal translation.   The Board pre-
fers, however, to commit such a sacred work, whenever
possible, to a committee rather than to a single individual.
In cases of difference of opinion its rule follows the principle
of democracy, considering the vote of a majority decisive in
cases where good men hold divergent views as to rendering
any passage in the original language.

Early in May, 1836, the Rev. Dr. Cone resigned his position as Corresponding Secretary of the American Bible Society and the same week became President of the " American
and Foreign Bible Society," a new organism established
to carry out the ideas which the American Bible Society
could not.   Of this Society the Corresponding Secretary
was the Rev. C. G. Sommers, who had been for some years
Secretary for Domestic Correspondence of the American
Bible Society.

Deeply as the members of the Board regretted this dis-
cord, they rejoiced in the sympathy of a considerable number of their Baptist friends.   Baptists then and ever since
have worked fraternally with the Auxiliary Societies and
have taken part in the management of the national Society as
members of the Board.   A number of years later Rev. Dr.
Francis Wayland published in the *Christian Watchman and
Reflector* [1] a review of this whole affair so far as he was
connected with it; and he closed his article with the declara-

[1] August 10, 1866.

tion: " I cannot perceive how, consistently with the principles of its constitution, the Bible Society could have adopted
any other rule. It is equally required by the dictates of
justice and common sense, and it breathes the spirit of
fraternal equality and Christian courtesy. It has, therefore,
my cheerful and unwavering support." Some years later
definite charges of unfairness were made in Baptist newspapers against the Managers of the Bible Society. These
charges were fully discussed and refuted in a paper published
with the Annual Report of 1841 (page 109) and this mention
must suffice in this place.[1]

[1] It is only proper to add that since these incidents the American
Bible Society has been glad, as ever, to make grants of money or of
Scriptures to Baptist Societies, missions and congregations.

CHAPTER XIX

A CAPITALIST in New York who invests in a gold-mining enterprise in Australia or even in Colorado will feel uneasy if the success of his venture depends in any degree upon a prospectus. The Board of Managers of the Society had now reached a point in its ventures abroad where it needed to be in closer touch with foreign affairs. The formal adoption of the fields of American missionaries in India, China, Turkey, and other lands piled responsibility high upon the shoulders of the Managers. As the central missionary idea of a Bible Society finds fuller expression, the idea itself grows like a living thing.

In the foreign field hitherto the action of the Bible Society had been more or less sporadic and its results had not been reported in much detail. In 1834 the Board reported that during the year just passed it had sent Scriptures into Canada, Mexico, different parts of South America, to France, Russia and Greece, to India, Ceylon, Burma, Java and China, to Africa and to the Sandwich Islands. About the same time another letter from Archdeacon Wix at St. Johns, Newfoundland, set forth the needs of the fishermen of Labrador, a grant was promptly made to him. Rev. E. Stallybrass, a missionary of the London Missionary Society, was printing an Old Testament in the Mongolian of Lake Baikal. He asked aid and the Board sent him one thousand dollars. So every now and then Spanish Scriptures were sent to Havana, to Mexico City and to Colombia. Each shipment was made in conscientious solicitude; but every one of those parcels of books was like a bullet fired at a venture. It was very hard to guess whether the mark was hit.

The Board of Managers was a good deal in the position of men making preparations for a journey to a far country.

There was need for study of the lands and their people, of economic methods, and of measures for securing steady progress. Equipment, resources and helpers must be looked after. The people among whom it was going to work, their environment and the conditions of life must be known; and then the Board found itself in the predicament of the wise man who said, "It is easier to be wise for others than for oneself." In fact the members of the Board were in appalling ignorance of the actual requirements of the task which had been given them. But they had faith, and in such a case wisdom comes " like waters that refresh the earth, some bursting forth from below but the best and purest coming down from heaven."

The reports of the missionaries which led to the decision to participate in foreign work gave a thrilling interest to this undertaking of the Society. Calls kept coming from regions entirely beyond reach for aid which would commit the Society to large expense, forecasts of which must largely rest on faith rather than on discretion. Money was to be furnished the missions for the distribution of Scriptures. Somebody must pick the men who would be sent out with Bibles to distribute. Somebody must be sure that men of a single purpose were selected so that no mingling of acts with mere good intentions should confuse the purpose of their lives. Distribution is a word easily said. In real action that word covers opposition and even violence from men who know not the Bible, together with triumphant conquest over self on the part of the workers and unspeakable weariness which faith alone restrains from the Slough of Despond.

Then again the Board of Managers must be assured, in giving money for translation, that those who are to translate the Bible are fit. It must be fully guaranteed against their having mistaken their calling through " being stung by the splendour of a thought." Life in man cannot be measured or defined; it is a wonder beyond analysis. So, beyond all analysis is the life pulsing in the words of the Bible; words transferred, still pulsing, from language to language when the translator is filled with his Bible and taught by the Holy Spirit, but motionless and shrivelled, like a cell of the body that has worn itself out, if any man goes at the work equipped solely with a grammar and a dictionary.

Even the mechanical work of printing Scriptures in a foreign land rested as a responsibility upon the Board in New York. Abroad there was then no such skill of printers that general instructions could end anxiety about the result. Carrying forward the work at home was like travelling on a smooth, well built highway as compared with the obstacles met in foreign lands while the missionary or Bible Agent hews his path through the tangled underbrush at every step.

A reason for the confidence of the Board was the thorough organisation of the forces at home. The Auxiliary system with its co-operative corps of travelling Agents, formed a frame work, a skeleton, if you please, upon which the organs of activity could find support and which insures some co-ordinate action. Through the Auxiliaries the spirit and purpose of the national Society was known throughout the land. The Auxiliaries served the Board of Managers as eyes to report needs and dangers, and as hands to apply the remedy instantly needed. The question now before the Board was, How can the Society have eyes abroad, going to and fro through all the different lands seeing needs, and hands abroad to provide the service of fellowship with all the different denominations, and to yield trusty reports of things done and even of things vainly tried?

The answer to this question was that carefully chosen agents sent to the different fields would serve the Board of Managers as eyes and hands. The agent must be ever on hand to follow into minutest details the execution of the plans made in New York. He must be a lover of God and of mankind; a man of penetration, of great prudence, of experience in dealing with his fellowmen. With fine polish of this sort an agent can effectively act for the Society. For as Richter says, " Men, like bullets, go farthest when they are smoothest."

The first agent sent out by the American Bible Society for this direct oversight of the distribution of Scriptures was the Rev. Isaac W. Wheelwright, appointed to the Pacific Coast of South America. Mr. Wheelwright sailed from New

York for Valparaiso, Chile, in November, 1833. His instructions were to make a determined effort to put the Spanish Scriptures into circulation in Chile and in fact in all the coast regions as far north as the western slopes of Mexico. In each place which he visited he was to sell as many books as possible. Only after supplying those willing to buy was he to give gratuitously to schools or to individuals.

Mr. Wheelwright was a man of thoughtful habit, judicious in his choice of methods, simple and economical in his tastes, and endowed with the virtue of perseverance. He took with him two hundred Spanish Bibles, twelve hundred New Testaments, besides five thousand copies of the Gospel of St. Matthew that he might have something to give to the children.

After the long and tedious voyage of three months around Cape Horn, Mr. Wheelwright reached Valparaiso in March, 1834. He had good success in disposing of his Scriptures. A good many of his books went into the schools. A learned priest who was a member of the Senate took an interest in his work and favoured the unrestricted circulation of the Bible. But after he went northward to Coquimbo an influential bishop opposed his work with might and main; and the Bible Society Agent was much chagrined to find himself obliged to take away from a native bookstore two boxes of Scriptures in order to save them from being burned by order of the Bishop. Elsewhere people whose influence might have hampered him were religiously indifferent; and a great many people refused to buy the Bible at any price.

After two years the Board put on record its faithful effort to furnish the Bible to the disturbed countries of South America, but noted that those countries offered little reason for the continuance of the Agency. Nevertheless, the Board decided to continue the experiment, probably because the Agent, in spite of all obstacles, more than once wrote home for further supplies of books. The agency came to an end, however, in 1837 and was not renewed.

In its twentieth report the Board took up the agency question as entirely new. " Hitherto," it announced, " appropriations for publishing foreign Scriptures have mostly been made through missionary bodies of different religious denominations. Great good has in this way been effected, and the same instrumentalities must be more or less resorted to in the future. It appears to the Board, however, that they should, as far as practicable, begin to establish agents of their own in foreign countries; men who shall co-operate with missionaries in preparing and distributing the Scriptures, and yet be responsible to this Board for their operations."

This decision of the Board was a natural step of progress in efficiency. No longer would the Society seem to be a mere money box upon which drafts could be made in sure hope of acceptance. Far more than this the Society, here-after, would be in intimate co-operation with missionaries everywhere. The needs of the missionaries would be its needs. The joy of the missionaries in seeing the power of the gospel of Jesus Christ would be its joy. As a mis-sionary Society the American Bible Society would now enter the realms of paganism and Mohammedanism, one in interest and aim with each of the denominations there labour-ing. It could do this feeling that the call had come from the missions. Missionaries gladly served when they could as distributors of the Bible, but to many of them keeping account of books sent and of dues to men who distributed to the people began to seem what serving tables seemed to the Apostles in the early mission of the Church. The work of preaching and teaching could not brook the distraction of energy implied in carrying Bibles far afield to reach the secluded, the isolated and the hungry. This pioneer work distinctively belongs to the Bible Society.

A vastly more important agency than the travelling com-mission given Mr. Wheelwright was established in 1836 in the fields of the American missionaries in the countries bordering on the Eastern Mediterranean. The Rev. Simeon H. Calhoun of Williams College was chosen to be the agent and sailed for Smyrna in November, 1836. His voyage by sailing vessel occupied forty-four days. Mr. Calhoun wrote a cheery letter from Smyrna, Turkey, telling of his cordial reception by the missionaries, the agent of the British and Foreign Bible Society, and other friends. He went almost immediately to Constantinople, the centre where American missionaries were engaged in translation. Smyrna was the location of the Mission Press. Printing material could be brought into the country more easily there, and more liberty was enjoyed in Smyrna than immediately under the shadow of the Sultan.

The Turkish Empire at that time extended from the frontiers of Persia and the Caucasus Mountains westward to the Adriatic Sea, and from the Persian Gulf and the valley of the Nile on the south to the borders of Hungary and Transylvania on the north. Its territories included all the lands which figure in Bible History, and its proud and self-satisfied rulers were fully assured believers in the religion of Mohammed. To Mohammedans in those early days insanity was the least opprobrious epithet with which they could characterise the wisdom of Christianity. The object of American missions there was, of course, influence upon Mohammedans; but at first the missionaries sought to arouse spiritual yearnings among the Greek and Armenian Christians of the Empire, long cut off from fellowship with the Christians of the West.

Mr. Calhoun's first letters justified the decision of the Board to send agents abroad. The American missionaries at Constantinople were translating the Scriptures into Modern Armenian, into Turkish as written with the Armenian alphabet, and into the Spanish jargon written with Hebrew letters used by the Jews of Turkey. In 1815 the Russian Bible Society had published five thousand Ancient Armenian Bibles and later two thousand Testaments in the same language. In 1822 with earnest solicitude to reach those who could not understand their ancient writings, it had published the New Testament in Armeno-Turkish.[1] During almost a score of years the British and Foreign Bible Society had been securing the publication of Scriptures in Armenian as well as in Greek. In 1819 Mr. Pinkerton while at Constantinople informed the British and Foreign Bible Society that he had arranged for one thousand Modern Greek Testaments, five hundred Testaments in Ancient and Modern Greek in parallel columns, and five hundred Arabic Testa-

[1] Turkish written with Armenian letters.

ments to be distributed among the pilgrims at Jerusalem without money and without price. The Board in New York might be puzzled to know why, with such seed ready for sowing, American missionaries urgently appealed for aid in providing new seed for the sower. Mr. Calhoun quickly learned that the existing versions had been generally in the ancient form, while those issued in the modern dialect which the people understood depended for accuracy upon the judgment of native translators, well-intentioned but little experienced in the use and interpretation of the Bible. Hence those versions in the local languages could not be permanent.

By having an agent abroad who was a keen observer the Board could see the actual needs and conditions of the fields where they were asked to work. In the educational work of the missions they quickly understood that the mission schools and the Bible Society are rooted in the same soil and bear the same kind of fruit. The mission schools make the Bible an important part of the course. The board could understand the utter weakness of the oriental Christian churches. The priests never preached. They were exactly like those described by one of the old prophets as " dumb dogs that cannot bark." They could not intelligently expound any passage of Scripture. The people led by such priests cannot understand why worship should demand thought. At one place during morning prayers a house servant was moving noisily about the room arranging the furniture. Afterwards Mr. Calhoun rebuked him for disturbing the worship. " Oh, what is the difference!" he said. His idea of worship was merely the making of the sign of the Cross, or the counting of beads, and no noise disturbs that.

It was of the greatest importance to the Board to know that the distribution of Scriptures at their expense was really efficient. Mr. Calhoun was able to show that the tide of interest in the Bible had risen enough in those regions to float the Bible Society ark over all obstructions and all shoals. For instance, Armenians could use the Bible without fear of penalty. Although the Greek patriarchs fiercely cursed those who circulated and those who read the Modern Greek Testament, large numbers of them were sold to the Greeks. Mr. Calhoun writes in 1839 that about ten thousand New

Testaments had been circulated in Greece through the bounty of the Society. " Some of them," he says, " were torn up and destroyed; but what of God's mercies are not abused by men? The most of them were kept and read by the people." When the Hebrew-Spanish version of Psalms prepared by Dr. Schauffler and printed at the expense of the Society was issued the Jewish Rabbis in Constantinople anathematised the book and stopped its sale. But Mr. Calhoun sent his edition to Adrianople, Brousa, and other cities, quickly selling a large number.

Had it not been for the Agent in the Mediterranean regions the Board of Managers might not have heard of the variety of demands for Scriptures encountered in Constantinople. Thousands of people seemed to be waiting by the table to pick up any crumbs which fell. It became necessary to get German Bibles in quantities from New York to supply the demand at Odessa. In Constantinople itself were English and French and Germans who demanded Scriptures in their own languages, and of course it would not do to say to such that the Bible Agent came to Constantinople merely to supply Armenians and Greeks. Mr. Calhoun received an appeal from Rev. Justin Perkins, American missionary far away in Persia. A Nestorian priest asked him for a Bible and as a test the question was put to him: " In return what will you pay for it? " The priest answered, " Silver and gold have I none, but I will pray the Lord in return to give you a portion in the Kingdom of Heaven." Mr. Perkins wrote, " I suppose that your Society will have no objection to receiving such currency as this."

It was also useful to the Board to understand the self-denials and dangers which their agent encountered in doing his ordinary work. Because the plague was ravaging Constantinople, when Mr. Calhoun went to Greece he was imprisoned in quarantine for fifteen days, during which time he was not allowed to see any friends excepting at a distance, separated by a wide hall. In travelling in Syria in 1839 he was attacked by Bedouin Arabs but happily his fleet mule out-distanced them. Various qualities of their Agent revealed themselves through such experiences. In Smyrna Mr. Calhoun took time to visit the hospitals and care for English sailors among the sick; and coming out of the hospital he wrote at once to the far away office in New York, "Send me two hundred English Bibles quickly!" When he was put in quarantine and cut off from his friends, his Bible was his companion. He received a new sense of the fitness of this companion; therefore he longed for greater earnestness in distributing it among the people whose awful fate for ages had been that the Bible was a sealed book to them.

The object of the Bible Society is none other than to offer slaves of evil the truth that sets men free. The fitness of the Bible to satisfy men's need was the ultimate reason compelling the Society to choose Agents for its foreign fields. Let the words of the Rev. John Breckenridge here express the hope and the belief of the Society at this epoch: "Under the present title and organisation the benevolences of the Society are absolutely unrestricted and universal. It is American in the spirit of enlargement, not of restriction. It expresses our Nation's philanthropy. . . . The history of the Bible is the history of liberty. The South American states are not free because they have not the Bible. Ireland is not free; unhappy Poland is not free; Spain, Portugal — all oppressed nations are not free because the people at large have not the Bible. Theirs is an erectness of principle, a mental and moral independence proper to and inseparable from the influence of the Bible. History has wrung a reluctant tribute on this subject from Gibbon. ' Philadelphia alone,' he tells us, ' was saved by prophecy or by courage. Her valiant citizens defended her religion and her freedom above four score years, and at length capitulated with the proudest of the Ottomans. Among the Greek colonies and churches of Asia Minor Philadelphia is still erect, a column in a scene of ruins.' Such a testimony needs no comment." [1]

[1] Rev. Dr. Breckenridge at the Sixteenth Anniversary of the American Bible Society. Monthly Extracts, No. 52.

CHAPTER XX

THE FINANCING OF THE BIBLE SOCIETY

On hearing interesting information about any benevolent enterprise some people regret a common practice which mingles with the story, appeals for money. They do not hesitate to communicate to others this regret. Efforts for the good of mankind should not be debased by association with money seems to be their thought.

But even Bibles cost. Sending them to the destitute implies expense. Even postage on the letters that convey news of free grants of Scriptures in the course of each year costs quite a little sum. So it comes about that obedience to the command " Go teach all nations," whether it takes the form of a missionary or a Bible Society is as inseparable from the problem of ways and means as is obedience to the law of love in the home circle. Like every undertaking which is worth while a Bible Society costs money in proportion to the breadth and depth of its influence in the world. In 1817 the work of the Bible Society was carried on at an expense of about $19,500. In 1841 the cost shown by the Treasurer's books was a little more than $118,000. There was nothing to regret in placing this fact of necessary cost before those who formed the Society for the benefit of the community and the nation. Appeals for the support of the work naturally belong with the narrative of its incidents.

Financing the Bible Society during its first twenty-five years was (as it ever must be) a great problem which generally absorbed the thought of the whole administration. So many potential supporters of the Society seemed dormant as to conscience ; so many people now knew not the founders of the Society ; so gingerly must the approach to them be made ; so hard was the choice of the opportune time for overtures ; so often did impending disaster cloud hope ; that the effort

153

to give some stability to the income of the Society would have been a mill-stone about the necks of men less able or less godly than this group of managers and officers. Yet on the whole this complicated and perplexing task in the retrospect offers situations of intense interest.

The main reliance of the Society for financial strength, as we have explained, was an enterprising and efficient Auxiliary system. So long as they maintained the spirit which animated them at the beginning, Auxiliaries would retain efficiency. A chain of branches of a commercial house succeeded upon this principle; their usefulness often depending upon spirited admonitions from the central office.

In 1841 there were nearly nine hundred Auxiliary Bible Societies. Of these about one-half could be relied upon for contributing to the general work so regularly that their contributions could form a part of the financial plans of the Society. One society in Western Massachusetts was inclined to congratulate itself that its donations for the general work of the American Bible Society during the whole twenty-five years exceeded one thousand dollars a year. Where the habit of giving is fixed, mere contact with regular givers brings others into the same category. The Washington City (District of Columbia) Bible Society was preparing a liberal donation for the American Bible Society, when one man rose in the congregation and said that he would pledge two hundred and fifty dollars a year for four years for this purpose. Instantly in another part of the house a second man sprang to his feet and said, " I'll give a thousand dollars on the same terms ! " This contagious interest made the donation of the Washington City Bible Society more than twice as much as its officers had thought of raising.

The Board urged Auxiliaries to remember the sacredness of the effort in which they were engaged; to hold meetings at central points throughout their field that people might be informed, and so to stir many hearts with desire to help. It later appointed agents to travel among the Auxiliaries in order to systematise both distribution of Scriptures and collection of money. After a time, the expense of maintaining these agents was found to equal about twenty-five per cent. of the money which they were able to raise for general work, and the Board began to hesitate as to whether the good work which they did in distributing Scriptures to the poor was justified at such a cost in money. So in 1839 the Board decided to diminish the number of these agents. Then Auxiliaries which were not regularly visited by agents with tidings of the great work began to lose energy; the wheels of their activity moved slower and slower, and finally stopped like the wheels of a clock that has been forgotten. In 1840 as already noted, the Board appointed a Financial Secretary, the Rev. E. S. Janes, D.D., to excite Auxiliaries and other friends to larger contributions to the Bible Society. By his efforts the Auxiliaries were to be encouraged and the finances of the Society improved.

Grants to distant fields complicated the problem of financing the Bible Society. Appeals as moving as the cry of a child lost in the darkness of night came from Asia, Africa and the islands of the Pacific. Of course the Managers in making appropriations to help the missionaries carefully examine the Society's average receipts of past years. This is the basis of the limit within which all appropriations must be brought. After it is fixed in deliberate council, the Board has to proceed as if the money were in hand, although at the beginning of every new year the Treasury be empty. Cautious business men who never relax their watch upon the mouth of the money bag were led, however, to take risks by appeals like the following copied from the records of 1838. Mr. Spaulding, Methodist Episcopal missionary in Brazil, thus begged for Scriptures: "Suppose one in twenty would receive the Bible, then two hundred and fifty thousand are now wanted — or one in fifty, then one hundred thousand — one in a hundred, then fifty thousand — or one in two hundred, then twenty-five thousand — or one in five hundred, then ten thousand — or even one in a thousand, then five thousand are now wanted. The country is open for their reception. The door may soon be closed, forever. Can the American Bible Society furnish us with what we want?" This appeal caused the Board at once (1839) to decide to print the Scriptures of the Portuguese version in New York.

From Madras came word that the American Mission Press had been enlarged, and to make its power felt by the masses all was ready except the money. "My dear Brother," wrote Mr. Scudder, "we must go forward, and you must in connection with the British Bible Society come up to our help or our hands must hang down. Will you come to our help? I, with such helpers as I need, will go forth and distribute the books when prepared."

The agent in the Levant, Mr. Calhoun, wrote of demands for Scriptures from American missionaries in Greece, Syria and Persia. These he supplied by buying from the British and Foreign Bible Society, whose agent, happily, did not refuse him as the virgins of the empty lamps in the parable were refused. From Dr. Grant of the American Mission in Persia came a moving appeal for aid to print the Bible in Syriac. Syriac Scriptures were scarce at Julamerk. "Nestorian children," wrote Dr. Grant, "are taught to read with the book bottom side up or turned on either side as well as held in the perpendicular position so that five or six persons may read from a single book around which they sit in a circle." Such a picture of destitution coupled with youthful eagerness to read remains on the tablet of the mind.

When the appropriation to aid work of any kind is once made, it becomes an agreement which cannot be recalled without notice. Men engaged for the work cannot be dismissed at the close of a day, even though the Society's income dwindles. Hence applications for grants were received at the point of the bayonet when people at home reduced their donations to the Society.

In 1835 the Board found that the census in the United States showed more than five thousand blind. It promptly decided that so soon as funds should be specially contributed at least the entire New Testament must be printed in letters which the blind can read. To Dr. Samuel G. Howe of Boston, then engaged in experimenting to find a practical system of raised letters, was granted one thousand dollars and later further sums toward the expense of printing the New Testament in raised letters. The Massachusetts Bible Society contributed for this work one thousand dollars, and the New York Female Bible Society eight hundred dollars more. "What," said a blind woman to Dr. Howe, "do you think I can read the New Testament which you are printing?

Then I can die in peace!" It was like a miracle of the Lord Jesus. The Board could not fail to take part in so blessed a work. And yet the agreement to begin this work was equivalent to a promise to carry it on. And so, year after year, many thousands of dollars have been expended by the Society in printing books for the blind.

Almost unconsciously, about the same time, the Board agreed to another permanent draft upon the Treasury. An application came from the American Sunday School Union for the terms on which it could be supplied with Scriptures, since it wished to cease printing Bibles. The Managers agreed cordially to put that Society on the same footing, as to prices, with Auxiliary Bible Societies; allowing it, more-over, six months credit. Later the Sunday School Union desired Testaments which it could sell at ten cents. They were furnished, although they cost the Society eleven and a half cents a piece. The arrangement meant a steady burden upon the finances of the Society, yet it was justified because the Sunday School Union distributed the books widely over the country.

The financing of the Society was complicated by the un-expected in 1836 and 1837. It then had to conduct work under the stress of a terrible financial panic. In 1836 the Board of Managers actually apologised to the public because of a small balance in the Treasury at the end of the year. It had promised to pay about forty thousand dollars to mis-sions abroad, and part of the money was left in hand to be paid after correspondence. The change from fulness to emptiness of the Treasury came with the appalling sudden-ness of a tropical storm. In that year naturally a slight diminution of income was to be expected through the forma-tion of the American and Foreign Bible Society. But be-sides this a crisis arose in commercial circles through the tariff and the removal of United States funds from the banks under President Jackson's financial policy. Strin-gency for money then began.

The year 1837 was an entire year of pecuniary embarrass-ment and suffering in every part of the country. Book sales were about five thousand dollars below the average in each of three next succeeding years. Collections of money for the Bible Society were difficult and sometimes impossible. Auxiliaries in many cases had to take payment in farm produce for Scriptures or for annual subscriptions toward the Bible Society work. Such contributions often spoiled in store because there was no transportation to a market. In the West when money was paid over, the treasurer of a local Society could not remit it to New York without a very heavy discount. Consequently money which ought to be in New York remained in the treasuries of Auxiliary Societies. Money that was sent sometimes lost its value on the journey to New York. The Treasurer's report for 1839 showed a balance in hand of $1,452.43, and frankly specified the elements of this balance to wit: Bills receivable not received, $562.43; broken bank and counterfeit notes, $142.50; Texas money not current, $747.50; total, $1,452.43.

As the time dragged along the stock of books in the depository was lower than for several years, but more Scriptures could not be printed because the receipts from sales had fallen off. The Board did not feel justified in borrowing money for printing, and was unwilling to plead importunately for money because of the suffering that blighted the whole nation. Like a noble ship driven by a hurricane, the Bible Society was thrust by each voracious wave nearer to a rocky coast. Money was not available to pay the appropriations for American Missions abroad. The Society was in debt to the mission in Ceylon, the missionaries having begun printing as soon as an appropriation was announced. In sheer desperation the Board considered dismissing the printers and binders in New York, and announcing to missionaries everywhere that it was impossible to furnish the promised money. Mr. Calhoun, foreseeing this, wrote from Turkey in 1838: "Your contributions have gladdened the hearts of the missionaries; will you now abandon them? If so my work will be short." Mr. Goodell at Constantinople wrote: "We cannot indulge for a moment the thought of the American Bible Society giving up its work in the Mediterranean regions. It would be unjust! The American Bible Society has been doing a great and good work here. If it holds on but three or four years longer it will complete the great things which it has undertaken, and then can retire with honour and with the gratitude of half the world." The Board of Managers when obliged to hear such reproachful pleading felt like a culprit before his righteous judge.

Before the end of 1838, as if in answer to the prayers of his distracted servants the Master had come to lead them to their desired haven, there was a sudden calm. Donations from Auxiliary Societies kept coming in until a total of twenty-four thousand dollars was reached. Such a sum had not before been paid in one year by Auxiliary Societies. Mr. James Douglass of Cavors, Scotland, without solicitation was suddenly moved to send a draft for one thousand pounds sterling, as a donation to the Society. About the same time some one bought a part of the land in Pennsylvania left to the Society by Dr. Boudinot fifteen years before, and this unexpectedly brought in two thousand dollars. Other legacies paid in 1837 and 1838 brought eighteen thousand dollars more into the Treasury. The lean years were ended; the relief seemed to be due to a divine intervention; the very printing presses hummed out psalms of thanksgiving. The missionaries in Ceylon received their belated grant; Scudder and Winslow in India beamed with happiness on receiving five thousand dollars at once to print books for the poor Tamil villagers; Agent Calhoun had solid comfort to spare for Goodell and Schauffler, the translators; and Siam, Africa and the Sandwich Islands received their allotted portions with joy. As for the men burdened with the problem of finding the means for all these important labours, they thanked God and went on with new courage.

It may be of interest to note, just here, the amount of receipts of the Society during the first twenty-five years. The aggregate of these receipts was $1,814,705. Almost half of this amount came from sales of books, and went to re-stock empty shelves. The donations of Auxiliary Societies during the twenty-five years amounted to $469,284. Donations from churches, societies, individuals, including Bible Societies not Auxiliary amounted to $391,475. Legacies received during the twenty-five years made a total of $103,410. About $24,000 were received from other sources such as rents, interest, etc. These totals made a very encouraging showing, when we remember the two or three years of financial panic and real poverty in almost all parts of the country.

The problem of providing means for a work like that of the Society was an inheritance from the fathers. The people who called the Society into being had mostly passed away at the end of a quarter of a century, and so to many the Bible Society seemed a case of spontaneous generation for the maintenance of which no one outside of its membership had responsibility. Such careless aloofness was due to ignorance and not to ill-will. Financing the Society required the Board in the executive officers to keep close to the people so as to remove ignorance, scatter information, and so to draw the sons to feel toward the Society as their fathers did. The Society was a living thing; therefore, it could not remain limited to the measure of its first activities; it grew, and growth means larger supplies of the means of support. The development of the object for which the Society was formed was a sacred trust committed to the Society by the last generation that the Board might hand it down to its successors. The Bible Society, like a great fruit-bearing tree, needs not only earth and sunlight and space to grow, but water and suitable nourishment in order to rejoice the people with abundant fruit. To provide these is a duty that falls upon the shoulders of each successive generation of our people, and to them, if they but appreciate it, such a duty will prove a veritable mantle of Elijah.

At the end of the first twenty-five years of its existence the Bible Society represented the definite purpose of a solid and influential part of the American people. It had a right to assume that all the people can be interested in learning its work, and can learn that it properly depends upon the people all over the land for the support of enterprises placed in its hands by the providence of God. When there is questioning, then, why the American Bible Society should stand at the door pleading for money, the answer is that the Board and its officers are bound to make these requests. This is not like some visionary scheme for drawing light and heat without labour or expense from coal as it lies in the mine. It is a skilfully directed missionary enterprise, which, in the providence of God, like all sane enterprises of His church, had direct and active relation to the whole progress of the race.

CHAPTER XXI

THE GAINS OF TWENTY-FIVE YEARS

On the 13th day of May, 1841, the American Bible Society met at the Society's house in New York at nine o'clock A. M., and after the routine business was transacted, at half past nine a procession was formed, consisting of officers, managers, guests, members, delegates, clergymen and others, which moved to the Tabernacle on Broadway. At ten o'clock the chair was taken by the President supported by six Vice-Presidents, and the meeting was opened by Rev. Dr. Milnor reading part of the 119th Psalm.

President John Cotton Smith delivered an address, emphasising the promise for the future found in the experiences of the past. Secretary Brigham then read a report of the operations of the twenty-fifth year. The issues were 150,202 volumes, making the aggregate issues of the Society in twenty-five years 2,795,698 volumes. The receipts from all sources amounted to $118,860.41; the aggregate receipts for twenty-five years being $947,384.06. The Scriptures had been circulated in about fifty languages and especially among the poor who would not otherwise have received the gospel.

The report of this meeting adds, " As usual the audience was immense and attentive, evincing unabated attachment to the circulation of the Bible." A part of this interest came from a dramatic incident. The Rev. Hiram Bingham, missionary of the American Board in the Sandwich Islands, and translator of the Bible, was called upon for an address. He brought forward and formally presented to the Society a copy of the Bible in Hawaiian, the result of fifteen years' labour which he said had been made available to the people by financial aid from the American Bible Society. A thrill ran through the audience like that which moved the multitude when Jesus Christ gave hearing and speech to the dumb. People looked their satisfaction into each other's eyes.

Mr. Bingham made a telling point in his address when he said that he had just learned that the Society had appropriated fifty thousand dollars to be given for Bible work among heathen abroad during the current year. " I cannot conceal my grief," he said. " If I were to express my feeling and that of my associates I would say to the Board of Managers, ' Take thy bill quickly and write five hundred thousand.' Would not this enlightened and Christian assembly approve the amendment? Just think of it; fifty thousand dollars for the whole pagan world!" The passionate entreaty was not lost upon the audience, although no action upon it could be hastily taken. During years they had given and had prayed that their gifts might advance the kingdom. The gifts and the prayers had been accepted and used by God as they desired! In Hawaii a newly Christianised nation was the result! Such an appeal emphasised as nothing else could the increased opportunity for service which marked these twenty-five years. Men went from that meeting convinced of the great possibilities which God has placed before the Society, and in it before all Christians.

One point of difference in the position of the Society in 1841 compared with its uncertain beginnings in 1816 is shown in its stable administration. The outstanding feature of its administration was its dependence upon the Auxiliary Bible Societies. Many of them represented mere good intentions without strength to execute; and the list of Auxiliary Societies had been in great measure cleared of the weaklings. Many dormant Auxiliaries had been revived, sometimes with a more simple organisation. All of the Auxiliaries were knit more firmly together through their union with the American Bible Society, and all knew that the plan of this combined action was a plan that would work. Aspirations like that for the General Supply or for work in foreign fields would have vanished like air-castles of other types had these Societies not been bound together by means of a national Society.

Another salient point of difference between the Society in 1841 and the Society in 1816 was its comprehension of its home field. The fact that distribution at home was a vital necessity, had become elucidated and fully understood. In 1816 the great work before the Society was to print Bibles. It is a great thing to print many Bibles, but in 1841 it had become a commonplace axiom that though the number printed be enough to bury the Bible House, the books would do no good unless carried forth to the needy. The Society had learned in some degree that people may eat at the same table, find shelter under the same roof, and yet be miles apart in their spiritual sympathies. It now included in its fields points in Europe, Asia, and Africa, but it appreciated the wrong which would be involved in thinking the needs of Turkey more urgent than those of Tennessee.

Its field at home had many pressing problems, the most grave of which was that after all the lavish supply there were still in these United States people handicapped by ignorance of the Bible. How could any one live without the Bible for one year? Members of the Board would almost as soon give up life as give up the Bible. The golden rule of a Bible Society is to do to others, even at home, as it would be done by. Some paragraphs in the report of May, 1841, showed both the need and the helpless desires of destitute people to find the Bible. One agent in the mountains of Kentucky said that hundreds and thousands of women in that state are anxious to get the Bible, praying God to let them have one, who never had and never would have so much as fifty cents of their own. One of these women said she loved the Bible; she had seen but one in five years, and that belonged to a friend living seven miles away. She would buy a Bible but she had no money. The agent gave her one. Tears came to her eyes as she said, " It is the most precious present I have ever received. Now instead of visiting on Sunday I can stay with my Bible and be happy." Another agent in southeastern Georgia told of a house which he reached by a log path; that is, a line of trees so felled that one touches the other, bridging a great swamp. In three families which the agent visited at the other end of this primitive path, but one person could read; but when that one person was given a Bible, the three families established the custom of meeting together every night and the one read aloud to them, stooping over the fire of pine knots which gave them light.   The Society had a right to insist that " demand for the Bible among the destitute proves that God both prepares their hearts to receive it, and calls upon us to circulate it more extensively."

In the early years of the Society some warm-hearted Christians feared the effect of giving to ignorant people Bibles without notes.   This fear was of the same quality as that of a grandmother who protests on seeing a grandchild fed meat for the first time.   But the dread of Bibles without notes slowly passed away.   As President Mark Hopkins strongly said in an address at the Anniversary in 1840 (which we cannot give in full), none should say there is harm in giving ignorant people the Bible without notes. The sun requires no artifical medium by which to transmit its light.   The free air of heaven needs no addendum of human perfumes to make it healthful.   No one hesitates to let his child see the works of God in the sky or in the rocks fearing lest the child's simple mind be disturbed by the controversies of geologists and astronomers.   The child's emotions of beauty and sublimity are called forth by seeing the grandeurs of nature.   So with the Bible.

The Biblical scientist may dig down through the strata of truth and adopt what pleases him; " but let the child and the unlettered feel the beauty and sublimity and moral power of the precepts and facts of revelation which God has made to stand out as great rocky mountains.   Love of truth helps one to comprehend truth."   And so it is lawful to place the light of truth in the benighted cottage; to give durable riches to the poor; to give the oil of joy to widow and orphan; to give the soldier, the sailor, and the immigrant an invaluable directory.   The Society had freely added all these to the privileges of its home field in twenty-five years of experience.

The Society's serious work in the foreign field was entirely the development of a decade, and that field in 1841 was no longer a vague expanse of unknown and unclassified paganism.   The American foreign missionary societies since the organisation of the Bible Society had sent men to spread the gospel in many foreign lands.   As soon as these mission-

aries realised the need of Bibles they cried aloud to the
American Bible Society for help, so that by the end of the
twenty-fifth year the work of the Society was linked to
that of missions in Asia, Africa, and Oceania besides those
in America and in Europe.   Hiram Bingham said truly, in
speaking of the Bible Society at the anniversary, that " the
Bible cause every year assumes new importance from the
indispensable aid which it furnishes the advancing cause of
Christian missions."   It seemed almost as if the whole question of a speedy evangelisation of the world might depend
upon the will of contributors to Bible Societies.

Another point of gain in the equipment of the Society in
twenty-five years was its increased command of languages.
In 1817 the Board had already arranged to purchase French
and German Scriptures, and expressed the hope that some
time to these it might add Scriptures in Spanish and Portuguese.   By the end of 1841 the Society had printed or aided
in printing Bibles, Testaments or portions in five languages
of the American Indians, seven European languages, five
languages of Asiatic Turkey, seven languages of India, besides Hawaiian, Chinese, and the Grebo language of West
Africa.   Moreover, in carrying on its work, it had found
it necessary to purchase Scriptures in twenty other languages.

This rapid gain sprang from the entreaty of missionaries
for aid not only in printing but also in translating the
Scriptures.   The American Board in those days was the
largest of the foreign missionary societies, and consequently
the larger part of these requests came from its missions.
Under its charter that Society was obliged to print Bibles
for its different fields when necessary.   In its first twenty
years it had printed the Scriptures in various alien languages.   In September, 1839, however, Rev. Dr. Anderson, Secretary of the A. B. C. F. M., wrote Secretary Brigham that appropriations had been made to its missionary
stations absorbing all its probable income; but that it had
not appropriated one dollar for printing Scriptures, leaving
this entirely to the American Bible Society.

The printing of Bibles for missions brought the Society
an important advantage in close personal relations with the

VETERAN TRANSLATORS IN TURKEY

Left to right: Rev. Elias Riggs, Rev. William Goodell, Rev. W. D. Schauffler

missionaries who knew their fields most thoroughly. They must have been men of strong initiative and endurance who in those days could venture to translate the Bible. Some of the names of the early missionaries of the American Board have been treasured in Bible Society records as well as in those of the missionary Society. We have room only to mention a few who were busy with Bible translation at that time: J. B. Adger, William Goodell, W. G. Schauffler, H. G. O. Dwight, and Elias Riggs, in Turkey; Hiram Bingham in the Sandwich Islands, and E. C. Bridgman in China; and among missionaries working in the United States, S. Riggs, Williamson, besides Dencke, whose was the version in the Delaware language first undertaken by the Society. These men put into the hands of the Bible Society a God-given power, for it takes several years to fit out one missionary in a single language, but in one year a Bible Society can make thousands of Bibles in many languages which when ready can be set in places reached by no living missionary.

A curious illustration of the importance of this power was seen in Bombay, India, when as a by-product of the Society's edition of the Scriptures in Marathi, Israel was enlightened. Numbers of Jews living in Bombay had forgotten Hebrew and had almost lost the principles of their religion. But they eagerly took up the study of the Old Testament in Marathi which was a revelation to them, and led to important reforms. So in this blessed work the very languages come bowing the neck to receive the yoke of the Son of God, lending themselves to the sower of the Word.

From all this it becomes clear that the Society had now reached maturity. Its bones were hardened, its muscles toughened, and its eyes trained accurately to observe. Much preparation is required to turn the recruit into a soldier; seasoned, cool and unflinching. The Society had found that a means used of God for securing his servants from unfruitful effort is often a plain blocking of the way. As Burke says, " Our antagonist is our helper." The fact is that men pray for quiet success too much. They would not seek the quiet that belongs to stagnation. Any life, to be tolerable, must have aspirations which spring from discontent with current conditions; leading perhaps to strife, but certainly to struggle. The Board of Managers probably much desired a plain and easy path, but looking back upon its course during these years, it saw that the progress gained could not have been gained by any who sit at ease in Zion.

The death list in the records of the Bible Society during twenty-five years includes three Presidents, twenty-three vice-Presidents, and seventeen members of the Board of Managers. As President John Cotton Smith said: " The virtues of the men who founded the American Bible Society are to be revered and emulated, but the places once occupied by those deceased associates in active duty have been successively filled by men capable and qualified for these onerous and responsible offices." The men now in charge of the affairs of the Society found themselves trusted by the people not alone because of the great men who had gone but because of their own good service, just as the soldier is rewarded on the battle-field; not for the rank which he holds but for what he has done.

A precious gain of the Society in its first quarter century was a larger appreciation of the power of the Bible to change men. We may not understand this power, but we can feel it and see it, just as we can live and grow without understanding how food is changed into blood, muscle and bone. Where the Bible is not read corrupt forms of religion prevail. It was the privilege of the Society in these years to see nations definitely influenced by the Bible in South America, in Turkey, and in the Sandwich Islands, besides noting its influence in different parts of the United States. In Latin America, whether in Mexico, West Indies or the different countries of South America, cases were repeatedly observed where the lives of men were lifted to a high plane through Bible study; and many were prepared for receiving instructions of the missionaries soon to establish themselves in those regions. In Greece twenty thousand copies of the New Testament had been scattered among the schools and the homes of the common people. This sowing was somewhat like that of the parable; much of the seed seemed wasted, and yet, there too, the seed which fell on good ground repaid all the expense and all the labour.

The Bible points out germicides which arrest moral and spiritual decay. No medical man or professor of bacteriology is as positively sure as this book in the indication of antiseptics that prevent blood-poisoning.

In Turkey before 1841 twenty-five American missionaries with their wives had established themselves in ten widely separated stations in different parts of the empire. Each one of these stations was a distributing centre for Scriptures furnished by the Bible Society. The stations nearest the coast were built upon foundations laid by Mr. Benjamin Barker, Agent of the British and Foreign Bible Society; but after 1836 they were supplied by the American Bible Society, some with books printed in Turkey on the mission press at its expense, some with Scriptures bought from the Agent of the British Society. By the close linking of the Society with the missions these Scriptures were distributed with a discretion and thoroughness which no single agent of any Bible Society could exercise; and the result, precious fruit of larger grants of the American Bible Society, was a general clearing of the religious ideas of Armenians and Greeks. Unsound thoughts leave the mind in the presence of the word of God as silt leaves the turbid stream, sinking to the bottom where it belongs, when exposed to the light and air of heaven.

A lesson of these experiences is that the Bible glorifies God. The Book was planted as an essential in the first American colonies; it moved men to make so rare a treasure known to the destitute; it thus assured in the midst of the nation a will to serve the purposes of God, and became fundamental in both Bible Society and missionary Society. Thoughtful men regarding the story of the first quarter of a century of the Bible Society were startled by evidence, withal, that God's hand directed its course. This guidance was seen in the time at which the organisation took place, just as immigration commenced to assume importance and as the vast territories of " Louisiana " received from Napoleon had begun to attract settlers. It was seen in the responsibility brought upon the Society for providing French, Spanish and German Scriptures to be used in the United States; it was seen again in the attention to needs in South

America forced by a logic like that of Joseph Hughes: if we can give Bibles to the aliens in the United States, why not to those using the same languages elsewhere? It was seen in the simultaneous invention by several Auxiliary Bible Societies of the plan of systematic supply of all destitute families in their local fields within two years' time, which plan men dared apply to the whole United States; and it was seen again in the echo from American missions abroad of the reports of this General Supply at home, that led to the momentous decision to supply all American foreign missionaries, so making the American Society a world Bible Society.

Thus the Board of Managers had seen a vision of God's hand beckoning and had heard His voice calling to the action for which He Himself had raised it up. Nothing had remained for them to do but to throw energy and persistence into their work, with thanksgiving for the privilege of a share in the divine purpose to establish His kingdom; and with every servant through whom from the beginning the kingdom has been in any way advanced, each member of the Board and every Secretary was moved to the utterance of the old song: " The Lord has triumphed gloriously, praise ye the Lord ! "

FOURTH PERIOD 1841-1861

CHAPTER XXII

AMONG DESTITUTE AMERICANS

A MOST commonplace axiom declares acts to be permanent in their results. On the other hand any great enterprise in these days has some date which men call its beginning, although the true beginning is not commonly sought. The American Bible Society came into existence in 1816; before that, however, the idea from which it sprang was rooted in many lands. Europe, with its turmoil of clashing religious and political systems; the Roman Empire, with its iron rigidity of organisation; the Jewish Commonwealth, with its glory and its shame, all nourished some roots of this great idea. The idea which took form in America in 1816 did not then have its beginning. Paul has planted, Apollos has watered, and the increase has followed in time from principles of uplift long unnoted.

Small events described in the first twenty-five years covered by this story have somehow become knit together in a complicated pattern. Since the story hereafter deals more clearly with results than with mere hopes and plans, mystery gives place to certainty that a Society " whose beginnings are eternal " does not end when men connected with it end their active life. An empire built upon force of arms begins with a man skilled in arms and bold in self-assertion, and it ends when his successors let it fall. The enterprise of the Bible Society abides because it plants in the minds of sincere Bible lovers, God's truth. Some of these will hand the Word down to children's children, and some will pass it on to neighbours who bequeath it to their children's children. The result is an ever widening circle whose centre is the truth which makes men free. An end to this extension cannot be imagined, any more than one can imagine the end of rare and beautiful flowers seen in Japan

or China or South America, and brought to our gardens.
No one discusses whether seed or flower came first, and no
one dreams of an end to the species, once established in the
soil.

The permanence of the plant once established was not
necessarily prominent in the minds of the Board as it faced
the question, How can the work of the Society advance in
this country with the growth of population? The first step
to finding the destitute Americans in the home field was appreciation, at last, of its immensity. The strongest Auxiliary Bible Societies were all within three hundred miles of
New York City; but by painful experience the Board had
learned in 1841 that its greatest problems lay beyond a circle
three hundred miles from New York. Sitting in New York
the Board heard appeals from the people and from its
Agents; some were five hundred miles away, some eight
hundred, some twelve hundred, and some almost three
thousand miles away, yet within the limits of the United
States. The efficiency of plans to increase the circulation
of the Bible at such distances rested upon the hearts of
members of the Board as constantly as the need to make
money hangs about the neck of one who has planned to acquire quickly a million dollars. And the urgency of these
appeals pressed upon the Managers of the Bible Society because without the Bible men, women and children of the
frontier districts would become hardened through following their own hot desires as the earth is hardened by the sun
in a weary land where no water is.

In this desperate condition were the people among whom
Agent Simpson of Kentucky worked in the late forties and
of whom he wrote. " They are often as careless and indifferent about spiritual things as the wild beasts in their
own mountains. No minister has ever had access to them,
and around them no moral restraints are ever thrown." Yet
these were full-blooded descendants of the early colonists.
The greatness of its task was forced upon the attention of
the Board by such reports as that one-fourth of the families
of Kentucky had no Bible; in several election districts of
Maryland the same ratio of destitution was found; in Potter
County, Pennsylvania, which had been supplied five years be-

fore, fully one-fourth of the families in the increased population were destitute. The need to save our own people
from dry rot, and the sense that it was for their sake, perhaps, that the Bible Society had " come to the kingdom,"
pressed ceaselessly upon conscience. The members of the
Board, the Secretaries, the Agents, the Auxiliaries, the explorers whom the Auxiliaries employed, their officers, and
the many branch Societies might have been found, therefore, in the twenty years before the Civil War breathlessly
working together for the one object of the Bible Society —
an instrument of uplift divinely supplied with pervasive
power.

By this time the American Bible Society had some thousands of Life Members and a very considerable number of
Life Directors. To these friends the Board looked for aid.
Life Members and Life Directors scattered over the whole
breadth of the country might distribute many Bibles. The
Board, therefore, decided in 1841 to let every Life Member
participate in Bible distribution by receiving without charge
one dollar's worth of Bibles or Testaments in each year.
The same cheap books to a larger value would be given, on
request, to each of the Life Directors. In the first year
after this decision about eleven hundred dollars' worth of
Bibles and Testaments were distributed among the poor by
Life Members and Life Directors. Later it became necessary once or twice for the Board to call attention to the purpose of enabling Life Members and Life Directors to be
agents of Bible distribution, for which this annuity of books
was allowed; but the purpose has been, to a large degree,
carried out, many and many worthy poor having received,
through Life Directors and Life Members, Scriptures which
they otherwise could not have obtained. The system was
as simple as the distribution of water from an irrigating
canal over a wide expanse of country by means of little
channels opened when needed by individual farmers.

Another method of widely distributing Scriptures which
suggested itself to the Board of Managers was enlistment of
the good offices of pastors. It seemed reasonable that the
destitute should be supplied with Scriptures by their nearest
neighbours, and the Board sent out circulars urging pastors

of churches to help the local Auxiliary Societies to reach
needs in their own fields.   No agency could equal churches
interested in the work and co-operating with the Society.
The pastor is one individual in a church, but by his leader-
ship the people are impelled to win others.   It was this great
influence which the Board sought to gain and did gain in the
sparsely settled districts.   As the churches became larger
and the cares of the clergy more complicated, it came to pass
in many instances, however, that pastors replied, when asked
to act as distributors and collectors for the Bible Society,
that with the duties of their charges and the supervision of
the many charities of the day they were taxed to the full extent of their physical powers.   When asked, at least to induce members of their churches to lend a hand in Bible distribution, many replied that laymen are so pressed with the
legitimate engagements of business as to have little time to
make personal distribution of Scriptures.   The country was
growing up; its people were fully occupied.   The Board
was forced to rely chiefly upon Auxiliary Societies for exploring the needy fastnesses of the West.

The Board at its station in New York regarded Auxiliary
Bible Societies five hundred, a thousand, or fifteen hundred
miles away as the natural outlet for the stream of Bibles
and Testaments continually issuing from the Bible House.
Many days' journey from that Managers' Room, where
reigned supreme the one desire to build up character in the
nation, somebody must seek out those careless about character.   Auxiliary Societies on the ground could most wisely
choose and direct explorers and Bible distributors.   So it
came about that the Board urged the six hundred or more
Auxiliary Societies beyond the Alleghanies to strengthen
their organisations, securing the co-operation of every church
and every individual.

The Auxiliaries of the Eastern States were caring for
their own fields.   The New York Bible Society was supplying the destitute in New York City and the immigrants as
they landed after the tedious passage across the ocean.
Through work among the merchant ships in the harbour,
the New York Society and also the Philadelphia Society
found means of getting Bibles into Spain.   This in the

fifties was an impossible feat if directly attempted. Spanish sailors in New York harbour, however, supplied with the Book which to them was a curiosity were careful enough to see that no custom house or police devices in their own land touched their own private property. The Massachusetts Bible Society, the New Hampshire Bible Society, the Vermont Bible Society, comparatively near at hand, were all busy with the distribution in their own states. The Pennsylvania Bible Society in the three years, 1841 to 1844, distributed one hundred and fifty-three thousand volumes in its own field. It built a commodious Bible House in Philadelphia but even this expense did not lead it to diminish the donation of some five thousand dollars which each year it attempted to place at the disposal of the national Society. The Virginia Bible Society, fully awake to the ignorance which was threatening the mountain regions of that state, effectively worked for Bible distribution, placing two or three thousand volumes each year in the most needy districts. But it was beyond the five hundred mile limit that the Board of Managers most felt its dependence upon Auxiliaries as channels of distribution.

Types of the distant but active societies linking remote populations with the warm sympathy centred in New York are worthy of notice. One was the Nashville Bible Society, of which General Andrew Jackson had been the first vice-President. This Society was the source of supply of all destitute families in Middle Tennessee in 1829, and twenty-five years later was busily distributing Scriptures not only in its own, but in many neighbouring counties. Another efficient Society was the Charleston Auxiliary in South Carolina which paid a part of the salary of the Agent sent by the Board to supervise Bible distribution in that state, and which showed marked activity until the Civil War cut off, for a time, communication between the New York Bible House and the Southern States. One of the last acts of the Charleston Auxiliary before the outbreak of the Civil War was in 1860 to send a donation of one thousand dollars to the American Bible Society while at the same time distributing 800 volumes of Scripture among the troops who were shortly to begin the attack upon Fort Sumter. Another of these more distant Bible Societies was the Alabama Bible Society which in 1852 built a serviceable Bible House stocked with Scriptures for the surrounding ten or fifteen counties. A thousand miles or so from New York was the New Orleans Bible Society. Here the American Bible Society kept a stock of about $5,000 worth of Scriptures in various languages for distribution among interior towns, and, during the Mexican War, in Texas and in Mexico. After the Mexican War the New Orleans Bible Society bought the whole stock of books belonging to the American Bible Society in that city and shortly took part in the organisation of the Southwestern Bible Society at New Orleans in which it was merged and which built a Bible House in New Orleans from which Bible workers throughout the Southwest could obtain supplies.

In 1857 the Southwestern Bible Society reported that during the six years since its organisation it had sent 42,000 volumes of Scripture into Louisiana and Southern Mississippi, and had explored territories which up to this moment had never been systematically examined. Equally important, but not quite so far away, was the St. Louis Bible Society whose efficiency was shown in the year of financial panic, 1847, by its visitation of ten thousand families in Missouri, of whom only three hundred destitute of the Bible refused to be supplied. Still within a circle of one thousand miles from New York, the officers of the Auxiliaries in Illinois took up enthusiastically the plan of establishing branch Societies in every township. In 1855 there were in that state six hundred and twenty-five Auxiliary Bible Societies and branches. In 1857 there were a thousand so well organised that there were fully one thousand local depositories in the state. At the outbreak of the Civil War in 1861, Illinois had one thousand two hundred and twenty-five Bible Societies which had issued fifty-five thousand volumes during the year; fifteen hundred ministers co-operating heartily in the distribution and forming a part of an effective army of ten thousand unpaid volunteers engaged in Bible distribution in the state.

Separated from New York by the whole breadth of the Continent, in 1850 an Auxiliary Bible Society was organised in San Francisco by the Rev. F. Buel, whom the Board had sent in August in 1849, by way of the Panama railroad, post haste to furnish Bibles for that wonderful region of gold which passed through no territorial childhood, but almost as soon as Commodore Sloat and Colonel Fremont had taken possession sprang into notice a full grown and amply populated country demanding admission as a state. Almost with its first introduction to the people of the Eastern States, Christian workers hurried to this wonderful new country. Churches were built and to the infinite satisfaction of the Board of Managers of the Bible Society, in settlements where no preacher had yet appeared, Bible depositories had been opened, stocked with Scriptures in almost all the languages of Babel. Two thousand miles west of New York was another distributing centre among the Mormons in Utah. At first Bible distribution was approved and the Mormons themselves organised little local Bible Societies; but in 1858 there is a record of the unhappy ending of the work so pleasantly commenced. In that year the Mormons expelled from Utah territory the Bible Society Agents.

Of course there were some idle and inefficient Societies which could not be moved by any high tension motors in New York, but in general the zeal and the efficiency of these distant Auxiliary Societies counted for much in solving the problems of the Board.

The various methods devised by the Board for the supply of the United States form a complicated whole sometimes described summarily as "machinery." But in Bible distribution on such a scale no system of mere machinery can achieve results. In this case action must be thoughtful and sympathetic or the object will not be attained for which the great Master of all work thrusts forth His labourers. As already mentioned, the Board employed superintending and advisory agents, especially in fields where the duty of seeking and supplying the destitute was neglected or imperfectly performed. Each Agent had under his supervision from forty to fifty counties, in each of which, theoretically, an Auxiliary Bible Society was constantly in action. In the districts of the West and Southwest, far from New York, it was found that Auxiliaries could do little unless

occasionally visited by an Agent to advise and to strengthen
their purpose of looking up and supplying the destitute.   An
illustration of the influence of the Agents marks a stage of
progress in New Jersey.   In 1848 there were in that state
forty-one Auxiliary Bible Societies.   Twenty-three of these
were absolutely torpid.   An Agent was appointed by the
Board to re-animate these local Bible Societies.   After five
years, returns from New Jersey showed that there was
hardly a single inactive Society in the state.   But the reports
of the national Society do not show the whole result of
such agencies, for a number of strong state Societies appointed and supported Agents of their own to advise and encourage the county Auxiliaries.

In 1842 the number of Agents employed by the American Bible Society was fifteen.   The number was gradually
increased until after four or five years, between thirty and
forty Agents were in the service all the time.   These Agents
were carefully selected for the work, since, like St. Paul,
they must count physical obstacles as naught.   In a newly
settled region the Bible Agent's condition resembles that of
the settlers whose log huts he visits.   His work is of the
same type as that of men newly occupying wild land.   It
is the work of taking out the tangled undergrowth, felling
trees, dragging together logs, chopping up branches, and
finally ploughing and harrowing the soil that it may be seeded
down.   Of a typical Agent it is recorded that " he sought
to organise a Bible Society Auxiliary in every congregation."   This was the Rev. Thomas Stringfield, of Tennessee
and Alabama, who afterwards became editor, the first editor
in fact of the *Southwestern Christian Advocate,* now the
Christian Advocate published at Nashville, Tennessee,
being the organ of the Methodist Episcopal Church South.
Our space will not allow us to characterise in details the
members of this noble body of Christian workers.

Nothing was ever achieved without enthusiasm, and therefore Agents must feel that they are called to the work, and
are doing that for which God has sent them.   They were
chosen for spiritual qualities as well as for those more ob-
viously needed which imply strength of body and of mind;
and it has been the experience of the Society from the be-

ginning that to be personally engaged in taking the Bible to those who do not know or do not want it is a means of spiritual growth which is not to be surpassed.

Sometimes the work of taking Bibles into the wilderness was costly on account of the sparseness of the population. Rev. J. A. Baughman, Agent in Michigan, some ten years after the territory had become a state, reported that the distance he travelled during the year was 2,723 miles, but the number of books which he put into circulation was only three thousand five hundred volumes. An Agent in one of the Southern States gives in his report a glimpse of other cares in this kind of life: "I have been separated from my family in special cases eight or ten weeks at a time, suffering many inconveniences, several times being upset in stages, more than once barely escaping drowning on the coast, preaching usually three times on Sunday besides addressing Conventions and Auxiliary Societies almost every day during the week. All these things combine to make the year one of toil and sacrifice; but I do not regret it." Rev. J. J. Simpson, an Agent partly supported by the Lexington and Vicinity, Kentucky, Bible Society had for the goal of his efforts a visit to every family in his district that could be reached on horseback or on foot. One adventure in seeking out the houses of settlers hidden away in the woods, included missing the road in the dark and finding himself in a ravine from which there was no visible exit. Providentially, at this crisis, out of the darkness, two rough looking but kind-hearted farmers came to his relief. The records of this class of labour also include tragedies. The Rev. H. J. Durbin, one of these Agents, while riding through a forest in a storm was killed by a heavy branch torn from a tree by the gale. Rev. Richard Bond, an experienced and efficient Agent in Missouri, was killed by the accidental discharge of a carbine brought home as a trophy from Mexico by one of the volunteers. In Indiana, Agent Mayhew was drowned in fording a river. While Agent Hatcher of Tennessee was absent from home on a Bible tour in 1850, his house, library and papers were burned. The shock of the home-coming can be imagined!

The expense of maintaining agents among the Auxiliary

Societies was a subject of constant anxiety to the Board. The average annual cost to the Society of an Agent was something like one thousand dollars; but no new discussion of the question disclosed means of avoiding the expense. It could not be a wise economy to save the cost of Agents and let Auxiliary Societies give up the struggle and die. The newly settled regions in the West must be supplied at all costs; and after the year 1848 the Board deliberately decided to treat distant western territories as the British and Foreign Bible Society treated countries in Europe and Asia where Scriptures were not easily put in circulation. Besides the Agents, Colporteurs were employed wherever Auxiliaries were feeble, and in districts where no Auxiliary had been formed, to act as explorers to unearth and supply families that were carelessly living without the Bible.

Under the influence of the Agents the number of Auxiliary Societies and especially of local branches of the county Societies increased. In 1860 there were between four thousand and five thousand local Bible Societies, counting the branches and village committees. This means that as many as one hundred thousand people were engaged in a cordial and self-sacrificing effort to place God's word in every part of the domestic field in co-operation with the Society.

The question has often been raised, whether Bible distribution on such terms is worth while. One has only to call to mind that it plants in every district of the home land a single idea new to many, but which is instantly adopted by some after studying the Bible. This idea, foreign to those who have not the Bible reading habit, is the need of every man to abide in obedient dependence on God. The work of the Board of Managers in New York was like the labour of Sisyphus, for the peculiarity of Bible distribution in a growing nation is that it is never completed. Nevertheless men are so closely in contact with each other that of necessity they bear one another's burdens and, to some degree, they share one another's gains and advantages. An atom is added to the common stock by each man who lives worthily. He passes away when his work is done, but his good deeds live in some degree among those who follow. The scattering of the word of God among the settlers on the frontier thus prepared a future for many a district now fully occupied, and so is to be reckoned a noteworthy factor in the development of the nation.

CHAPTER XXIII

ONE peculiarity of any missionary society's relation to its enterprises is that feeble and helpless people can shape its use of the apparatus in hand as effectively as though having authority to command. The more helpless such people, the more clearly relief is due. The last chapter dealt with methods of Bible distribution developed under pressure of a general prior claim of the home field upon the Society. From beyond the accustomed range of the home field thousands of people now newly came into view who caused enormous increase in the responsibilities of the Board, until it almost attained the standing of a foster father to orphans. The events which brought forward these creators of new responsibilities were the Mexican War and a period of unrest in Europe.

In 1846, thirty years of peace was broken by war with Mexico. Like the most of such conflicts, this war was the explosion of fiery elements that had smouldered, out of sight, during years. Americans had settled in Texas before 1830 in considerable numbers. In 1836, after seeking in vain from the Mexican government some amelioration of its arbitrary rule over the American settlers, the Texans declared independence, and were recognised as an independent republic by the United States, and later by the most of the European governments. Proposals to admit Texas to the United States were opposed throughout the North because, if granted, the large territory added would favour slavery, and the weight in Congress would be increased of those with whom the North was in ceaseless controversy. Moreover, Mexico, framing a species of " Monroe Doctrine " for herself, had declared that if Texas were annexed by the United States, that act would mean war.

In 1845 President Polk, supported by the Secretary of State, John C. Calhoun, and the southern delegations in Congress, considered it wise to grant the request of the republic of Texas, refused during several years, for annexation to the United States, and Congress by joint resolution voted the annexation. Mexico at once broke off relations with the United States, and, a detachment of the United States Army being in Texas at this time, its troops in April, 1846, attacked this little force under General Taylor near the Rio Grande. Congress immediately voted war measures, and during the next two years the United States Army was fighting, while, American fashion, hurriedly preparing to fight. About a dozen serious battles took place; in September, 1847, the city of Mexico was captured, and on February 2, 1848, the conquerors dictated the terms of peace. The acquisition by the United States of lands about equal in area to the thirteen original states of the Union was one great result of the Mexican War. For this conquered land fifteen million dollars were paid under the Treaty of peace. The home field of the Bible Society was thus increased by a region which, roughly speaking, corresponds with the states of California, Utah, New Mexico, Arizona, and a part of Colorado.

The outbreak of war brought new demands upon the Bible Society. Calls from Texas for Scriptures and the establishment of Auxiliary Bible Societies there had already brought the Society into cordial relations with the people of that little-known province of Mexico. The men of the United States army were supplied with Bibles and Testaments, and the advance of the army into Mexico opened access to the Spanish speaking people of Mexico. Scriptures were issued for troops as they marched from home by the Cincinnati Young Men's Bible Society, by the New Orleans Bible Society, by chaplains at Vicksburg, Mississippi, to the officers of the army and to the troops sent west to occupy California; a thousand volumes were sent to the Texas Auxiliary Bible Societies, and the local Auxiliaries in New York, Boston, Pittsburg and Charleston, South Carolina, were energetic in supplying troops passing through these cities. So it came to pass that a large proportion of

the soldiers going to Mexico took with them Scriptures issued by the Society.

The opportunity to reach Mexicans also was seriously
taken in hand by the Board in 1847, when it decided to send
as its Agent to Mexico the Rev. W. H. Norris, formerly a
missionary in Buenos Aires, who had learned the Spanish
language and had proved himself throughly efficient.
Equipped with some thousands of Bibles and Testaments
in English, Spanish, French and German, Mr. Norris reached
the United States army in Vera Cruz toward the end of
the year. His power for meeting the difficulties of his
rather perplexing mission lay in his thorough belief in the
old saying that "one man with God is in the majority."
This agency was successful at least in placing the Bible in
the hands of many Mexicans who read it carefully and
were thus prepared to give a cordial reception to American
missionaries in after years.

During this period questions reared themselves unexpectedly, sometimes north and sometimes south of the
line, out of the institution of slavery. Like a wild grass
in a lawn, that sends out roots underground to invade choice
flower beds, each fragment of root endowed with persistence
of life that seems to defy eradication, the institution showed
itself on every side. The Mexican War was probably inevitable; but its outbreak at the time might be laid to the
eagerness of slave-holders to insure their influence in Congress. In hope of calming the controversy over the proposal
to annex Texas, the American Government just at this time
secured from Great Britain a treaty acknowledging the
rights of the United States over the territory of "Oregon,"
later carved into the states of Oregon, Washington and
Nevada. This gain it was hoped would, by balancing the
addition of Texas to the South, satisfy the North. The
addition of so immense a territory to the home field was
to the Bible Society a discovery of great communities who
are famine stricken, and therefore compel attention and
succour. These great Spanish speaking populations and
Indian populations were generally ignorant of what makes
men worth while, ensures a tranquil life, and is the basis of
mere business prosperity. Thus the backward Mexicans

COLPORTEUR AMONG THE SOLDIERS IN TEXAS

and the Indians, as well as the settlers in all the new territories, unseen and unknown to the Board at New York,
unwittingly compelled it to supply with Scriptures masses
of people not before included in the plans for the domestic
field.

Meanwhile the two sections of the country were steadily
drifting apart.   An antagonism grew up akin to those class
antagonisms where each body in the social order considers
its vested rights to be unjustly attacked.   In the North
Southerners were regarded as devoid of elementary moral
sense, while in the South the people dreaded any extension
of the notions of the " Yankees " as they dreaded Northern
frosts which untimely destroyed their crops.

The central figure in this fateful antagonism was a man
or woman who had no rights, so that social and political
authorities were free from obligation to humanize the master
of slaves when his conduct seemed other than humane.
The life of the slave, at its best, left little room for aspiration and development.   The field hands, especially, divided
their life into three unequal portions : toiling in the fields,
eating, and sleeping.   Few of the slaves could read.   Many
of their masters were unwilling to let them learn to read
because a slave rebellion was the Southern planter's bogey.
Among the house servants, in some cases, a few were permitted by the master or mistress to take lessons in reading
from the warm-hearted children of the manor.   The great
body of the slaves of the plantations, however, were looked
upon by people of the New England States as groaning
by reason of bondage, like Israel in Egypt.

Many good people in the Northern States thought that
the Bible Society ought to send Bibles to comfort the slaves.
In 1834 the Board of Managers had stated its principle of
supplying every race destitute of the Scriptures ; leaving
responsibility for the details of distribution in the United
States, however, to the wisdom and piety of the local Auxiliary Societies, aided, if need be, by grants from the Bible
House.   In 1845 the Board had to re-publish the statement
of 1834, again pointing out that co-operation in this good
work belonged to the Board, while the detailed measures
of distribution were the privilege and duty of the local

Auxiliaries. It later called attention to an example of work for slaves in which the Society had engaged in a small way. A missionary supported by a church in one of the northern counties of Alabama among the coloured people asked the Bible Society for books. He was furnished a grant of thirty Bibles and four hundred Testaments, the more gladly since he could discover the coloured people who could read. All such opportunities the Board was glad to use.

New agitation in the North led in 1848 to the formation of the Free Soil political party; and again requests showered upon the Board for a general distribution of Scriptures among the coloured people in the South. Individuals in the Northern States undertook to raise a large fund which would embarrass the Bible Society should it not undertake to furnish all slaves with the Scriptures.

The subject was of grave importance, but seemed to be imperfectly understood. The Board, therefore, issued a frank statement recalling previous demands of the same tenor, and the Society's desire to furnish the Bible to all classes able to use it. The statement cited the original plan by which the Society was expected to distribute Scriptures mostly through local Auxiliaries, some of which were large state institutions organised before the national Society, and becoming connected with it as do all Auxiliaries by two simple pledges; namely, to circulate the Scriptures without note or comment and to pay over surplus revenues to the general Society. In all other respects they were more independent of the general Society than the several states in the Union in relation to the federal government. This relation to Auxiliary Societies, the Board added, it would not disturb even if it had the power. If the Board were to intervene in the fields of Auxiliary Societies, a great number of them, overshadowed like grasses under a spreading tree, would sink into torpor and soon become extinct.

As to the question, how far local Auxiliaries should reasonably be expected to supply the coloured people of the South, the Managers declared that " no Bible Society in any place is bound to perform all sorts of duty. It is an institution with one great object. It is not formed for purposes of education, or missions, or the correction of civil laws; but it is formed for the purpose of circulating the word of God as far as practicable among all classes and conditions of men who are capable of using it. So far as there are coloured freemen or slaves within the limits of an Auxiliary who can be reached, who are capable of reading the blessed word of God, and are without it, they should unquestionably be supplied with it, as well as any other class. This duty is plain and imperative; so plain that the Board knows not a Bible Society in the South which calls it in question."

As to the question whether collection of money would simplify the problem of Bible work among slaves, the Board said that there was an almost universal inability among slaves to read, and an indisposition to instruct them equally extensive. Funds in the hands of any Bible Society could not remove these obstacles; and distributions on any considerable scale could not usefully be made before their removal. If numerous slaves in the South able to read the Bible were yet without it, and their holders consented to their being supplied, then collections of money would help to meet so important a demand. By formal and unanimous resolution the Board declared its policy to be the use of every opportunity for furthering Bible distribution among the slaves but it asked those who contribute to the Bible Society to consider " whether it is wise to restrict contributions to an object which can only be attained gradually; the funds for which remain in part unexpended, while elsewhere people equally destitute and more accessible are left unsupplied." This agitation over the slavery question was hardly more than a summons to be ready for labours sure to be called for some day, and from this time another expansion of the Society's responsibilities at home was foreseen.

Another such expansion began in a small way in Oregon. The first settlers were hunters and trappers, who established themselves on the coast to collect furs, and opened friendly trade relations with the Indians. The whole country was occupied by tribes of Indians who gauged the value of the region from the standpoint of the game-warden. They were nomad hunters, each tribe owning a certain strip of land valuable as a game preserve and a fishing privilege. The Indian's title to the land was the tomahawk, promptly used on any stranger who seemed to be a competitor. On the other hand the white men who flocked into the country after its recognition as a part of the United States, valued the land from the standpoint of the farmer and the industrial worker. Even the streams had value in terms of water power.

The Indians and the whites, then, differing as to the purpose for which Oregon existed, were pretty sure to clash as soon as they faced each other without interpreters able patiently to explain good-will as understood by the two parties. Consequently the story of the relations between the settlers and the Indians is unpleasant. In one part or another of this great region the settlers were at war with the Indians from 1845 almost constantly until 1855, and again in 1858. In fact, taking into account the Shoshone War and the Modoc War, that region was not free from bloodshed until the Indians were confined to reservations about 1875.

Missions to the Indians of Oregon were established by the Methodist Episcopal Church in 1834 and by the A. B. C. F. M. in 1836. Grants of Scriptures were made by the Bible Society to these, the American Home Missionary Society, and other missions.

The Oregon Auxiliary Bible Society was organised, where Portland now stands, in 1850 and the Clatsop County Auxiliary, near the mouth of the Colombia, in 1851. Rev. Mr. Phillips was sent to Oregon as Agent of the American Bible Society in 1853. He reported that the sturdy adventurers on the Pacific coast often showed real delight on finding the Society represented there by its Scriptures. Having suffered in the long, weary journey and many having lost their Bibles with other goods, would fain replenish their stock. The larger part of the Scriptures sent to Oregon in this period went into the hands of settlers.

In 1847, 250,000 immigrants landed in the United States, in large part fugitives from the famine in Ireland. They were worn with fatigues of the long voyage, but eager to find the work which would put them in a position better

than they had ever known. In 1848 other immigrants began to pour into the country in consequence of the con-
vulsions which shook the monarchies of Europe. From
1849 to 1853 an average of one thousand immigrants landed
every day. Every sailing vessel, brig, bark, or stately ship
which took the long voyage of six to eight weeks across
the ocean from European ports, brought numbers of dream-
ers that El Dorado lay within the growing republic. In
1850 ten new states had been added to the Union since the
Bible Society was organised, and these ten states had acquired a population almost equal to that of the whole country in 1816. The Society had already provided itself with
Scriptures in various languages, and had supplied, either
directly or through the local Bible Societies and the general
home missionary societies, immigrants in New York State,
Pennsylvania, Ohio, Illinois, Missouri and Wisconsin. In
1854 the Southwestern Bible Society at New Orleans distributed 10,000 volumes in thirteen languages obtained from
the American Bible Society. In 1858 it placed Testaments
or portions of Scripture in the hands of people from thirty
different nations speaking twenty languages. The New
York Bible Society made it a point, as far as possible, to
meet every man as he landed with a Testament in his own
language, obtained from the national Society and offered
to him by a man of his own nation. Hon. Samuel J. Walker,
former Secretary of the United States Treasury, prepared
a resolution which was adopted by the Washington City
Bible Society and forwarded to New York, urging the
preparation of a Testament in Spanish and English for use
among the multitudes of Spanish speaking citizens in California and the other territories acquired from Mexico.
This was done, and Testaments were printed in German,
Italian, Dutch, and Norwegian, with the English version
in parallel columns, so that the newcomers might be helped
to acquire the English language. These people maintained
their roots, so to speak, in many foreign lands. Only a
small proportion of the immigrants knew anything about
the Bible, even as a rule of ethics. Many rejoiced in the
idea that liberty is freedom from restraint of law.

These strangers, left like neglected apple trees to follow

their own nature, would be sure, notwithstanding a show of prosperity, to become morally debased, corrupt and corrupting.   Chancellor Ferris, of the New York University, who was chairman of the Distribution Committee at this time, drew a contrast between the expectation of friends of the Society in past years and the actual situation.   A few years ago, he said, it was thought that the country would soon be completely supplied with Bibles, so that there would be little for the Society to do in the United States.   But he pointed out, now that God is pouring upon the land a multitude of immigrants from the old world which is certain to increase, all Auxiliary Bible Societies, all churches, all Christians should rise to the emergency and supply the Society with funds for the great extension of its labours clearly foreseen.

It is hard to realise the burden which at this time rested upon the souls of the members of the Board and the Secretaries.   All felt that these people must be encouraged to read the Bible since it is the will of God, and since that book helps men to be law-abiding citizens.   Among the immigrants some were prepared to accept new ideas of life and growth.   The members of the Board knew that if the Society could increase the circulation of the Bible among these strangers, no matter whence the alien might come, he would surely be a blessing to the land.

Besides the principles which had always urged activity in the work of Bible distribution, the occurrences mentioned in this chapter brought to light a principle equally fundamental with the others, that destitution has in itself a claim to be supplied.   This is a natural requirement like the demand of the heart that tenderness be shown to infants on account of their helplessness.   Wherefore the extension of labour always awaiting a Bible Society is immeasurable.

CHAPTER XXIV

A VISION OF PERPETUAL GROWTH

In 1846 the Society at its annual meeting was greatly stirred by the prophetic vision of unlimited progress now opening before the Society. It directed the Board of Managers to arrange to print at least seven hundred and fifty thousand volumes during the year ending with March, 1847, and to plan for at least one million volumes of issues in the next year.

The Board abandoned the contract system of printing its books; bought new and improved presses; considerably reduced the cost of books; but at the end of the year found that notwithstanding these efforts, the issues from the press were more than one hundred thousand volumes less than had been called for by the Society. They also discovered the reason for this shortage. The Society's House was too small to receive the presses required for so great editions.

A daring flight of imagination was needed to believe that more space was necessary than the existing House, by an enlargement, could be made to yield. The great expansion of the field described in the last chapter, however, stirred the Board of Managers like a revelation. Members of the Board began to perceive the scope of the duty laid upon the Society from its very birth, and they decided to build a new house in accord with the thrilling vision. In July, 1847, a lot was contracted for on Chambers Street extending through to Reade Street which would accommodate a building almost twice as large as the Society's House in Nassau Street.

Disappointment came to the Board when it was compelled to give up the purchase of the Chambers Street plot on account of unsatisfactory surroundings and a doubtful validity of title. Yet it was perfectly clear that the demand for Scriptures would soon exceed the possibility of supply with the existing equipment. From 1836 to 1841 the average annual issue of Scriptures was 160,000 volumes. In the next five years the annual average was 340,000, and in the five years ending in 1851 the annual average of issues was 600,000. A committee was appointed to find a suitable site, if possible near Broadway between Canal and Bleecker Streets. This limitation, however, was afterwards removed, and early in 1852 land for the new Bible House was bought; a great plot of three quarters of an acre between Third and Fourth Avenues, Ninth Street and Astor Place at Eighth Street. The Committee had to explain, however, that they bought so large a lot because a good site downtown could not be found; the owners would not divide this plot, but after building a house which would accommodate the growing work of the Bible Society, any excess of land could easily be sold. The men of the Bible Society received their sight gradually like the one at Bethsaida who before seeing clearly had a dim stage when men seemed like trees.

When the Society began its operations John E. Caldwell, the first Agent, kept the depository at his office in an upper room at the corner of Nassau and Cedar Streets. Later the books were removed to a building on Cliff Street occupied by Mr. Fanshaw, who had the contract for printing and attended to the shipment of books. The books were issued from a room measuring nine by twelve feet. Later a four-story building was hired for the printer in Hanover Street, adjoining the Exchange. Here the Agent had his office and a rear room twenty feet square for the depository. In a moment of optimism he expressed his belief that he would yet see that room entirely filled with Bibles. In 1823 the Society's House in Nassau Street was finished and occupied. It contained a depository capable of holding one hundred thousand Bibles, and here the work of the Society was done, the building having been twice enlarged, until 1853.

After some hesitation about so great daring, the Board decided that three quarters of an acre would be an area none too large for a Bible House to serve the United States and American Missions abroad. This decision of the Board was never for a moment regretted.

THE BIBLE HOUSE
Astor Place, New York

The cornerstone of the Bible House in Astor Place was laid in the presence of a large assembly. The list of articles which the cornerstone contains is worth transcribing: one of the first Bibles published by the Society in 1817; one of the last edition of the Bible published in 1852; the thirty-six annual reports of the Society; the Bible Society Record from 1849 to 1852; a catalogue of the Society's Biblical Library; a copy of the report of the Versions Committee on the collation of the English Bible; the rules of the Board respecting principles to be followed in translation; a programme of the exercises at the laying of the cornerstone, and a copy of President Frelinghuysen's address.

The new Bible House had 741 feet of street front, was six stories high, with a floor space of about three acres besides the cellars and vaults. At the time of its completion it was one of the finest business houses in New York City. Its cost, with the land, was $303,000; but it was not built with money given for Bible distribution. The proceeds of the sale of the Society's House in Nassau Street were $105,000; more than twice the original cost. Fifty-nine thousand dollars was derived from special subscriptions made by friends in the city. The remainder of the cost of the building, $140,000, was borrowed upon mortgage, and the rents during the first year amounted to $20,000; more than twice the amount of the interest on the mortgage. As the rent roll increased it finally paid off the mortgage without further special subscriptions.

The records of the Board contain a definite mention of the belief of its members that the plan for the new Bible House was commensurate with the importance of the Bible cause by providential direction. When the new site was finally secured the Managers remembered almost with awe their disappointment at losing the land contracted for in Chambers Street, and they felt that the hand of the Lord was in it. When they found that the land now acquired on Astor Place had been assigned three several times to other purposes by the owners, and three times the purchase proposed had been given up, they were confirmed in the feeling that an over-ruling providence had reserved this land for nobler purposes.

The Building Committee, too, in its report referred to the narrow boundaries within which the Board was content to confine the Society at the outset, and compared that limited area with the commodious spaces of the new Bible House as showing how even the most sagacious of the Managers fell short of any conception of such a result as providence had realised for them. Though the expenditure for this great building was large and was entered upon without specific action of the Board, discussion of the amount to be expended, or of whence this money could be supplied, in no one instance was a properly audited bill presented a second time for payment. But like the widow's cruse of oil, the supply in the Treasury had been found equal to every call, ceasing only with the demands of the Building Committee; and this without the use, even temporarily, of one dollar of the ordinary contributions of the Society.

In February, 1854, the Building Committee made its final report and received the warmest thanks of the Board for its work. On the suggestion of Rev. Dr. S. H. Tyng of the Protestant Episcopal Church, Rev. Dr. Gardiner Spring, Pastor of the Brick Presbyterian Church, offered a prayer of thanksgiving to God for His gift to the Bible Society of this spacious and commodious house; imploring God's blessing upon it that it might ever continue to send forth leaves from the Tree of Life for the healing of the nations. All the members of the Board felt that the call to build this house had come as all God's calls come, arousing His servants to action by revelation of a great need, even as the vision of the man from Macedonia revealed new fields in Europe to St. Paul.

Christians believe that they hold the Bible in trust for the world. If this is true, to have failed to build this house under the existing circumstances would have been to condemn the Bible Society to a small and fruitless future. The Board, expecting great things from God, committed itself to a work whose length and breadth had not been imagined. In the year of their full occupation of the new house the issues of one month were more than in any one year of the Society's first eleven years. In the five years from 1846 to 1851 the average issues of each year were

600,000 volumes.   In the next five years, 1851 to 1856, the average issues were 940,000 volumes.   This quick expansion seemed instantly to justify the daring of the Board.

Many of the men who had laboured nobly to build up the strength and efficiency of the Bible Society, like Moses and Aaron as they led the people toward the Promised Land, fell out of the ranks before this great epoch was reached, and new workers took their places as do the reserves of an army whose front ranks are thinned.

By the election of Rev. Dr. E. S. Janes, Financial Secretary, to be a Bishop of the Methodist Episcopal Church, the Board had to regret in 1844 a great loss to the Society. As a successor to Dr. Janes the Rev. Dr. Noah Levings, pastor of a Methodist Episcopal Church in New York, was chosen financial Secretary.   Dr. Levings was well qualified for his work.   At the time it was said that he had no superior as a platform speaker in his denomination.   But in January, 1849, while returning from a journey for the Society to the South, he was taken ill and died at Cincinnati, greatly regretted by all who knew his diligent and efficient services as Secretary of the Society.

In April, 1845, the Bible Society was called to mourn the death of Rev. Dr. James Milnor, for more than twenty years a Secretary of the Society and a leader in many of its great decisions.   Dr. Milnor had ceased to perform the duties of a Secretary some years before, but he was active in all the affairs of the Board of Managers; in fact, he had served as chairman of the Anniversaries Committee in preparing for the annual meeting of the Society held about a month after his death.   His legal training and familiarity with business methods fitted him to render services in the Board from which many ministers would shrink.   He was remarkably free from small prejudices.   When questions difficult of adjustment arose in the Board, they were approached by Dr. Milnor with a frankness and sincerity that showed how earnestly he sought truth and right, and this habit secured for him the confidence of his associates.   His devoted and scriptural piety made him rejoice in discovering the image of Christ under any outward form.   In the Bible cause this noble spirit had ample scope.   The last sermon which he preached in St. George's Church two days before his death was on Christian union. All of the members of the Board, as well as the Secretaries of the Society, felt his death as a personal loss.

In December, 1845, the Hon. John Cotton Smith, for nearly fifteen years President of the Society, closed his useful life at the age of eighty-one. He was appointed a Vice-President of the Society at its organisation, and became President in 1831. He was an abiding patron of sound learning and a consistent advocate of the doctrines and duties set forth in the Holy Scriptures.

The large development of the Society in the Western States seemed to make it desirable that one of the Vice-Presidents residing in the West should be chosen as the next President, and the Board unanimously elected for this office the Hon. John McLean of Ohio, one of the Justices of the Supreme Court of the United States. Justice McLean expressed regret that his duties in court in each month of May would absolutely prevent his ever attending an annual meeting of the Society. For this reason he declined the office of President.

Vice-President Theodore Frelinghuysen, Chancellor of the University of New York, was then elected and became President of the Society in April, 1846. Chancellor Frelinghuysen at the age of twenty-five had commanded a company of soldiers in the War of 1812. Later he had become Attorney-General of New Jersey, and in 1829 was elected United States Senator from that state. While still President of the Bible Society he was chosen President of Rutgers College, New Brunswick, N. J. His fitness to stand at the head of the Bible Society, and the important services which he was qualified to render to it, were clear to its friends in every part of the country.

Vice-Presidents Alexander Henry, Peter G. Stuyvesant, John Griscom, who represented the Society of Friends in the Convention of 1816 which organised the Society, Hubert Van Wagenen, who had been connected with the Society for thirty years, and Judge Duncan Cameron of North Carolina, passed away during this period. Among members of the Board of Managers who finished their work about this time the name of John Aspinwall is to be noted. He became a member of the Board of Managers in 1816 and his name was signed as auditor to every one of the Treasury accounts from the organisation of the Society up to the time of his death in 1847.

Before the next Annual Meeting of the Society the Hon. John Quincy Adams died. He was chosen Vice-President in 1817, and later filled the high office of President of the United States during four years. He was a hearty and unswerving friend of the Society until the time of his death on the 23rd of February, 1848. The esteem with which he was regarded was shown by the expressions of bereavement which came from thousands in widely separated regions.

The increase in the amount of correspondence, due, perhaps, to the great extension of the Auxiliary system, made it necessary to appoint more Secretaries. In January, 1849, the Rev. S. I. Prime was elected Secretary. He was a pastor of Presbyterian churches in the state of New York until 1840, when throat troubles compelled him to give up preaching. After some strenuous tours for the Society a return of the same throat troubles obliged Secretary Prime to resign his position after one year of service. In 1849, the Rev. Joseph Holdich, D.D., a prominent Methodist Episcopal minister who was at the time Professor of Moral Science in Wesleyan University, and in 1853 Rev. James McNeill, a Presbyterian pastor from North Carolina, were elected Secretaries to fill the vacancies caused by the resignation of Mr. Prime and the death of Dr. Levings.

The Rev. Joseph C. Stiles of Savannah, Ga., a Presbyterian Evangelist in the South and Southwest, who in 1848 became pastor of the Mercer Street Presbyterian Church in New York, resigned his pastorate on account of ill-health, and in 1850 became Secretary of the Society with special reference to work in the Southern States. He resigned this office in 1852 and returned to the pastorate.

The burden of correspondence grew more and more heavy as the years went by, and in 1855 the Board decided to relieve the Secretaries of the duty of attending General Conferences and Synods of ecclesiastical bodies. The Rev. Moses L. Scudder was appointed General Delegate to represent the Bible Society at such meetings of the church courts.

In spite of perplexities on every side the addition of territory and population to the United States expressed a clear command to the Society as a missionary organisation. The annual meeting on the 8th of May 1856, therefore, formally resolved that for the second time the Society should undertake to place a Bible in every destitute family throughout the United States which was willing to receive it. A general circular was issued calling upon the people to co-operate in this work, noting that the population of the country had been doubled since the first general supply, and was now more than twenty-six millions. The circular insisted that this work must not be slighted as a mere enterprise of men. It was an undertaking to which God Himself called His people. Every Christian should aid by assuming some definite part of this task. Happily, this appeal furnished a good illustration of the pervasive quality of Christian principle which drives men into action even as St. John was forced into action in the vision when he ate the book, although warned beforehand that later it would bring bitterness.

On account of the vast extent of the land and its widely scattered population, more than four years were occupied in the work. It was pressed with earnestness, and 3,678,837 volumes were distributed to those willing to read the Bible. In 1856 the states and territories which existed when the supply began had been pretty thoroughly supplied, and by 1860 territories which at the beginning of the undertaking were unorganized had received thousands of copies. The great fact of this distribution was that the multitude newly affected and animated by the teachings of the Bible would give tone to generations yet to come. From this point of view the most exigent and possibly the most fruitful field of the Society was and 's the domestic field; without neglect, however, of the foreign field wherever American missionaries labour.

CHAPTER XXV

A CLEARING HOUSE FOR NEEDS

EACH year the Bible House in New York became more surely a clearing house for the wants of people of diverse tongues. As immigration increased, Scriptures in the European languages were printed in the Bible House in New York instead of being imported in small quantities. During the whole period from 1841 to 1861 the Spanish version of the Bible took a large place in discussions of the Committee and of the Board because of the dislike of Spanish speaking Americans for the quaint and obsolete terms found in the Valera version. Various attempts were made to improve this version. In 1860 the Board finally announced that a new edition of the Spanish Bible would have the advantage of all revisions which had taken place during previous years. The Portuguese Bible which had been purchased from the British and Foreign Bible Society was now so much in demand that a set of plates was ordered from London, and Portuguese Scriptures began to be printed at the Bible House in New York. During this same period a Welsh Bible with references, a Hawaiian Testament with English in parallel columns, and a German Bible for which new plates were made from the best edition of the Canstein Bible, were printed at the Bible House. In 1858 the Bible in Modern Armenian was electrotyped and printed there. The type was set up by compositors, some of whom knew not a single letter of the Armenian alphabet, the eminent linguist and missionary, Elias Riggs, the translator of the version, giving close supervision to the work.

From its first year the Bible Society had taken interest in the welfare of Indians throughout the country; work for them being classed by common consent with work for " foreigners." In 1834 a grant was made to the American

Board's Missionaries, S. R. Riggs and Williamson, for print-ing portions of the Scriptures in the Sioux or Dakota lan-guage for the use of missionaries of two or three denomina-tions.   About the same time the New Testament of the Ojibwa (Chippeway) version, translated by the Rev. Sher-man Hall of the American Board, was printed at the Bible House, and the good missionary expressed the hope that the Scriptures in Ojibwa and those in the Dakota language might break down the fierce enmity between Sioux and Ojibwa Indians.   In 1844, a grant of some seven hundred dollars was made to the American Board for the expense of printing parts of the Bible in Cherokee, translated by Rev. Mr. Worcester.   Shortly afterwards grants were made to the American Board for printing Scriptures in Choctaw.

That there was benefit in the dissemination of the Bible among the Indians was clear from the fact that the missions were successful.   Bishop Kemper of a Protestant Episcopal Mission on the borders of Canada, in writing for a grant of one hundred copies of the Book of Isaiah in the Mohawk language, casually mentioned as though it was nothing sur-prising that in his mission among the Mohawks there were ninety-nine faithful Indian communicants; and the Board was astonished and delighted a few years later to receive ap-plication from Choctaws and from Cherokees for recogni-tion as local Bible Societies, auxiliary to the American Bible Society.

All this work of preparing versions in different lan-guages was in the same vein as the labour spent upon books for the blind; for what is translation of the Bible into the spoken language of any people but opening the eyes of those who cannot see the truth?

The condition of the blind, cut off from sharing the life of the nation, isolated both by their own impotence and by the dulness of many who are not able to feel the meaning of blindness, is always a silent appeal for sympathy.   The Board of Managers had helped Dr. Howe in his splendid work for the blind, and in April, 1843, the stereotype plates in line letter for the whole Bible were at length finished at a total cost of ten thousand dollars.   Within the next ten years about four hundred volumes of Scripture had been distributed to blind persons. Some of these books went to the West Indies, some to Central and South America, and some to Turkey. They went into thirteen states of the Union; this kindly help being rendered without noise or pride although each person who received the Book rejoiced as much as if on a ship in mid-ocean he had received a wireless message from a dear friend at home.

From all parts of the country and for many kinds of supplies, applications as eager as the pleas of men in a "bread line" came from Christian workers. These were dealt with under the general rule that, where possible, Auxiliary Societies should do what ought to be done. This rule, however, did not serve where no Auxiliary could be found. All requests and suggestions from such districts were dealt with sympathetically and thoughtfully in the Board Room. Of this latter class was the proposal to put Scriptures in hotels in different parts of the country. Many travellers would be pleased to find the Book in their rooms. The Board decided in 1846 that any hotel would be supplied with Scriptures on payment of half of the cost of the books. At the suggestion of the Hon. S. Wells Williams, who had travelled, perhaps, by the overland route from California, the Board freely granted Bibles to be placed in each of the overland stage stations.

The cholera epidemic of 1849 and the opening of California to gold seekers both brought difficulties to the brave workers in the Western States struggling to do their share in Bible distribution. By the immense emigration to the gold regions many districts were almost stripped of the more active part of their population. Hundreds on whom the Bible Society relied for help were taken off as by a tidal wave. Letters to officers of the Auxiliary Societies many times brought no answer or came back marked "gone to California." The Auxiliaries found themselves in difficulty, too, because much ready money was taken out of the community by those undertaking that tremendous journey across the plains and the mountains to the new El Dorado.

The San Francisco Bible Society had to deal with many different nationalities. Thousands of Chinese were pouring into California, stopping in camp at San Francisco for a short time, and then scattering through the mining regions. Efforts were made to reach this nomad crowd with portions of Scripture, Mr. Buel, the Agent for California, and some of his assistants committing to memory a sentence or two of Chinese that they might show friendliness to these wanderers from the Far East and help them to understand the aim of the book that was placed in their hands. San Francisco quickly became a strategic point with reference to the long stretch of the coast and the regions beyond the Pacific. Accordingly, in 1853, the San Francisco Bible Society built a Bible House which would serve as a depository for the Board in New York. Orders would come to the San Francisco depository in the same day, perhaps, from Oregon and from the Sandwich Islands. At that time an order sent from the Sandwich Islands to New York might be expected to bring a consignment of books to Honolulu in about one year. On the other hand, a well-assorted stock at the Bible House in San Francisco would ensure that those ordering from the Sandwich Islands would receive the books in two months' time. A similar promptness of supply was registered by the Agent in Oregon when he ordered Bibles from San Francisco.

In the midst of the great labour imposed upon the Board by the multitudes of immigrants and settlers moving into the Western land, it was with satisfaction that the Board received applications from the American Tract Society for grants of Scriptures to be distributed by its colporteurs. Such applications soon became so frequent as to call for a definite understanding with the Tract Society about the methods of its colporteurs. Valuable as was the help rendered by these men outside of the field of an Auxiliary Bible Society a careless tract distributor might easily interfere with the work of the Auxiliaries, if not advised to avoid competition. Difficulties were found to arise from the confusion sometimes created in the minds of the people when Tract distributors offered to sell books of the Bible Society. Overlapping seemed inevitable, when Tract Society workers unintentionally entered the field of an active Auxiliary. After some discussion between the two Societies, the officers of the Tract Society expressed entire agreement with the

BIBLE DAY AT SAN FRANCISCO PANAMA EXPOSITION

rules for the use of grants laid down by the Board of Managers and considerable numbers of Scriptures were at that
time distributed by Tract Society colporteurs in those parts
of the great western region which was yet unexplored by the
agents of the Bible Society.

Such efforts as the Society was making throughout the
land could hardly fail to excite enemies of the Bible.   In
1842, the Champlain Bible Society, a branch of the Clinton
County, New York, Auxiliary Society, finding many French
Canadians settling in its field, distributed French Scriptures
among them, which were well received.   In November of
the same year Father Telmonde, a Jesuit priest from Mon-
treal, suddenly appeared at Corbeau, one of the French
settlements in the Champlain township, and raved like a
madman against the Protestants who had supplied the
Canadian settlers with the Bible.   He seems to have forgotten that he was a visitor in a free country and scared
Roman Catholics by an arrogated authority until he succeeded in collecting about one hundred of the Bibles.   These
he brought together at Corbeau, tore off the covers and gave
them to the men to use in stropping their razors, and burned
the books in a rather barbaric public ceremony.   Having
thus violated the peace of an American village, he escaped
to Canada unpunished.   To Protestants, of course, the act
was sacrilegious, and aroused anger by its arrogance.   It
was an insult to the American people, as well as an outrage
on the immigrants who gave up books which they prized.

However, Father Telmonde did not check Bible work.   It
is always better to overcome opposition than to be spared it.
Professor Deems of the University of North Carolina,
speaking on another subject, mentioned the objection raised
by some people that if the Bible Society scatters Bibles
promiscuously, many will sell them and take the money to
buy whiskey.   " Let them sell them ! " said Professor Deems,
" the Book is still in existence, still full of heavenly energy
for any who will read it."   The truth of this philosophical
remark was vindicated at Corbeau.   One woman, even when
threatened by Father Telmonde, flatly refused to give up her
Bible, saying, " It is the best of books."   And she kept it.
Many of the Roman Catholics were indignant at the outrage ;

for they recognised robbery when they ruminated over the action of the priest. After a few years it was discovered that the man foremost in assisting the priest in the Bible burning, stirring up the fire with a long pole in order to make the books burn more thoroughly, became conscience-smitten for what he had done, abandoned the Roman Catholic church, and joined the Protestant mission at Grande Ligne in Canada. In the little settlement where the Bibles were burned, three of the families left the Roman for the Protestant church, and one of the men became a Bible colporteur among his own people in consequence of the violence which woke him up, much as a man asleep on a bank by the side of a brook may be wakened by a hailstorm, unpleasant, but useful as sending him to shelter before a heavy rain.

A chief element of the strength of the Bible Society is, of course, the warm interest of the numbers who support it with their thoughts, their prayers, and their gifts. Every now and then a kindly word of sympathy from a man high in the councils of the nation, brings encouragement to those engaged in the ceaseless labour of the Society.

In February, 1844, a general Bible convention was held in Washington, the place of meeting being the hall of the House of Representatives. In that crowded hall ex-President John Quincy Adams presided as senior vice-President of the American Bible Society. In an address full of fire he set forth the value and power of the Holy Scriptures, and his own affection for the Society which labours to extend their circulation.

General Zachary Taylor, fresh from the Mexican War, in 1849 became President of the United States. In 1850 some ladies of Frankfort, Kentucky, presented him with a Bible beautifully bound with the constitution of the United States. President Taylor revealed his opinion of the Bible in his letter of thanks. He said, " I accept with gratitude and pleasure your gift of this inestimable volume. If there were nothing in that book but its great precept, ' All things whatsoever ye would that men should do unto you, do ye even so to them,' and if that precept were obeyed, our government might extend over the whole continent." In June of the same year a Presbyterian Sunday School in Paterson, New

Jersey, made a contribution constituting President Taylor a Life Director of the Bible Society. His letter of acknowledgment written on the fifth day of July, after the commencement of the severe illness which, to the grief of the nation, proved fatal a few days later, contained these words: " I accept with the liveliest emotions of gratitude this complimentary testimonial which has associated my name with an institution so comprehensive in its usefulness and efficiency as a means of good as the American Bible Society. Believing that our prosperity and greatness as a nation, no less than our happiness as individuals, is in direct proportion to our observance of the teachings of that Book in which the holy religion is revealed, I cannot be indifferent to those labours which tend to diffuse its instructions and render it more accessible to all."

Reports of Agents and colporteurs during this period give glimpses of the influence of the Bible upon the nation. The book went among men and women too busy to pray or to think of God except when in pain or terror, qualified perhaps to be attractive as flowers in a well-kept garden, but starved in their souls like a rosebush choked with weeds. In a town in Illinois one hundred and two persons who had been indifferent to religion, hardly knowing the name of Christ except as profaned in assertion or threat, during 1848 became warm-hearted members of the church, after a Bible Society Agent had sold in that town one hundred dollars' worth of Bibles. In Wisconsin a Roman Catholic woman, very religious in her fashion, showed some annoyance when her husband let a belated traveller lodge in their house. After the stranger had retired for the night the woman took up one of the books which he had laid on a shelf, curious to see what made people buy them. It was a Bible. She had never heard of the Bible and she looked into it. The beautiful words held her fascinated until the day dawned. That chance access to the Bible changed the woman's life, and some months later the Bible colporteur had the satisfaction of learning that she had cast in her lot with the neighbouring Protestant church.

Among the immigrants were some easily interested in Bible work. Picture, for instance, a German widow in

Ohio, with her four unmarried daughters, weaving, spinning, sewing, selling butter and eggs, for one great purpose. They worked for their living, but the purpose was not fully rounded out until they had each given thirty dollars for a Life Membership in the Bible Society. A German farmer in the same district dug out of the ground, as it were, Life Memberships for all the members of his family, amounting to $210 altogether. Another German woman who had settled in Auburn, New York, begged the Agent to write her message to the Society. " I want to tell them," she said, " how much thankful I am for the Bible. I wish I could tell how hungry I was for the Bible and good books in German; so hungry, not for bread and water, but for the Bible. And after I got it, I be so glad!"

Professor Deems of the University of North Carolina wrote to the Bible Society in 1843 of a settlement in Wake County called Flat Rivers. This place for eighty years had been infamous as a Sodom. The people were unclean and profane, fearing not God nor regarding man. In 1830, during the first General Supply, a Bible Society colporteur went to Flat Rivers, visited thirty-four families, gave away thirty-three Bibles (for in one house he found a Bible), received in return forty cents, paid more than one dollar for board and lodging, and went away. Thirteen years after this visit the place had entirely changed, and in every one of the houses where a Bible was left some, at least, of the members of the family were pious, God-fearing people. Professor Deems remarks on two points concerning Bible distribution which are worth carrying in mind. In the first place Christians may so neglect neighbours who have not the Bible that an entire settlement close at hand may become degenerate; and in the second place, where the Bible is used by any family or community, it quickly lifts them to a higher plane.

A significant feature of the story of the Society has been the support given to it by thousands of day-labourers. There was a little Auxiliary Society in New York known as the Fulton County Auxiliary. One day a plainly dressed woman came to the annual meeting of that Society. She said she had come six miles to attend the meeting and mentioned that her home was five or six miles from any meeting house. She had neighbours who lived without the Bible and she wanted to supply them. Eight dollars and fifty-four cents she had brought with her and she was furnished with Bibles and Testaments.

The next year the same woman appeared at the annual meeting with fifteen dollars and thirty-eight cents. During fourteen years this woman acted as a branch Bible Society, herself long being the sole member. She came every year bringing small sums of money, part to pay for books that she had distributed, and part as a donation for the Society. After a time two younger women came with her to the Bible meeting to take up the work of Bible distribution. A number of years later the Fulton County Bible Society found that these poor women, moved by love of Christ like the woman who poured the precious ointment upon His feet, had paid into the Treasury of the Society altogether $813.62. If every district in the country had Bible workers of this earnest, persistent type, the whole world would soon be filled with Bibles.

CHAPTER XXVI

TURBULENT EUROPE

THE year 1848 was notable for upheavals in all Europe. Where nations simultaneously break the bonds by which kings have shaped the fortunes of the people, we may look for great rational causes in vain. Small material troubles like famine and high prices lead the people to think their rulers incapable, as is probably the case. At all events, in France poor harvests and the cost of living in 1847 led the people of Paris in February, 1848, to drive away Lafayette's "Citizen King" Louis Philippe, like the manager of an estate dispossessed while sure that his position has placed him above criticism. This outbreak of the Parisians kept the country unsettled throughout the year. In December Prince Louis Napoleon was elected President of the Republic of France, and laid plans for ruling, as soon as might be, as Emperor.

The expulsion of Louis Philippe from France was an object lesson to the rest of Europe. Fire applied to a boiler makes no change in the appearance of the water for some time. Then a single bubble of steam appears at some point, and shortly with sufficient heat, the whole mass of water may be converted into steam at once, and rend its restraining iron with a tremendous explosion. Something of this sort followed the suggestion that it is possible for a people to tell a king to get out of the way of their progress. Before the year 1848 was through, Ferdinand, Emperor of Austria, had been driven from Vienna and gave up his throne; the Pope had fled from Rome in terror; the King of Prussia barely escaped being sent away from Berlin; several of the small states into which Italy was divided drove out their grand dukes and princes, and insurrection everywhere seemed on the point of expelling monarchy from the continent.

North Italy, that is, Lombardy and Venice, revolted against the king of Naples; Mazzini proclaimed the Italian Republic at about the same time that the French Republic was declared. Under Louis Kossuth the Hungarian people made a bold dash for freedom from Austria, and marched their army upon Vienna.

March, 1848, brought with it insurrections in Vienna, in Budapest, in Berlin. Then the tide turned and with it kings came back. Before the year was through French troops had occupied Rome for the Pope; Francis Joseph had taken the crown of Austria, succeeding his uncle Ferdinand. By the middle of 1850 the Austrians again oppressed northern Italy; the Pope had abolished the liberal constitution in Rome; Kossuth had fled to America, and the dream of liberty for European peoples faded like other dreams.

These facts have a place in this story, because an impulse like that of the Good Samaritan drew the American Bible Society into close relations with the sufferers in troubled Europe. In France the revolution naturally brought opportunity for a wide distribution of Scriptures. Even a careless, pleasure loving people becomes thoughtful when the whole social structure seems to be falling to pieces.

But the disturbances which made the opportunity cut off local means of using it. Who should furnish means but the American Bible Society? There were no cables, no telegraphs, no quick steamers across the ocean in those days, and so a special messenger was sent from the French and Foreign Bible Society to New York to tell the story of its dire need. This messenger, the Rev. Mr. Bridel, addressed the Annual Meeting of the Society in May, 1848. He said that the French Bible Society had been in successful operation until the recent political movements reduced to poverty some of the wealthiest friends of the Society, and had thus wrecked its resources and crippled its hands. Printing was suspended, colporteurs had been discharged. France, now a republic, like a younger sister appealed for help.

The Society at its Annual Meeting voted " that it is the clear and palpable duty of this Society to listen to these calls, and that the Managers be therefore advised to raise and remit to France the sum of $10,000 this year and a like sum for the succeeding year." Rev. Mr. Kirk of Boston strongly supported this resolution, referring to the unusual crisis when all have heard the rolling of the awful chariot wheels of God whose hand sways the nations. Rev. Dr. S. H. Tyng remarked that a gentleman in New York had offered to give a thousand dollars if the Society would raise ten thousand. He himself would agree to raise five hundred more, and he hoped pledges would quickly follow for the whole ten thousand dollars. Mr. Kirk promised one hundred dollars. Secretary Brigham called attention to the well established custom for the Society to act through its Auxiliaries, and doubtless prompt action of the Auxiliaries in this matter would be secured. As a result $10,000 was sent to France during the year.

Difficulties were met in raising the second instalment of $10,000 to be sent to France during 1849. In fact, only $1,000 was sent out during that year, and the French Bible Society wrote piteous entreaties for a speedy payment of the amount promised. In consequence of the assurance of this aid from America, it had incurred obligations, and found itself in serious difficulty; $3,500 were sent in response to this appeal but a sort of paralysis seemed to have smitten the sources of revenue. As is often the case, many who might have given, assumed that others would certainly pay, for the whole country sympathised with needy France. It was not until the year 1851 that the whole of the promised amount was remitted to the French Bible Society.

In 1849 the French Government curtailed liberties which had flourished after the establishment of the republic. Departments of France in which the clergy had strong influence were for a time entirely closed to Bible colporteurs. No one was permitted to distribute the smallest printed leaf unless authorised by the prefect of the Department, and the obtaining of such authorisations became more and more difficult. But in spite of these obstacles, authorisations in sufficient number were granted to enable the Bible missionary in some places to continue his operations on a large scale. In other Departments the authorities, recognising the peaceable character of the people employed in Bible distribution, and perceiving good effects from their labour, relaxed their rigour in the matter of granting the authorisations. Furthermore, Rev. Dr. Monod reported, general interest in circulation of the Bible was seen to increase in proportion to the bitterness of the opposition to it. Many people who in calmer times would have cared little for the Bible now sought it with eagerness; and many booksellers who would never have kept the Bible in stock at other times were compelled by the reading public to give the Scriptures a certain importance in their trade.

The Society has had by repeated grants to the French Society an important share in the development of the Protestant movement in France. It should be remembered, however, that the British and Foreign Bible Society had then, as now, an able Agent in Paris, and from time to time made grants of money and books to the Protestant Bible Society of Paris as well as to the French and Foreign Bible Society. Thus the British and the American Societies have touched shoulders in aiding evangelicals to cultivate the moral and spiritual sense of the brilliant and attractive French people. During the twenty-eight years from 1833 to 1861 the grants of the American Society as aid to Bible work in France amounted in all to something more than $40,000.

Disturbances in Austria and Germany during 1848 very much restricted the operations of the German Bible Societies. After the overthrow of the revolutionists in Hungary and in Austria, an agreement was made between the Emperor Francis Joseph and the Pope by which all religious instruction, and, in fact, all education throughout the Austrian Empire was surrendered to the Roman Catholic clergy, controlled by bishops in the appointment of whom the Austrian government had no voice. This " Concordat," as it was called, became an effectual barrier for many years against general Bible circulation on the Austrian domains.

In Germany, Baptist and later Methodist missionaries, supported from America, finding multitudes of people without the Bible, applied to the Society and received aid in books and especially in money for printing in German. Up to the year 1861 the money grants of the Society for printing Scriptures in Germany amounted to $33,000. The Rev. J. G. Oncken of the Baptist Publishing House in Hamburg, applying for help in 1856, gave some idea of the extent of his work. He then reported that since the year 1829 he had put into circulation 600,694 volumes. These grants for printing Scriptures supplemented the efforts of the German Bible Societies, which, being commonly quite local in character, left considerable stretches of country without systematic Bible supply.

The American Society had at various times granted Scriptures for distribution in Italy. In 1849 the Rev. G. Hastings, American Seamen's Chaplain at Marseilles, was allowed to go on a United States ship-of-war to Sicily. He took with him all the Italian Bibles he had and got a further stock from the British and Foreign Bible Society and sold 700 volumes in Sicily, besides receiving commissions for 2,100 volumes more. The avidity with which the Sicilians seized the Bible at that time suggests a hunger for the Word of God often found among the most unlikely people.

In Italy the chief supply of Scriptures came through the British and Foreign Bible Society. In the few months of the Republic of 1849 more Scriptures were circulated in Italy than in six hundred years before. Four thousand New Testaments were even printed in Rome, for the first time in history. But after the return of the Pope the most stringent measures were adopted in central Italy against the Bible and all religious books not authorised by the Roman Church. Men of first rate education and high standing in society felt obliged to deposit their Bibles, obtained during the republic, with English residents, saying that they could not feel safe with the Book in the house. These people were not cowardly, but they had no armour that could repel the fierce attacks of the inquisition. Count Guicciardini of Florence had been known as a Protestant for three or four years, but on the return of the Grand Duke of Tuscany from exile, the Count was arrested. Six other Protestants of Florence were also arrested and condemned to exile in the Marremma, the most unhealthy marsh-land that the Tuscan government could find. Happily, the influence of Guicciardini was sufficient to save them from going to the marshes when they promised to leave Tuscan territory. But in exterminating the Bible by force the priests commended it to the people. Arbitrary proceedings have a wonderful tendency to open men's eyes.

When a Protestant Committee was organised for Bible distribution in Northern Italy, it received aid from the American Bible Society. Between 1855 and 1861 grants of money to the Italian Committee at Florence amounted to $9,700, and the plates of the Italian Bible made at that time served for years in furnishing Scriptures for use in Italy. It was almost ten years after the restoration of the Pope to the Vatican that freedom dawned for any considerable section of the Italian people. With the expulsion of the Austrians from Lombardy and Venice in the summer of 1859, a new era of religious liberty began.

During this period the Society was also aiding Bible work in North Russia. Mr. William Ropes, an American merchant living in St. Petersburg, brought to the notice of Secretary Brigham the desperate condition of the Protestant Esthonians in the Baltic regions, and also an extraordinary dearth of Scriptures in Finland where Protestant Christians searched in vain for Bibles. The British and Foreign Bible Society had made some grants during several years to a Bible Committee in connection with the Anglo-American Congregation in St. Petersburg, whose place of worship, by the way, received its Government license as the Chapel of the American Legation on request of James Buchanan, then United States minister. After Pastor Knill, pastor of this body, died, he was succeeded by the Rev. John C. Brown and application was at once made to America for money to supply the destitute Protestants. This was the beginning of an important work of the Society of which we shall hear later. During the twenty-seven years from 1834 to 1861 money sent to the St. Petersburg Committee (composed of Messrs. Ropes, Gillibrand, and Miricles) amounted to $18,800. Mr. Brown wrote to Dr. Brigham that he had a list of Lutheran clergymen in the Esthonians who would encourage every attempt to benefit their parishioners by Bible distribution. A young theological student of his acquaintance would be exactly the man to supply every family with a copy of the New Testament at a low price or gratuitously. This done the young man would supply the parishes of Lutheran clergymen who were unlikely to co-operate energetically in the work, and when those were supplied he would go into parishes where the ministers were so rationalistic as to oppose Bible circulation. Beyond that he hoped to do something for Livonia and Finland.

Mr. Brown's plan was attractive, although exacting. Ideas come lightly into the mind, whence we know not, which may prove solvents of difficulties or bearers of fruit to an unheard of degree. Then it becomes evident that the same idea occurred to many. As we say of the wind, concerning which, after millenniums of study none can tell whence it comes or whither it goes, we can only say in this case that we receive the impression; its source transcends our apprehension. Of this class of ideas was the plan of helping European Protestants. The Society felt it a duty to give aid to Bible lovers crippled by anarchy or stifled by tyranny; and lo, the thought was seized with eagerness in all directions. It was one of those God-given ideas that everybody knew to be in his mind before it found expression. " Of course it is our duty ! "

The influence of such a campaign widens like the circle where a pebble has fallen into a still pool. Men who have been moved by the old Bible make it live in a new soil, with new applications and perhaps new interpretations. And so the sum of the work accomplished tells upon generations to come. It is worth while to have done such a work. In every undertaking of this class God's truth becomes spread in many directions like the beams from a lighthouse guiding ships which approach from north or south or east.

Rev. Dr. F. Monod, a Secretary of the French and Foreign Bible Society, reported early in 1850 that up to the end of 1849 the aid of the American Society had permitted the printing of 102,000 volumes, besides making new plates for an octavo and a duodecimo Bible in French; plates for the New Testament, with the Psalms in each of these sizes, and a set of plates for the four Gospels and the Acts bound together. Of the books printed, 62,625 volumes had been put in circulation during the year. The colporteurs of the French Society reported that this Bible distribution was warmly welcomed. Again and again village people who received the Scriptures afterwards said, " I read that book constantly; the religion of the Bible shall be my religion henceforth forever." The colporteurs also reached a multitude of political prisoners held in durance, and their Testaments rejoiced both prisoners and guards.

In any upheaval of society not the richer class, but the great mass of the poor is the decisive factor. In the work of the Society in Europe the rich and highly educated were not neglected, but it was among the masses, the despised common people, that the influence of the Bible was most strongly felt. It was among them that the numbers of Scriptures scattered abroad could be seen to have influence because these books, read in private, attack the habit of evil thought and act in its lair. Single sentences out of thousands found in the Bible tend to fix in mind attractive ideals like the words of the Psalmist: " I will set no base thing before my eyes." In the long run the circulation of the Bible slowly but surely modifies national character. What these ignorant and oppressed peoples have always needed and still need is instruction in free manliness and its precious worth. That instruction they can find compressed into the pages of the Bible. The Society could not work out the rebuilding of these broken nations, but using every opportunity to give them the Book, it has helped them to learn how they could do it themselves.

The appeal to the Board from distressed Europe led President Frelinghuysen to say in his address at the Annual Meeting of 1850, " The Word is ordained in its course among the nations to bring the whole family of man into one blessed brotherhood, bound to God and to each other by the ties of love." Obedience to the command of Jesus Christ respecting the instruction of all nations is justified by all the experiences of the Society. The faith and foresight of the members of the Board and its executive officers has always tended to the extension of beneficent influences. One generation profits from the struggles, the faith, and the progress of those who are gone, but its profit is a sacred trust received for the betterment of many other generations to come. So it was meet that children of Europe who brought the Bible with them across the ocean to the new world, and there proved its power to make life fruitful, should hasten, when they saw European nations suffering through igno-rance of Bible teaching, to carry back, for the good of their old fatherland, the great Book of Life.

CHAPTER XXVII

NEIGHBOURLY feeling is a most natural and praiseworthy emotion. The Orientals say: "When you buy a house don't look at the house, look at the neighbours!" In regard to Latin America it was perfectly natural that the Society and its supporters throughout the United States should have a most kindly regard for the welfare of these neighbours who spoke only Spanish or Portuguese, and yet one of the great problems of the Society was how to reach them. There was a barrier like a steel wall separating Anglo-Saxon America and Latin America. The cause of this separation was not distance, not difference of race and language, not even lack of roads; it was a total difference of atmosphere. The Latin American countries had only slowly commenced to emerge from a cloud of ignorance and superstition. The very governments of the different republics were unstable, replaced in some regions by anarchy; and a considerable plausibility attaches to the theory that this was largely due to the church which, finding its material interests attacked when the different colonies revolted from Spain, steadily struggled against the progress of the masses toward political liberty.

The Society cherished no enmity against the Roman Catholic Church. By experience, however, the Board was obliged to regard it as a partly political organisation endowed with the ideals of militarism while armoured with the sanctities of religion. It seemed to have for its object in Latin America the absolute control of mind as well as of soul in its adherents in order that the church might be built up. The people were in a state of bondage. The outward forms of religion were strictly and pompously performed, but there was little inward searching out of defects in motive or conduct. Any crime might be committed by a member of the church and within an hour be fully forgiven at the word of the priest. To the masses of the people religion had for its chief function deliverance of the individual from hell. This was deemed impossible unless each individual held aloof from intercourse with heretics as though they were infected with leprosy.

On the other hand warm-hearted Protestant Christians of the United States felt responsibility for the betterment of all within their reach, since it is God's will that his people should be efficient instruments for the uplift of the race. In the eyes of the Protestants of the United States it was clear that God's revelation of the rules of the universe had not reached the people of Latin America. Those people were suffering for lack of knowledge of the elements of prosperity and peace. The impelling principle which led the Board continuously to strive to circulate Scriptures among these people was that expressed in the old proverb, " Go slowly to the banquets of a neighbour, but haste to his afflictions."

During the first forty years of the Society's activity, its plans for supplying Scriptures to accessible places in Latin America was what the French might call " opportunist." When any person from those lands of Spain's might and Portugal's adventure appeared in New York, or wrote from any island, district, or commercial mart promising to circulate Scriptures in languages of the Latins, the Board was ready to respond. In this casual and uncertain way during the twenty years of the period from 1841 to 1861, 42,000 volumes of Scripture were distributed through local friends of the Bible, not connected with the Bible Society, with much travail of soul and in many places, from the West Indies and Mexico to the southernmost tip of Patagonia.

As missionaries of different denominations were sent out to the Latin Islands of the West Indies, the Board took pains to supply every call for Scriptures. These calls came sometimes from missionaries, sometimes from the chaplains of the Seamen's Friend Society, sometimes from merchants, sometimes from United States Consular officials, and they reached San Domingo, St. Thomas, Porto Rico, Cuba and

Hayti. The Island of Hayti attracted special attention through the religious liberty said to obtain there, and serious efforts were put forth by missionary Societies and the Bible Society in that domain of French speaking coloured people. Religious liberty in Hayti, however, proved to be more or less of an *ignis fatuus,* for it alternately appeared and disappeared whenever the officials of government became careless of the priests, or on the other hand saw reasons for prostrating themselves before those intelligent white men of strong will.

In 1850 the Rev. Mr. Pierson was sent to Hayti as an Agent of the Society. He found a field hungry for the Bible and was cheered by the numbers who rejoiced to read it. Mr. Pierson found that there was more freedom, more education, and more open detestation of unworthy priests than he had expected. He found missionaries in different parts of the country, and he urged the Society to increase its force because expenses were so small. The Haytian dollar was only one-fourteenth part of an American dollar and yet had about the same purchasing power as the dollar at home. He soon found himself in difficulties, however, for Father Cessen, a leading Roman Catholic priest, a native of Corsica who had travelled much and had lived in the United States for several years, began a campaign of sermons against Mr. Pierson and the work of the Bible Society. General La Rochelle, a leading member of the Haytian Government and a Roman Catholic, had welcomed Mr. Pierson because of the great need of moral training among the people. But Father Cessen warned the people that Mr. Pierson and the missionaries were really political agents of the United States Government, that they were paid from the Government ten dollars a head for every convert, and fifty dollars for every child born to these converts, and thus they were expected to overthrow the Haytian Empire. Father Cessen won the Empress to his opinion of the dangerous influence of the Protestants, and shortly the government went to the extent of forcing into the army all young men whom they found in possession of the Scriptures. Agent Pierson had little opportunity for Bible distribution after this fierce outbreak, and much disappointed, he withdrew.

Mexico was the nearest neighbour to the United States among the Spanish republics. Its needs excited warm sympathy; but a certain stubborn prejudice repelled every expression of sympathy. The people of Mexico were patriotic and because of their patriotism were quite ready to use their knives upon those whom they considered enemies of the country. At the same time one could not consider the nation as happy. It was composed of an aristocracy, mainly Spanish, ruling with a rod of iron a labouring class chiefly Indian; and this proud, Spanish, aristocratic rule persisted with but little basis of intellectual primacy. The country was almost constantly in political upheaval, like the lake of lava lying at the bottom of a crater, boiling, belching noxious gases, and sometimes bursting forth to destroy itself as well as the surrounding regions. The country was in so disturbed a state even as late as the French invasion in 1862, that a resident Bible Agent from the United States could hardly escape violence.

During the occupation by United States troops, Rev. Mr. Norris, the Agent of the Society, placed Scriptures in some hundreds of families in Vera Cruz, Jalapa, Puebla, and Mexico City. But he left with the Army in 1849. The Rev. B. P. Thompson was appointed Agent in 1859 to distribute Scriptures among the Spanish speaking people along the Rio Grande. Miss Melinda Rankin, a missionary living at Brownsville, Texas, also distributed Scriptures faithfully among the Mexicans within her reach. Mexicans from the interior often wished Scriptures but roving bandits often made it impossible to reach such applicants and impeded Bible work even on the border line.

In Central America the Rev. D. H. Wheeler, Seamen's Friend Society Chaplain at Aspinwall, had been cordially helpful to the Society during more than two years in distributing Scriptures on the Isthmus of Panama, along the line of the Panama railroad, and he had placed books also in the hotels at Aspinwall, Gatun, and Chagres. In July, 1856, he was commissioned as Agent of the American Bible Society for Central America, and sent to Nicaragua, where there seemed to be an opportunity for Bible distribution. "General" William Walker, with his filibusters, had succeeded in getting possession of a part of the country, and in this region Mr. Wheeler was expected to work. In October, foreseeing, perhaps, but not afraid, Mr. Wheeler wrote that the Nicaraguans seemed determined to drive out Walker and his government and to exterminate all Americans residing in Nicaragua. He remained, however, in Granada. While a battle was proceeding a few miles away between Walker and the Nicaraguan troops, some Nicaraguan cavalry made a raid upon the city. They ordered every man capable of bearing arms to go out and join the Nicaraguan troops. Mr. Wheeler and two other Americans who occupied the same house refused, on the ground that they were Americans and neutrals, to take part in the battle. The cavalry-men immediately seized the three men, took them out of the city and shot them. It was a terrible end of an agency most hopefully undertaken. Mr. Wheeler was a delightful man and a devoted Christian, always ready to sacrifice personal interests for the sake of winning men to Jesus Christ. A few weeks later Walker burned the city of Granada. This, of course, made it impossible for the Society at once to send another Agent to Nicaragua.

In 1854 Rev. Ramon Montsalvatge was appointed Agent of the Society for Spanish South America with instructions to begin work in Venezuela and go on to New Granada, a re-public nearly corresponding with Colombia of to-day. Mr. Montsalvatge was a Spaniard, a Roman Catholic by birth, and a truly converted man. He landed at La Guayra, Venezuela, where he distributed in a very short time a thousand volumes of Scripture mainly by sale, but before long he found that some of the priests did not think well of him. A priest in La Guayra bought a Bible and a Testament of him and expressed interest in his work, saying that the American Bible Society was doing the town a great benefit by sending the Scriptures in Spanish there. A day or two later the bishop, accompanied by two of his clergy, called on Mr. Montsalvatge, and upbraided him for selling Protestant Bibles. He went off, leaving a canon to labour with the "renegade." This labour took the form of offering Mr. Montsalvatge a round sum of money for ten boxes of Bibles which were in the custom house and which would be put where they would do no harm. Mr. Montsalvatge declined to sell Bibles for this purpose, whereupon the canon went off raging noisily. Mr. Montsalvatge also visited Caracas and some other places with considerable success in Bible distribution, finally establishing himself at Cartagena until directed from New York to go to Bogota. He chose the route which follows the Magdalena River, but before long announced that the steamer in which he was ascending the river with his family had been destroyed by an explosion and he had to return to Cartagena. He then began to preach to a small congregation of Protestants and was very kindly regarded by this congregation; but he gradually gave up work for the American Bible Society after the arrival of Mr. Duffield, the Agent of the British and Foreign Bible Society.

Chile, pointed out in 1825 by Dr. (then Mr.) Brigham as a notable centre for Bible distribution, and occupied in 1833 by Mr. Wheelwright, the first Agent sent abroad by the Board, began to attract attention again a score of years later. The Rev. D. Trumbull, a young minister sent in 1846 by the American and Foreign Christian Union and the Seamen's Friend Society of New York, to work for foreigners and seamen at Valparaiso, was from the first a regular correspondent of the Society, receiving considerable quantities of Bibles in Spanish and in other languages for circulation by his own hand and by a colporteur locally supported. Mr. Trumbull believed in selling the Scriptures whenever possible and yet his labours aroused sincere and enduring interest among the people. His name became known along the whole coast and orders for Scriptures came to him from many distant places.

Another attempt to open systematic Bible distribution in Spanish South America was made by the Board in 1857, when the Rev. V. D. Collins, a missionary of the American and Foreign Christian Union in Brazil, was appointed Agent of the Society for Spanish South America. Mr. Collins was acquainted with the Spanish as well as the Portuguese language, and he was instructed to begin his work at Buenos Aires and then to cross the river into Paraguay and visit Uruguay and such other republics as he found it convenient to reach.   Mr. Collins arrived at Buenos Aires in October, 1857.   He laboured earnestly and persistently and put in circulation in different parts of the South American continent a considerable number of Scriptures.   From Uruguay he went across the great plains and crossed the Andes into Chile.   Encountering somewhat strenuous opposition and finding little encouragement on the Pacific coast, Mr. Collins resigned his commission in 1859 and went as a missionary to China.

By this time the American missionary societies had begun to send men into different parts of South America.   The Bible Society was thus enabled to proceed more confidently as it responded to requests from missionaries, sending Scriptures to Rev. H. B. Pratt at Bogota, Colombia, to Rev. Dr. E. D. Carew at Buenos Aires, to Rev. F. Crowe at Guatemala, and others.   It also came into relations with the Moravians in Guiana for whom it published a version in Arawack of the Book of Acts, the translation having been made by the Rev. Otto Tank.

Rio Janeiro must always bring to mind the disastrous result of the attempt of French Huguenots in 1555, to establish a colony of refuge at this point.   The leader of the expedition was a man of some distinction in the French Naval service, named Villegagnon.   The colonists went to Brazil because, as one writer remarks, there was every reason to hope that the Reformation would take root there and fill the South as well as the North with Protestant people.   But upon the arrival of a large force of Portuguese with orders to seize the country, Villegagnon suddenly threw off a mask, commenced to persecute the Protestants, and the result was that the little colony disappeared.   Some returned to France after suffering terrible hardships, some were freed from the treacherous enemy by death, others apostatised in order to escape implacable and cruel hatred.   The French court was too busy destroying Huguenots in France to think of those in Brazil, and those fellow believers at home who should have supported the colony beyond the ocean were fully occupied by an untiring enemy which threatened everything dear to them.   So the whole country became Portuguese and Roman Catholic.

Methodist missionaries to care for seamen went to Brazil about 1836, and both Rev. Mr. Spalding, and Rev. D. P. Kidder, who later joined Mr. Spalding, gave much time to circulating the Scriptures in Portuguese furnished them from New York. Mr. Kidder travelled extensively in the interior and wherever he went he carried the Bible with him. The priests opposed this work, but their unreasonable and fanatical obstruction stimulated curiosity in their followers, and sales increased. The books sent out from Rio Janeiro were not by any means without result. Mr. Kidder remarks: "While subsequently travelling in distant provinces I found that the sacred volumes put in circulation at Rio Janeiro had sometimes arrived before me, and wherever they went an interest had been awakened which led the people to seek for more."

The first organised agency in Brazil was established in 1854, when the Rev. J. G. Fletcher, an English gentleman long resident in that country, was appointed agent of the Society. He distributed many Bibles in the interior provinces, but in 1856, on account of illness in his family, he resigned and returned to England. Mr. R. Nesbit, who had already done good service for the Society in the valley of the Amazon, was appointed Agent at Para in July, 1857. After about one year's earnest and successful service, while on a journey up the Amazon River, Mr. Nesbit contracted a fever and died.

By this time the American missionary societies were beginning to send missionaries into Brazil. The Rev. Mr. Holden of the Protestant Episcopal Missionary Society, sent to Para, received Scriptures from the Bible Society to distribute in connection with his work. The Rev. Messrs. Simonton and Blackford, missionaries of the Presbyterian Board established at Rio Janeiro, for several years acted as agents of the Society, distributing the books over large expanses of country and everywhere finding friends glad to receive the Scriptures in their own Portuguese language.

The British and Foreign Bible Society had ceased systematic labours in South America for a decade or more. In July, 1856, however, the reports of Mr. Fletcher, the American Bible Society Agent, made its Committee the more eager to attempt something again in what the Secretary, Dr. Bergne, regarded as " a field of immense extent which both Societies can but imperfectly occupy." Dr. Bergne therefore informed Secretary Brigham that two Agents had been appointed to take up work in South America, one at Cartagena, Colombia, and one at Rio Janeiro. He expressed the hope that the American Society would hail the British Agents as fellow labourers instructed to maintain the most friendly intercourse with its Agents, and to engage " in such plans of joint operations as may be practicable." This was the beginning of organised labour in South America on the part of the British and Foreign Bible Society.

From all this work of the Society in South America, one may learn the nature of the Bible distribution. Its nature is to reach more and more individuals, and the truths which even the most unlearned can acquire from Bible reading make interest in the Bible spread as the light of dawn spreads over a dark valley. A fruit of the work of a Bible Society which appeals to all classes of the people is discovery of the value of the Bible as an instructor in liberty; for the Book teaches men how to escape the bondage of their own evil habits and furthermore how to claim their rights if they are held in bondage by others more powerful than themselves. In this way the Bible among the masses of the people slowly modifies national character. Missionaries going into South America found in repeated instances that the Scriptures sent out by the Society had prepared their way; and the missionaries, vigorously taking hold of the work of Bible distribution, in turn prepared a way, as the work grew, for the appointment of permanent Agencies of the Society in different parts of the neighbour continent and its islands.

CHAPTER XXVIII

ENVIRONMENT and atmosphere have a large place in the difficulties of Bible distribution, as we have seen in Latin America. The control of men's minds and conduct in the Mohammedan system which prevailed throughout the Levant Agency at the beginning of the nineteenth century was remarkably like the Roman Catholic control of thought and action at the same period in Latin America. The Mohammedan religious body, like the political Christian church of the Middle Ages, stood for militarism armoured with all the sanctities of religion. Mohammedanism has a form of godliness; it insists on reverent worship of the one true God. Its weakness lies in teaching men the habit of carefully performing outward forms of religion without insisting on the inward moral allegiance that is an essential of belief that God is. Any crime, excepting blasphemy, committed by a devoted Mohammedan, as soon as committed is forgiven by the merciful God. Social intimacy with Christians was in 1820 and to some extent still is, to a Mohammedan, contamination to be avoided with vigilance. The aim of the religious hierarchy in Mohammedan society was absolute control of mind and soul. The people lived in bondage, for the Sultan as vicegerent of God always had a " Thus saith the Lord " with which to check tendencies toward individual liberty of judgment.

Among a people manacled in this way the Bible Society could have small opportunity, were it not that the Oriental Christians subject to the Mohammedan government and scattered throughout its domains were tolerated, allowed to maintain their own worship and their own social customs. Nevertheless these Christians also at the beginning of the nineteenth century lived in bonds of ignorance and superstition.

American missions in Turkey were commenced in 1820 by the Rev. Pliny Fisk and Rev. Levi Parsons of the American Board, who made a beginning of mission work at Smyrna, at Beirut, and at Jerusalem. A complete printing outfit was sent from Boston to the mission, being first established on the island of Malta beyond the reach of Turkish officials. There the printing of Scriptures and tracts in the languages of the Levant was quickly commenced.

Among the Armenians of the Levant there was a strange readiness to receive the Bible not found among Greeks or Jews, and of course not among Mohammedans. This brought the missionaries into close relations with them at the outset. It will be remembered, as was intimated in the nineteenth chapter, that about 1815 the Russian Bible Society published the Bible in Ancient Armenian, and in 1822, for those who could not understand the ancient language, an edition of the New Testament in Armeno-Turkish, and the next year the British and Foreign Bible Society published a version of the Testament in modern or colloquial Armenian. These Testaments were widely circulated, although both had defects in style and sometimes in rendering. Later some publications of the American Mission Press at Malta found their way to Constantinople and stimulated questioning as to the need of reform in the Armenian Church.

During the first fifteen years of the American Mission, forty-one choice missionaries, men and women, were sent by the American Board into regions to which the Bible Society in 1836 sent Rev. Mr. Calhoun as Agent. Fifty-four new missionaries were sent out during the eight years of his agency, but of these ninety-five missionaries, thirty-eight in the meantime had been taken from the field by failure of health or by death. At the close of the forty-one years ending with this period of our history (1861) 251 missionaries (including wives of missionaries) had been sent by the American Board to this great field. But the stress of forty years' labour had reduced the whole number by 125 invalided home or removed by death. This missionary host was established in twenty-five widely separated strategic points in Turkey, Greece, Syria, and Western Persia.

Every missionary station in this broad area was a centre of Bible distribution which looked to the American Bible Society for books. The duties of the Society's Agent were not by any means trivial in such a field.

In the Levant were many sincere souls whose gropings for truth stirred sympathy. Bibles distributed by the first American missionaries deeply influenced such persons. In 1832, Mr. Goodell visited Nicomedia, the former capital of Bythinia, and the occasional residence of Diocletian the Cruel, of Constantine the Great, and other Roman Emperors. Here Mr. Goodell left with an old priest a copy of his Armeno-Turkish New Testament. He gave to some Armenian boys in the street some tracts in the Armenian language, one of which fell into the hands of another priest. These two priests were soon saying to themselves and to each other, " If this is religion, we have none ! " Six years later, Mr. H. G. O. Dwight found in Nicomedia sixteen Armenian followers of the Bible who had never seen a missionary, who appeared to be truly converted men, and who afterwards became the nucleus of a flourishing evangelical church.

One of the tracts issued in Armeno-Turkish from the mission press at Malta fell into the hands of an Armenian pilgrim at Jerusalem in 1826, and was taken home to Marsovan in Asia Minor. The tract introduced the pilgrim to the New Testament and the New Testament showed him Jesus Christ. That tract sent out at a venture by the earliest missionaries of the American Board was the first messenger of the Gospel in a place which since 1852 has been a noble station of the American Missionaries and a centre for the widest distribution of the Bible. Such works were the Lord's doings !

One of the graduates of Peshtimaljian's Armenian school in Constantinople, named Der Kevork, particularly interested the missionaries Goodell and Dwight, who attended his ordination at the Armenian Patriarchate in 1833. This young priest's after history illustrated the preparation among the Armenians in those days for study of the Bible. He was assigned to the parish of Haskeuy, Constantinople, and for long years he kept up friendly relations with the missionaries and, as the priest of that parish, he taught his people to study the Scriptures, and shape their conduct by the divine light. About half a century after this ordination a missionary called upon Der Kevork, who was still priest of the Armenian Church in Haskeuy. The old man, dressed in white, was bolstered up with pillows. His long beard was white as snow and his thin hands and kindly face were white and bloodless, for he was soon to pass from earth to the presence of the Saviour whom he loved. On a little stand at his bedside was the Armenian Bible of the American Bible Society, and on a shelf nearby were commentaries, a Bible handbook, and other books in Armenian printed by the American Mission. When the missionary was leaving that saintly presence, the venerable priest took his visitor's hand and, with warm emotion, said, " And so you are the son of my dear friend, Dr. Dwight: God bless you! " And he kissed the missionary on both cheeks. That affectionate benediction was a precious testimony to the worth of the Bible brought to Der Kevork by the early missionaries, to be a light to his path from his ordination to his grave.

The relation of the Bible to the work of the missionaries in the Levant was set forth by the Rev. William Goodell, translator of the Bible into Armeno-Turkish. He wrote to Secretary Brigham in 1842: " Our whole work with the Armenians is emphatically a Bible work. The Bible is our only standard and the Bible our final appeal. Without the Bible we might say one thing and the priests and bishops could say another, but where would be the umpire? All our efforts would be like beating the air. . . . And so we ourselves, with the Bible in our hands and in the hands of the people, seem to be standing on the Rock of Ages and building for eternity; but without it we build on the sand and our house is exposed to be blown down by every storm that sweeps by. These remarks I thought it important to make as an apology, should any be deemed necessary, for having devoted some eight years of my life to this work of translating the Word of God."

Mr. Calhoun threw his whole heart into his Agency. Hardly more than a dozen years before he went to Turkey in 1836 he had been an unbeliever and a mocker at the Bible. It seemed to him a great privilege now to help take the book back to the lands whence it issued. His agency field included almost all the territories mentioned in Bible history and it was, perhaps, the most attractive and promising of all the fields then occupied by the American Board of Foreign Missions.

Armenian Bible lovers in this field attracted the sympathy of many Europeans as well as Americans, when in 1839 the Armenian Church commenced a systematic persecution of those who persisted in reading the Bible. The persecution of these Evangelical Armenians continued until 1846 with some intervals of relaxation. The Armenian patriarch at Constantinople being allowed by the Turkish Government to use the Turkish police to maintain ecclesiastical discipline, banished many men, who had become enlightened through reading the Bible, to distant parts of the country, among them Mr. Calhoun's chief assistant in the Bible distribution. The trade unions expelled those who refused to give up the Bible, so that hundreds could get no employment. Even the butchers and bakers were forbidden to sell food to these unfortunate people. They were anathematised and excommunicated by the Armenian Church and it was not until 1846 that the British Ambassador, at the instance of the American Missionaries, obtained the interference of the Turkish Government in behalf of men persecuted for conscience' sake. This was the origin, entirely unexpected and unsought, of the Protestant Evangelical Community in the Turkish Empire, and of this body Mr. Calhoun said in one of his letters, " A truly religious, spiritual community, by the grace of God, has been created in Constantinople which would have done honour to the Church of Christ at any period of its history."

Mr. Calhoun did not withhold aid from regions bordering upon the Turkish field. Some hundreds of thousands of Protestant German colonists were scattered through the southern provinces of Russia and in Walachia and Moldavia, who were eager to have Bibles. At his request the Board of Managers granted funds and sent German Bibles for distribution among these people, who were in part directly reached, and partly through Mr. Melville of Odessa, afterwards Agent of the British and Foreign Bible Society, and through the Rev. Mr. Fielstedt of Bucharest, missionary of the Church Missionary Society. Protestants lived in Hungary for whom under the Austrian laws the Bible could not be imported. Mr. Calhoun caused to be printed in Vienna two thousand copies of the Testament and Psalms in German for these poor people, books printed in Vienna not being interfered with by the laws that checked importation.

The Board of Managers was always sensitive about using for salaries funds of the Society. Its hope was that missionaries would be able to care for Bible work, so that Agents would not be permanently needed in mission fields. In 1842 it notified Mr. Calhoun that his appointment would be continued for two years, but its renewal would then be an open question. Mr. Calhoun had set his heart upon labour for the people of Turkey and now he arranged to become a missionary of the American Board. But he urged the continuance of the Bible Society Agency. His reasons were, first, that Bible work in the Levant was largely in the hands of the American Bible Society. Second, all the missionaries looked to the Society for a supply of Scriptures but they were too busy with their own growing enterprise to supervise Bible work and make out regular and accurate reports of distribution. Third, the field is the most important that the Bible Society has or can have; the people are accessible and responsive, and it is an honour to carry the Bible back to the ancient Bible lands.[1] In 1844 he resigned, joining the mission in Syria, and the Board of Managers decided not at once to appoint another Agent for the Levant. To the end of his long and fruitful life Mr. Calhoun gladly co-operated with the Society in the distribution of Scriptures among the mountains of Lebanon where the impression of his faithful labours and his holy life persists to this day.

All this time Mr. Goodell was carrying on his translation of the Bible into Armeno-Turkish. In the early months of 1842 the Old Testament was finished, being printed at

[1] Letter of S. H. Calhoun to Secretary Brigham, May 9, 1842.

the expense of the American Bible Society, and in January, 1843, Mr. Goodell wrote to Secretary Brigham that the Armeno-Turkish Testament was also finished and was being printed by the British Bible Society.   He joyfully added: " In the hands of the Armenians who use only Turkish is now all the information that has ever come from Heaven for their benefit."

During the eight years of Mr. Calhoun's Agency, 35,000 volumes of Scripture had been printed at the expense of the Society chiefly at the Mission Press in Smyrna, 12,275 volumes had been supplied from the Bible House in New York, and 28,436 volumes had been purchased of the British and Foreign Bible Society for the use of the American missionaries.   The books sent out by the Agency were in seventeen languages, from Syriac and Persian in the East, to Albanian, German, Italian, French and English in the West.

In 1853 began a quarrel of Russia with Turkey over the question whether the Greek or the Roman Catholic Church ought to have custody of the key of the Church of the Nativity in Bethlehem.   In the war to which this quarrel led, the Western Powers of Europe became involved.   This concentrated attention in America as well as in Europe upon the Turkish Empire and Constantinople which Russia hoped to capture.

In the month of July, 1854, the Rev. Chester N. Righter, who had lately returned from a tour through Syria and Western Turkey, was appointed Agent in place of Mr. Calhoun.   Mr. Righter wrote pleasantly of his reception at Constantinople, and of the organisation of an Auxiliary (to the British and Foreign Bible Society) in that city which united British missionaries to the Jews and American Missionaries to the general population in one body under presidency of the Hon. Carrol Spence, the American Minister.   The stirring events of that time were emphasised during the first annual meeting of this Auxiliary, held in the hall of the principal hotel, when speakers were repeatedly interrupted by the thunder of guns from the English and French fleets saluting the Sultan as ship after ship, in full view from the windows, passed up the Bosphorus to attack the Russian fortress of Sebastopol.

Mr. Righter made a visit to the armies in the trenches before Sebastopol, distributing Scriptures among the soldiers, and in Constantinople he worked among soldiers as well as among the people of the city.   In fact, the Crimean war brought facilities for Bible distribution such as had never before been known in Turkey.

By this time the American Board had added to the number of its stations, and Mr. Righter wished to see for himself the men sending to him for Scriptures.   After visiting Greece and Egypt, in 1856 he set forth with an English missionary Secretary on a long tour on horseback to the stations occupied by adventurous missionaries of the American Board in Eastern Turkey.   He visited Tocat, Sivas, Arabkir, and Diarbekir, and proceeded to Mosul by a raft built in antediluvian style on inflated goat skins.   Thence he went to Mardin, where he was taken ill.   His companion brought him to Diarbekir with great difficulty.   Every effort of Dr. Nutting, the resident missionary physician, failed to check the disease, and Mr. Righter died at Diarbekir in December, 1856.

The blood of martyrs is the seed of the Church.   Mr. Righter's body, lying in the Syrian cemetery at Diarbekir, is a perpetual reminder to the evangelical congregation in that city of the self-sacrifice which brought them the Bible, and to the American Bible Society of its sacred duty to stand by that distant missionary station.   In this field every Testament taken into a village or town lying beyond the missionary centers, created a demand for many more.   Thus in these northern parts of Mesopotamia it was American enterprise which as early as 1850 discovered the opportunity, took permanent residence among the squalid houses of the people, and, mission and Bible Society always co-operating, scattered the seed of an abundant harvest.

A co-labourer with the Bible Society, the Rev. Dr. Eli Smith, translator of the New Testament into Arabic (the version chiefly used in evangelising Diarbekir), finished his earthly service in 1857.   In 1848 Dr. Smith had been set apart for Bible translation by the American Board, the Bible Society providing the salary of his assistant. On receiving intelligence of Dr. Smith's death, the Board of Managers honoured his memory by formally assuming the duty of supplying funds to complete the translation of the Bible into Arabic as soon as an able man was found for the work. This able man was another missionary of the American Board, the Rev. C. V. A. Van Dyck, who taking up the work of Dr. Smith revised it and completed the translation of the Bible in the most masterful manner.

An obvious necessity of the existence of a Bible Society is that missions anywhere sustained by churches which help to support the Society should receive aid for printing and distributing Scriptures. The Rev. I. G. Bliss, a former missionary of the American Board at Erzerum in Eastern Turkey, was selected for Mr. Righter's post and arrived at Constantinople in January, 1858.

Mr. Bliss had special qualifications for this position. He knew the land, its languages, and its needs. Being acquainted with a large proportion of the great missionary body he could sympathise with and help them as a stranger could not. Having an energetic habit he would press Bible distribution to the utmost. The time was propitious, for diffusion of the Bible always creates demand for it. Orders were constantly coming from all parts of the Levant for Scriptures. This demand came from all nationalities and from people of every rank. In Constantinople the Mussulman official of high standing could be seen reading the Bible and discussing its contents with a despised Protestant peasant from the far off highlands of Ararat.

Until 1836 nearly all the Scriptures used by the American missionaries in the Levant were obtained from the British and Foreign Bible Society, the bills for their cost being generally paid by the American Bible Society. This fact raised a curious problem. These Scriptures were naturally included by the British and Foreign Bible Society in its reports of issues. That Society rejoiced that it had supplied the Scriptures which the American missionaries used in beginning their remarkable campaign in Turkey. On the other hand, the American Bible Society of course reported among its issues books for which it had paid and which it sent to the missionary stations. For a time, therefore, the figures of Bible circulation in Turkey suffered from a double entry not observed perhaps by either Society. Such an infelicity was less liable to occur after a permanent Agent had the work of the American Society thoroughly in hand.[1]

One year after his arrival in Constantinople Mr. Bliss wrote to Dr. Brigham that during three months "more copies of the Scriptures published by our Society have been sent forth from the Depot in that city to different parts of the Empire than during the whole of the last year." One order was for 100 Bibles from Bythinia. A week or two before this eight boxes of Bibles were sent to Harput, reached by pack-mule caravan from a Black Sea port 300 miles east of Constantinople. The following week six large cases of Scriptures were despatched by ox-cart to Philippopolis in Bulgaria. An unexpected desire to read the Bible seemed to have been awakened among the Christian sects of Turkey and even among the Mohammedans. The enthusiasm shown by Mr. Bliss in these early months of his Agency continued fresh and undiminished during thirty years.

[1] The American Bible Society began in 1827 to make remittances for Scriptures to the missionaries of the American Board in the Levant, and from that time to 1861 it had granted for printing or for payment of the bills of the British and Foreign Bible Society for books supplied to American missionaries $110,816; the books being in Armenian, Armeno-Turkish, Arabic, Syriac, Hebrew-Spanish, Greek and some other languages.

CHAPTER XXIX

LIGHT FOR THE DARKER LANDS

GLORIOUSLY was the Nineteenth Century of church history ushered in by the great missionary movement. This movement both prepared a way for taking Bibles to almost every part of the world, and produced Societies to furnish the Bibles. The earliest American missions in purely pagan lands were established in India. Even before any formal decision to supply American missions abroad, the Society, as already mentioned, began to send money to missions which needed Scriptures as a foundation for their work. To American missions on the continent of India and in the island of Ceylon during its first twenty-five years the Society granted more than $35,000 for Bibles.

The confidence of the Society in making these appropriations largely rested upon the qualities of American missionaries. In India, for instance, the American Board had established itself in different parts of the country, and later other American missionary societies opened work in this strange, and in many respects beautiful land. Beginning with 1813 the American Board placed a missionary station at Jaffna in Ceylon and at Bombay and as the places seemed to invite occupancy, it also formed a station at Madras and later one at Madura. It sent out printing presses and printers to Jaffna and to Madras in order that the missionary might reinforce the spoken word with printed arguments.

We talk about India as if it was a single country and its people a single nation. We read that 300,000,000 people inhabit that land. These numerals, however, convey little impression, being no more interesting than the formula of a problem in Algebra. When American missionaries went into India, educated, refined, loving the good, hating the evil, they found themselves in the midst of different races, separated by language and by lines of caste as well as by walls of religion, yet in several respects alike. The masses of the people lived in darkest ignorance. They were unable to read, their minds seemed utterly vacant; a sort of animal instinct held them to the ways of their fathers, whether as to place of abode or its quality, whether as to religious belief or its outward expression. No aspiration for improvement brightened any life, and no curiosity was aroused when improvements were offered by others. With ten or more varieties of gross paganism to be studied and mastered, in the very place where Satan's seat appeared to be, a missionary in India had occasion, if ever man had, to doubt the duty of including India within the Saviour's command to teach all nations.

Possessed by the devil of egotism, the Brahmins, men of the highest caste, educated for the most part, unceasingly turned the ignorance of the masses to their own personal gratification and gain. Power to oppress was their birthright; the corruption of the people was the surest defence of their influence. Like the ancient Pharisees they would not touch with their finger-tips the heavy burdens which they laid upon the people. Their spirit appears in the cold unfeeling attitude which they held at this time toward their sacred Vedas. They restricted the use of these to members of the Brahmin caste. Lower castes might not possess or read the Vedas, nor even hear them read. The Pariahs, people so low in the social scale as to be outside of any caste, they regarded as not worthy to drink from the same well as Brahmins, nor entitled to own any space upon earth. Missionaries coming into the country, as though personally attacked, deeply felt this oppression of the masses of the people. The kind of sensitiveness toward injustice which burns as fire until a remedy is found, is what God always shows in His messages to men. A holy indignation fairly drove the missionaries into efforts to help the poor and ignorant and despised. Influence by which they could move such degraded people does not spring from genius, but from humble service in the name of Jesus Christ.

At the beginning of the second quarter century of the work of the Bible Society these missionaries, hidden as it were like leaven in a great mass of meal, had been labour-

ing for a score of years.   In the mission schools some people had learned to read; in limited circles the missionaries
were recognised as men of a new species.   An American
missionary did not tell lies.   He could not be convinced
of self-seeking, and he preached a religion which lived in
his heart.   Such traits of character, utterly at variance with
those prominent in India, led the common people little by
little to take interest in what the missionary taught.   Character, so to speak, was the thin edge of a wedge that cleft
the apathy of the people toward moral principle, toward the
circumstances of daily life and toward everything save the
daily scraping together of food enough for the day.

With a heat like that felt by those who have discovered
families dying from starvation, the missionaries cried to
the Bible Society for help and the Board hastened grants
of money for Bibles.   During the twenty years from 1841
to 1861 grants to the American missions in India amounted
to nearly $120,000.

The greatest value of these grants of money was that the
missionaries were thereby enabled adequately to publish
translations of some importance.   In Ceylon the Tamil
Version existed long before American missionaries acquired
the language, but the American Mission Press became for a
time a centre from which some English missions also received Scriptures in Tamil, since the Americans improved
the clearness and accuracy of the old translation.   It seemed
wise to the English and American missionaries to work together in this, and the Jaffna Bible Society, Auxiliary to
the British and Foreign Bible Society, was organised.   Before long we find American missionaries suggesting to the
American Bible Society that grants of money for Ceylon
be made directly to the Jaffna Auxiliary instead of to the
American Board of Boston.   The Managers granted the
request, and as a natural result, the fruit of the seed sowing by the Society was lost to sight in the reports of the
Jaffna Bible Society.   This was simply another illustration
of a fact which has close relation to the spiritual growth of
every Christian worker; namely, that God's way of advancing His kingdom is to have one sow and another reap the
fruit of the sowing.

The revision of the Tamil Bible was afterwards trans-ferred to Madras, where the American Mission Press was also occupied with work in Tamil, and where the advice and co-operation of English missionaries was more readily obtained. The Madras Auxiliary of the British and For-eign Bible Society took general charge of the printing, but in this case the rule was followed of dividing the editions in proportion to the money furnished by the two great Bible Societies. In 1845 the Rev. Mr. Winslow sent a beautiful letter to the Board of Managers accompanying a specimen of the first edition of the Bible in Tamil to be brought within the compass of a single volume.

Some of the grants for India during this period were made to the Rev. A. Sutton, an English Baptist missionary in Orissa, who confessed to Secretary Brigham that four of the missionaries in that field were English and only two Americans. " But then," he added, " four of the wives of missionaries are Americans and only two English. If I myself have not the honour of being American, yet I feel it difficult to admit that I am less interested in the pros-perity of your institution than a lineal descendant of the Pilgrim Fathers." Naturally this frank and friendly avowal secured for Mr. Sutton several grants of money for Scriptures in the Uriye language.

In the north of India as American Presbyterian Missions were established in the Lodiana District, money was fur-nished by the Society for translation, printing and distribu-tion in the Hindi and Urdu and later in the Punjabi lan-guage. The Methodist Episcopal mission at Lucknow re-ceived grants for Bible distribution almost as soon as it had fairly taken up its work. And later on the printing of Scriptures in Urdu at Lucknow was supported by funds from the American Bible Society.

It was during this period that the Indian mutiny oc-curred. It was a terrible insurrection in North India last-ing more than a year from May, 1857, which was intended to destroy the troops, establishments and other appurte-nances of the East India Company. From the missionary point of view a part of the significance of this terrible mutiny was the revelation which it made of trust in God and devoted bravery animating missionaries who stayed by their posts. This gave them influence among some classes of the people. The mutiny also resulted in the transfer of the British civil and military organisations in India from the East India Company to the British Government. Bible distribution, evangelistic efforts, and education made steady forward progress after this bloody episode of Indian history.

Mention has already been made of the early work of American missionaries upon the Marathi Version. Before 1850 the mission co-operated with the Bombay Auxiliary of the British and Foreign Bible Society, using the funds sent by the American Society to pay for printing Scriptures, and also for purchasing Scriptures in other languages than the Marathi which the missionaries used in their general evangelistic work. Mr. Allen, one of the missionaries of the Board in this field, mentioned a curious result of the Bible work. By the activities of Bible Societies, Mohammedans seemed to have been stirred to print the Koran, which had always before been written out by hand. They even went further than this in printing favourite chapters of the Koran separately in little booklets which, like those from the Mission press, could be sold for a very low price.

Another early mission of the American Board was in Siam, having been commenced by David Abeel in 1831 and continued until about 1850 when the missionaries were withdrawn. During the time of their stay at Bangkok the missionaries set up a printing office, manufactured Siamese type, and with money granted by the Society issued in Siamese the New Testament and some books of the Old Testament. Rev. Charles Robinson, one of the missionaries, wrote to the Board describing the work, and incidentally this letter illustrates what we have already mentioned — the importance of early editions of a new version as a foundation for permanent translation of the Bible. Mr. Robinson says, " This mission has introduced in your books the division of words in printing, as is done in other languages. The Siamese generally acknowledge that this makes the book much easier to read than those printed in the Siamese method which runs words together." The

American missionaries, also, introduced marks of punctuation, being rather cautious about this however, for fear of criticism; but the Siamese seemed to be pleased after they understood what was being done. "Hundreds and perhaps thousands," said Mr. Robinson, "in this kingdom have read portions of the word of life. Although buried long in dust, we trust the good seed will at length spring up." When the American Presbyterian Church opened its permanent mission in Siam, the hope of Mr. Robinson came true.

At the time of which we are writing, Africa was on the maps chiefly as a picture of a guess. The ignorance of the West concerning the interior of the great dark continent was hardly more gross than that of the people who lived in it concerning America. Excepting in the northern and southern extremities of the continent, which had been touched by civilisation, the very idea of writing had not yet reached the minds of the people. They were without an alphabet and of course without books. Among the various missionary societies attempting to enter the continent from the East and from the West, American societies had commenced work on the West coast in Liberia, and farther south near the mouth of the Gaboon River. Great Britain occupied Port Natal on the southern part of the East coast in 1842. The American Board sent missionaries into that region about the same time and it was not many years before the Bible Society was beset with requests for aid to print the Scriptures in African languages.

Intellectual giants only could enter that dark continent, discover means of talking with the people, acquire a vocabulary, decide upon an alphabet suitable for writing the language, and within a decade or so begin cautious translations of portions of Scripture. The old Romans did many things by which the Christian world still profits. Their alphabet has been the instrument of bringing intellectual and spiritual life to many a black tribe left generation after generation without the power of writing.

In 1847 the Society printed in New York the Gospel of John in the Grebo language, translated by a missionary of the American Episcopal Church in Liberia. In 1849 the missionaries of the American Board in southeastern Africa announced that they had completed a translation of one of the Gospels into the Zulu language, and the Society furnished them the means of printing it on their own press at the mission headquarters. This was the beginning of a great African version of which some 250,000 volumes have been printed at the Bible House in New York. In 1852 one of the first works undertaken in the new Bible House was the printing of the Gospel of John in the Mpongwe language, spoken by tribes in the district of Gaboon, in West Africa, Rev. Mr. Bushnell, one of the missionaries of the American Board, having supervised the proof-reading in order to insure accuracy. This work for darkest Africa, as we shall see later, has had the result of showing that the black men have the same difficulties and the same yearnings for better things as do the white men who often despise them.

In China the real beginning of advance in missionary work was prepared by treaties at the end of the war with England in 1842 commonly called the Opium War. Temporarily only, before that time, could missionaries find lodgement in Chinese cities. Singapore with its large Chinese population was a famous mission station, and the Portuguese island of Macao also had an important place in early missions to China. But after losing Canton in the war with England the Chinese government made peace and opened to foreign commerce five important seaports. These ports were quickly entered as mission stations. Incidentally the cession of the island of Hong Kong to Great Britain gave missions a secure base for operations in the Chinese Empire. After the second war with England new treaties gave access to several additional cities, some of which were in the interior of the country. China was open to the Gospel.

American missionaries in China received, from 1833 to 1836, $19,500 from the Society for printing revisions of Dr. Morrison's Chinese version. In 1843 the missionaries of several different denominations conferred in regard to Scriptures for China. The conference was unanimous on the necessity of promptly supplying missionaries with the Bible in Chinese, the necessity of revising the existing text, and the impropriety of independent action by the missions, which might produce several versions of the Chinese Scriptures. It was agreed, too, that missionaries of all denominations should participate in the revision, a portion being assigned to each station and afterwards passed around for comments before being taken in hand by the delegates composing the general revision committee. Along with the earnest desire for a union version, and a general agreement in principle, curiously enough this conference brought to light difficulties of translation which proved unexpectedly stubborn. Not only did the old question of rendering the Greek word *baptizo* prove a stumbling block, but the selection of terms to represent the Deity and the Holy Spirit in Chinese encountered irreconcilable differences of opinion, although Morrison's Bible, which used the term *Shin* for the Supreme Being, had been in use for twenty-five years. The conference voted in both cases to leave those questions for later settlement, in the meanwhile expecting the different missions to fill the blanks in the manuscript with the term by each preferred.

In June, 1847, the Committee of Delegates having received suggestions made by the different stations began its revision of the Chinese New Testament. Then began also a series of discussions in Committee lasting through three or four years concerning Chinese terms properly to be adopted for the name of the Deity and of the Holy Spirit. Some general principles of Bible translation also became topics for warm discussion. Discussion ripened into controversy; and quite a library of letters, pamphlets, and other documents were interchanged between the different parties and submitted to the Bible Societies in London and New York for their judgment, and sometimes even for their guidance.

When the New Testament was ready to be printed in 1850, the Bible Societies not having been willing to make a decree, as two hundred years earlier the Pope had done in a parallel controversy among Roman Catholic missionaries, the question of "terms" very definitely divided the Committee of Delegates. In the meantime the Committee of the British and Foreign Bible Society, in its eagerness quickly to supply Scriptures for China, had given to the London Missionary Society $5,000 to enable it to send a cylinder press to Shanghai, and had decided to furnish any amount of money that was necessary promptly to bring out a revised Chinese Bible. It informed the American Bible Society of its action and offered to let it participate in the expense. The American Society, also feeling very deeply the needs of China, appropriated $10,000 to be used by the missionaries of the American Board in bringing out the revised Chinese Bible whenever it should be ready. The New Testament was printed, the places left blank for the revisers, being filled by each party according to preference.

Throughout this controversy the letters from Dr. Bridgman, Dr. S. Wells Williams, and other American missionaries to Secretary Brigham showed a yearning to put the Bible into the empty hands of the Chinese which was pathetic. Again and again they begged for prayers in behalf of a speedy solution of the obstructive problems. Nevertheless, in August, 1851, when the " Delegates Committee " began to revise the Old Testament, it was almost immediately disrupted by divergent opinions respecting essential principles of Bible translation, Dr. Medhurst and Messrs. Stronach and Milne of the London Missionary Society following their preference in the revision, and Dr. Bridgman, Mr. Culbertson and Bishop Boone, American missionaries, carrying on a revision according to the principles for which they had contended. Instead of a union version, two versions of the Chinese Bible were therefore issued, one more elegant in style and the other more accurate in rendering. Neither could be accepted by all the missions. Perhaps because the Chinese themselves have thought the Supreme Being too far above man to be mentioned excepting by suggestion, the Chinese term to be used where " God " is named in the Bible is still unsettled. The Bible Societies must hope that the Chinese Christian church rather than missionary scholars will one day end a controversy which has endured through two generations.

In all of this work of Bible translation and publication while American missions were at their beginnings, the early translation perhaps of a single Gospel with all its imperfections proved a work of permanent value when made by a true scholar. There may be much retracing of steps as the translation is revised again and again, but the first serious impression upon the new language is commonly found in the earliest form of the version. Upon this foundation the finished structure of a more accurate and less crude translation is erected.

CHAPTER XXX

STORM CLOUDS

VEXATIOUS troubles, which the Apostle admits to be in one sense grievous, he more than once assures his disciples are matters for rejoicing. Patience, for instance, he counts among things worth gaining, like gold dust from a sand bank, out of carking cares and afflictions. He reminds one that when a person has acquired patience in this way he is a gainer also of the experience of various good things that come to him who waits. Another of the Apostle's postulates is that after gaining the experience of good in the midst of trouble, a permanent condition of optimism is apt to result — a hope which will not fail.

Notwithstanding the really remarkable successes which had attended the efforts of the Society both at home and abroad, the last few years of the period before the Civil War brought to the Board of Managers a series of perplexities which sometimes seemed to be harbingers of greater evils to come. In 1857 three harassing problems together had to be dealt with by the Board. In the first place, while the Society needed a considerable increase in the amount of money available for its expanding work, a financial panic destroyed confidence and made values shrink to such an extent that the donations for the work of the Society were diminished by some tens of thousands of dollars in one year. In the same year a perfectly innocent attempt to secure the Bibles published by the Society against typographical errors had result in an attack of threatening violence upon the Board and the Society. By a curious coincidence, in 1857, also, the Supreme Court of the United States made a sweeping decision on slavery which aroused fierce indignation in the Northern States and strengthened in the South the foreboding that a terrible conflict might

246

soon spring from the controversy about slavery. With-drawal from the Union seemed the only means of escape. Clearly, this political disturbance also threatened the Society's great undertaking. As the people of the whole country became absorbed in personal losses, in doubts of the Society's wisdom and in political quarrels they would forget the daily needs of the Bible Society. Such forgetfulness would be in effect like that of men at an air-pump on which depends the life of a diver hard at work out of sight under ten fathoms of water.

It is the lot of the Bible Society to be continually in anxiety between increase, on one hand, of demands from needy districts and needy people, and on the other hand, of difficulty in raising money to satisfy these demands.   In 1841 the Board appropriated $50,000 for the supply of the foreign field, but when the financial year came to a close it was found that the donations from Auxiliaries, the chief source of supply, amounted to less than half of this sum. In 1842 the receipts of the Society were $8,000 less than in 1841, and one half of the appropriations to the foreign fields could not be paid because of the lack of money.

The available money in the treasury was reduced by a habit fallen into by some Auxiliary Societies of ordering books in quantity without thought of the obligation to pay for them or of raising money for the purpose. Any Auxiliary might thus hamper the general work of the Society. In 1844 the Board was besought to cancel a number of such debts and it had to write off $27,355 from the book account, passing that amount to the account of books granted. In 1852, $46,373 were thus taken from the assets of the society and credited as free grants to Auxiliaries. The Board had no reserve fund to draw upon for such unforeseen grants. In a year or two, besides such calls, its regular grants of money for home and foreign work were barely covered by receipts, financial disturbances throughout the country having reduced contributions.

In 1857, beginning with the collapse of a number of business houses in Ohio, the Board's sources of supply seemed to vanish like a brook dried by the hot summer sun. In August of that year business failures seemed to become epidemic. Some 5,000 firms and companies failed in a few weeks with $290,000,000 of liabilities. The recourse of the Society in desperate need was the banks which would loan needed money. But in Philadelphia the banks generally suspended payment during the latter part of September, and in October there was a general suspension of payments by banks in New York. The Board and the Secretaries, who can cheerily hold their minds to the increase of Bible circulation when material means of increase have taken wing and gone, must have stalwart trust in God's purpose of good to the Society.

The Society was then engaged in its second general supply of the destitute. This work ceased as if struck by lightning. The Auxiliary Societies engaged in the distribution could not raise money even for the freight on books from New York. The dearth of money seemed about to close a large part of the work of the Bible Society. The busy presses at the Bible House appeared to be on the verge of permanent stoppage. Donations fell off until the total for the fiscal year was less than a hundred thousand dollars. Long before the year ended the Society had noted as the greatest hindrance to gifts for its current needs a general impression that since all churches in the land contribute, the decision of one church to omit its collection can not make any great difference to the Society.

Perhaps a wide-spread revival of religion which left a permanent mark on the nation in 1857 had something to do with the relief of the anxieties of the Board. Although the receipts from donations in 1857 were $33,000 less than in 1856, the legacies received by the Society, which had averaged less than $20,000 a year, were $152,000 for the three years 1856, 1857 and 1858. The Managers and the executive officers had looked to God for help. As a result Secretary Brigham wrote in the Annual Report, " By God's favour every financial obligation was met and at the end of the year the Board owed nothing except gratitude to God." Again all friends of the Society rejoiced with thanksgiving for a most wonderful deliverance from terrible calamity.

At this same time the hostile criticisms of old friends greatly harassed the Board. In 1847 complaints from many sources had set forth that the Bibles published by the Society differed in small particulars. Some editions had typographical errors; some varied in the spelling of words; some did not conform to any rule in the capitals, in the italics, or in the punctuation.

The feelings of the Board would revolt against the most trifling alteration of the authorised text of the Bible, but good intentions could not guarantee infallibility. Accordingly it directed the Committee on Versions to make a careful collation of the Society's Bibles with the best editions of the Queen's Printers in England, and to prepare a Standard edition to which all future Bibles printed by the Society would conform.

The Committee on Versions was composed of scholars of national and even international repute. One notable figure in the Committee was the Rev. Dr. Edward Robinson, Professor of Biblical Literature in Andover Theological Seminary and afterwards in the Union Theological Seminary in New York; a man honoured in two continents for his profound knowledge of the Bible and his high standing as a scholar. Another member of the Committee was the Rev. Dr. Samuel H. Turner, Professor of Biblical Learning in the General Theological Seminary of the Protestant Episcopal Church, a sound and able commentator on the Bible. Another member, the Rev. R. S. Storrs, Jr., D.D., was pastor of the Pilgrim Congregational Church in Brooklyn, great in intellect, in power of expression, in oratory as well as in manly character. The chairman of the Committee was the Rev. Gardiner Spring, D.D., one of the founders of the Society and a pastor of great experience and influence.

In three years and a half this committee finished its weary task of collation, and in 1851 presented to the Board of Managers a detailed report of the work accomplished, explaining that it " had no authority and no desire to go behind the translators." This report the Board approved and published. It seemed to meet with general approval; and the Board issued its Standard Bible that year — a standard because carefully conformed to the authorised version, as required by the constitution.

The Society's Standard Bible was circulated for six years, apparently without objection. Then an unheralded storm of criticism burst upon the Board. The Maryland Bible Society, the Pennsylvania Bible Society, and other Auxiliary societies pointed out changes in the text which they said affected the integrity of the version. Many good people refused to use the Standard Bible and sent it back to the Bible House because it contained changes dangerous and unauthorised. Ecclesiastical bodies added their protests against the action of the Board of Managers. Religious periodicals and last of all the secular press took up the cry, with careless and ignorant comments. The Versions Committee had stated that Rev. Dr. McLane, the collator, had found twenty-four thousand discrepancies between the six old editions compared, one differing from another in punctuation or in the use of capitals or italics. Newspapers immediately declared that the Versions Committee had made twenty-four thousand changes in the Bible; pens always ready to emphasise human weaknesses declared that the Board had "violated the sanctity of the Bible"; that the Versions Committee had "butchered the sacred writings and apparently gloried in the mutilation"; learned men of renown cried out in horror and alarm. The perfidy of the Bible Society was brought before the Presbyterian (Old School) General Assembly with the petition that it "find a remedy for such doings or make one." Happily, the Assembly was wise enough to wish to learn the facts, and referred the whole matter to the General Assembly of the following year. Nevertheless the tribulations of the year 1857 seemed to the Secretaries burdens heavier than their strength could withstand.

The Board could not neglect the outcry of its friends and fellow-workmen in different parts of the land. It knew the value of the labours of the Versions Committee and had a high opinion of the patient diligence of Dr. McLane, who had made the collation and endured the drudgery of noting discrepancies even to commas and parentheses. It feared that it had made a mistake in acting without close examination of the details of the Committee's work, being led by confidence in the scholarship of the Versions Committee to sanction unauthorised emendations. But the Committee was charged with exceeding its mandate. Alterations, it was said, had been made in the text where the King James translation had seemed to them to be incorrect. The Committee had also made new headings to chapters, having justly regarded these as no part of the Bible, but a sort of index prepared by any one superintending the printing. Eminent clergymen wrote to the papers that the Versions Committee " objected to criticism as if they were acting by divine authority instead of being mere intruders meddling with the oracles of God." The actual facts of the Committee's action must be set forth where they would inform critics; otherwise these discussions might agitate the Society for months. The Board accordingly referred the whole mass of complaints and criticisms to the Versions Committee with instructions to report upon the whole subject.

The report of the Committee was presented to the Board in November. It defended in general the decisions of the Committee but recommended that the headings of chapters in the Standard Bible should be brought into accord with those in former editions. This would remove some objections that had been made, but would not soften criticisms concerning changes in the text of the Bible which savoured of revision. The Board, therefore, referred the report back to the Versions Committee for consideration from this point of view. The Committee, however, did not wish to change its report and returned the papers to the Board. The Board was now perilously near a volcanic explosion. But Rev. Dr. Storrs suggested the appointment of a special Committee of nine, made up from nine different denominations, to be arbitrators, as it were, in this delicate emergency. According to usage in such cases, Dr. Storrs as proposer of the plan was made Chairman of the Special Committee.

In January, 1858, the special committee of nine reported resolutions for adoption in which Dr. Storrs did not concur, he urging in a minority report the adoption of a different set of resolutions. The controversial topic brought to the Board by these two sets of resolutions was in essence the question whether or not the Society has a right to revise the King James Version of 1611, Dr. Storrs urging the right to revise. His resolutions proposed that changes in the text of the Bible be approved where they are authorised " by some edition heretofore accepted in this country or in Great Britain, or by the unanimous consent of Christian scholars affirming their correctness."

Feeling was intense, and calm deliberation was essential to any useful action. Upon the decision of the Board would depend the peace of the Society and perhaps its very existence as a national institution. The Board therefore deferred consideration of the resolutions for two weeks, and on the 28th of January, 1858, the fateful decision was taken. Eighty-three persons entitled to vote in meetings of the Board of Managers were present. After a full and somewhat warm discussion, the Board adopted by a very large majority the resolutions offered by the special committee of nine, as follows:

" RESOLVED, That this Society's present Standard English Bible be referred to the Standing Committee on Versions for examination; and in all cases where the same differs in the text or its accessories from the Bibles previously published by the Society, the Committee is directed to correct the same by conforming it to previous editions printed by this Society or by authorised British presses; reference being also had to the original edition of the translators printed in 1611; and to report such corrections to this Board, to the end that a new edition, thus perfected, may be adopted as the Standard Edition of the Society.

" RESOLVED, That until the completion and adoption of such new Standard Edition, the English Bibles to be issued by this Society shall be such as conform to the editions of the Society anterior to the late revision, so far as may be practicable, and excepting cases where the persons or auxiliaries applying for Bibles shall prefer to be supplied from copies of the present Standard Edition now on hand or in process of manufacture."

The resolutions adopted sustained the principles on which the Board had always interpreted the first article of the constitution and on which it had always acted in respect to the English Bible. The dissenting resolutions, on the other hand, admitted the principle that Bible Societies, " on the unanimous verdict of Christian scholars," might revise the Bible. This theory, if carried into execution, would be almost certain to break up a Society which different denominations sustain. It was well, therefore, that the question was then permanently settled, since the revision of the English Bible was destined to be undertaken a score of years later.

The by-law which specifies the duties of the Versions Committee says, in so many words, that its action is to be " subject to the approval of the Board." Six of the members of the Committee, however, signed a protest against the action taken and asked to have it entered on the minutes. This the Board, of course, refused to permit. The six signers of the protest, Rev. Dr. Storrs, Rev. E. Robinson, Rev. S. H. Turner, Rev. Dr. Vermilye, Thomas Cock, M.D., and Rev. Dr. Floy, immediately resigned membership in the Versions Committee. Rev. Gardiner Spring, the Chairman of the Committee, only remained to carry out the decision of the Board. The Committee was reconstituted by appointment of nine new members, and proceeded to complete the Standard Bible of the Society in accordance with the resolutions of the Board. Quiet was at once restored.

Meanwhile in this same year of financial panic and of the attack on the Society for attempting a revision of the English Bible, the Supreme Court of the United States made a decision which profoundly affected the country and therefore the Bible Society. The case was that of Dred Scott, a slave who had sued for freedom. The decision of the Supreme Court was, in the first place, that a slave, not being a citizen, cannot sue in the United States courts, and in the second place, slavery being a national institution, it is the duty of Congress to protect the property of slave-owners, even when the slave is in free territory. In the North it was felt that this decision carried the world back twenty centuries, for it upheld an ideal of citizenship as exclusive and aristocratic, and a theory of slavery as heartless, as that of the Roman Empire.

All these things added to the anxieties of the Board, although they did not directly affect the Society. The simple and beneficent work of the Society steadily went on, the

Board, following St. Paul's rule of thinking no evil and patiently enduring affronts, while political agitators were rushing about the country making orations full of fire which increased the bewilderment of a people travelling an unknown road in a fog.

In 1859 John Brown of Kansas, with a small band of armed followers, seized the arsenal at Harper's Ferry, Virginia, with the idea that he could induce the slaves to rise against their masters and gain freedom by insurrection. It was a mad scheme, for originating which John Brown was hung; but it filled the hearts of Southerners with a sense of danger not only to their property but to themselves. The feeling grew that the whole of the Northern States were in a conspiracy to stir up insurrection among the slaves in the South.

For the first time the possibility of war between the two sections took definite form in the minds of clear-headed men. The approach of war, though as silent and stealthy as that of a tiger toward its prey, shakes the social system to its foundations, and throws upon trade a creeping paralysis. The difficulty of raising money for benevolent work steadily increased, although the Southern Auxiliaries, as a rule, loyally sustained by cordial approval and by material gifts close relations with the Society. During the uncertainties of the time a pleasing equilibrium existed in the Society's relations throughout the country; but an equilibrium is always uncertain since even a feeble effort may destroy it.

In July, 1861, the South Carolina Bible Convention in its annual meeting at Sumter passed a most cordial resolution: " That the American Bible Society merits the confidence and sympathy of the whole American people in view of the principles on which it is founded and the wisdom, economy, and efficiency of its management. It shall have our earnest co-operation in its plans and efforts for the supply of every family in our own and other lands with the oracles of God." The Convention then renewed its pledge to send to the Bible Society $5,000 during the year for its foreign work.

Four months later Abraham Lincoln was elected President of the United States by the vote of all the Northern States excepting New Jersey.

It seemed to the people of the South that the unanimity of this election meant a definite purpose on the part of the Northern States to wrest slaves from the hands of their owners. After six weeks of hurried consultation, South Carolina responded to this vote by passing with enthusiasm an ordinance of secession from the United States. During the next five months one after another the Southern States followed the lead of South Carolina, and organised a new Union as " the Confederate States of America " with Jefferson Davis as President.

Fear of calamity is of the same quality as calamity itself, but is apt to be more exhausting to strength. The men at the Bible House had at this time to contend with much the same feeling as the soldier who is carried forward with his regiment toward a clash with hostile forces, not knowing at what moment, nor in what place, nor in what guise the battle will begin. But no one at the Bible House flinched. The point most sensitive to such portentous events is the Treasure chest of the Society. From the Treasurer's point of view the nation is divided into two classes, the one consisting of people who contribute to the Society and the other of those who do not. Because of the secession movement and its uncertainties, receipts gradually became less. In the spring of the year the Board had appropriated for work abroad $43,439.90, and had notified the different missions that they would receive this amount. Of this sum $22,283.90 had been paid over. " The remainder," said the brave, calm and trustful men of the Board, " shall be sent out as soon as collected."

The forty-five years of which the story has been told up to this point have shown a steady increase of the influence and power of the Society. The Board had learned the lesson of expecting, in the spirit of the " bread petition " in the Lord's Prayer, to have the needs of the Society supplied one day at a time. It had no reserve of money laid up; there was nothing whatever that it could call its own except the Bible House and the fine equipment for printing books whenever there was money to pay for printing. But to men of devotion and experience and prayer storm-clouds cannot possibly destroy the calmness of hope in God. Political disturbances cannot be a hindrance to work for Him any more than the soldier's anxieties before the battle can in any way hinder his throwing his whole power sturdily into the struggle which his general directs.

In the midst of the forebodings caused by the secession movement, came from Florida a declaration that " all will rally to the support of the American Bible Society which knows no North, no South, no East, no West, but only one needy world." Another encouragement to unshaken confidence was a message from Charleston, South Carolina, after the secession ordinance had been passed, remitting to the American Bible Society $1,000 as the Charleston Auxiliary's share of the $5,000 promised at the State Convention.

On the 12th of April, 1861, the Southern troops began the bombardment of Fort Sumter, the United States fortress in front of Charleston. Mr. Lincoln immediately called for 75,000 volunteers to defend the property of the United States. That meant Civil War.

Twice the Society suffered heavy loss before a shot had been fired. Secretary James H. McNeill, a Presbyterian clergyman from Fayetteville, N. C., continued at his post, framed the resolution for the supply of Scriptures to all troops in all parts of the country, and on behalf of the Committee presented it to the Board, which unanimously adopted it. A week later North Carolina formally seceded from the Union, and Mr. McNeill, like many officers of the United States Army, decided that he must go with his State. He accordingly resigned on the 6th of June, after eight years of faithful and self-denying service of the Bible cause.[1] The second loss was of another class. It was not until some time had passed that the Board realised that on the day when

[1] Later the officers of the Society were saddened by the tragic result of this decision of a loved associate. Mr. McNeill returned to North Carolina, where he acted for a time as chaplain in the Southern army. He later became a Major and afterwards Colonel of the Fifth North Carolina Cavalry Regiment. He distinguished himself in various battles throughout the war, was severely wounded at Gettysburg, and just one week before the surrender of General Lee at Appomatox, he was killed in action, April 2, 1865, near Petersburg, Va.

the war commenced it lost in the seceded States 653 of its Auxiliary Societies.

It was perfectly clear to all that the rending of the Union menaced the existence of the Society. Never before had disaster seemed so imminent, the Society so defenceless; but the Managers and the executive officers quietly continued their work, unfrightened by the possibilities of this great crisis. In the annual report presented to the Forty-fifth Annual Meeting, in May, 1861, the Managers, with a hope born of experience, spoke these brave words: "Amid the political excitements and financial revulsions of the last four months we had reason to expect a large diminution of the Society's operations. This expectation has been realised, yet not to the extent that might have been anticipated. . . . Convinced more deeply than ever by events in this and other lands that without the controlling and sanctifying influence of the Bible there can be no permanent security for aught that is valuable to the individual or to the community, it behooves the Society to address itself with new earnestness and new hopefulness to its blessed work."

FIFTH PERIOD 1861–1871

CHAPTER XXXI

THE BLIGHT OF CIVIL WAR

A DECLARATION of war can impede the progress of a nation, and it can also brand as a crime love of kith or kin which reaches across a line drawn on the map. For when war has been declared, to love the enemy is far more criminal than to kill him, and to give him food is treason. A demand that men shall hate their fellows, then, is the first stage of the blight of war. In a civil war this blight assails the higher ideals and finer sentiments of men who are inseparable because they have walked together in Christian fellowship.

Something of this nature befell the Society in the spring of 1861, when a part of the people of the United States sought to rend the nation in twain while a larger portion determined at any cost to preserve its integrity. Foresight in detail of the blind hates and other harrowing features of civil war did not at first impress the minds of men because the secession of Southern States was gradual. Beginning with South Carolina December 20, 1860, five more states seceded during January, 1861; Texas seceded on the 1st of February; Virginia did not take the fateful step until April, after Fort Sumter had been bombarded and occupied by the Southern troops. Arkansas and North Carolina followed, and Tennessee did not yield to the public opinion of her neighbours until the 8th of June, 1861.

The majority of the soldiers called to the colours in the North had no hostility whatever toward the people of the South. Far from conspiring together to free the coloured people in the South, the most of these men would not have enlisted to free the slaves by violence. Their one motive in taking arms was to prevent division of the patrimony which their Southern brothers had demanded in order to take an adventurous journey by themselves.

A mature Christian experience, like accurate acquaintance with any branch of secular knowledge, reveals itself in words and acts. In such a mighty catastrophe as that which the Society faced in 1861 there was nothing to do but to pray. The very pause to ask God for help is at such a time a clearing of the mind and a revelation of the solid standing place for effort found in God's inexhaustible loving kindness and wisdom. So it might be said of the Managers at this time that like the Psalmist, " in the multitude of their thoughts, God's comforts delighted their souls."

President Frelinghuysen could not believe that a merely political disturbance could break the ties between the Society and its Auxiliaries. At the Annual Meeting, May 9, 1861, he said: " While there is much to alarm and afflict us in the political agitations of our country, one thing is our special comfort in the cause of the Bible Society: We are still one, bound together by the bands of Christian kindness, animated by like hopes, earnest in like purposes and cheered by the same sympathies." He doubtless remembered that General Stonewall Jackson of Virginia had long been a warm friend of the American Bible Society, sometimes going himself from house to house to collect money for the support of its work. Mr. Frelinghuysen, like the most of the members of the Board, thought that old ties uniting them with friends of the Bible in the South could not be broken by command of any meddler who had chanced to attain power.

It is always the difficulties hard to measure which lure Christian people to momentous decisions. Without reserve of money to make good a decision for enlargement, depending like Israel in the desert upon food that came each morning and could not be kept until the next, one of the Secretaries wrote at this time: " God has left us no choice here; we must open this book to those who have it not." To the eternal credit of the Society and its officers they could not conjure up hatred of the South such as war demands. They saw only the fact that war would prevent the relief of many poor people destitute of the Scriptures.

Deliberately but unanimously the Board adopted the principle of cordial regard for all needy ones in the land without question of their attitude toward the government of the United States. In May, 1861, it sent to Auxiliary Societies and Agents throughout the land, North and South, a circular which suggested the need of Bible consolations natural to those facing imminent danger and urged that every soldier who enlisted be supplied with a copy of the Scriptures; the Board would grant books freely in every case where money lacked for this great undertaking. Three months later Auxiliaries in several Southern States having ordered Scriptures without remitting money to pay for them, the Board unanimously agreed that no cause existed to make any alteration whatever in its practice as to the supply of Auxiliaries that need the aid of the Society.

For some time it seemed possible that the Society might preserve its ties of fraternity with the Southern Auxiliaries. Not until the middle of August, 1861, did the President declare the Southern States in insurrection. During the year ending March 31, 1862, thirty-six new Auxiliary Societies were recognised in nine of the seceding states. These Societies still ordered books from New York and the report shows that during the year Southern Auxiliaries paid the Society more than $3,000 for books which they had ordered.

Notwithstanding these pleasant relations it became evident in 1862 that a number of the Southern Auxiliaries had withdrawn confidence from the Society. A Confederate States' Bible Society was shortly organised at Augusta and the Auxiliary tie gave way entirely. In spite of the hopes and the initiative of the Society, intercourse with some 600 Auxiliary Societies in the seceded states then ended. Throughout the border states bitter animosities severed national and Christian ties which had bound the people together. People looked askance at each other as though the Dark Ages had returned and had laid whole communities under ban of the major excommunication. Some of the Auxiliaries in the border states held loyally to the parent Society and suffered for it. In Franklin County, Kentucky, the Auxiliary bravely kept at work although its members and all the surrounding people were held in constant fear for months because guerrillas from the South continually made raids into their fair county. At Buckhannon, in one of the central counties of Western Virginia, a detachment of Southern cavalry raided the town and a part of their plunder was the whole stock of Bibles in the Auxiliary depository. At Martinsburg, Virginia, near the Maryland border, the lady in charge of the depository more than once, finding troops moving to attack the town, was obliged to carry her Bibles into the cellar. After the enemy had departed she would laboriously restore them to the shelves again.

A little later in the history of the war the Agent of the Society in Missouri briefly tells of the desolation wrought in that state, although it did not secede, by the tides of war flowing back and forth across its fertile fields. " Several clergymen," he said, " of different denominations have come into St. Louis for safety. From them I learned that many Sunday Schools and many churches in this state will be closed for months to come." In Virginia, after battles on battles had been fought in the Shenandoah Valley, one of the Society's Agents reported, " In this valley of Virginia, church edifices are nearly all appropriated for hospitals and other military uses. Ministers are gone, congregations are broken up, the Sabbath, even, to a great extent is forgotten."

In war-time, railroad trains, steamers, wagons, carts and pack-horses headed for any point in the enemy's territory are stopped at some river or some pass in the mountains where stands a man, with a rifle and fixed bayonet, whose vocabulary contains but the one word, " Halt! " Men have been shot for trying to carry messages or even medicine to the enemy. After the President's proclamation in August, 1861, the stern fiat of martial law made intercourse with " the enemy " unpardonable. The greater the desire to benefit men in a hostile army, the greater the criminality of him who feels that emotion.

Since a closed door guarded by the bayonet confronted the peace-loving men in the Managers' Room at New York, the Society might perhaps have given up its plan to send Bibles to the soldiers of the South. But responsibility for influence on men's souls could not be thrown off. The Society was bound to do all that it could to check irreligion among soldiers separated from religious ties and so huddled together that evil devices would become epidemic. The Board had determined to place a Bible or Testament in the hands of every soldier both North and South. All the resources of the Society should be used to give effect to this determination.

The decision of the Board was confirmed by a marvellous occurrence. When Bibles were sent South to nourish the souls of the men of the Confederate Army, the guards did not order a halt. Generals and their subordinates on both sides of the line let the Book travel under a sort of " Truce of God." Through this unparalleled respect for a holy enterprise, some three hundred thousand Bibles, Testaments and single Gospels during the war passed from New York, through the firing lines, to comfort the Southern soldiers. Such a situation was beyond hope.

Possibly the slow stages by which peace gave place to war led up to this novel situation. From Maryland, with its long border touching Virginia at all points, and its easy water communication with the Virginian shores of Chesapeake Bay, throughout 1861 it was possible to send Bibles around the flanks of the hostile armies which were gathering. Packages of books went from Baltimore to the Virginia Bible Society at Richmond, at the very time when the New York newspapers were hurling at the Northern Armies along the border the war cry: " On to Richmond!"

Immediately after the first impulsive decision of the Board, in May, 1861, Secretary McNeill wrote to the Virginia Bible Society that the Southern Army would be supplied with Scriptures as well as the Northern. The first books sent in the West were held up as contraband of war. Early in 1862 Federal officers at Cairo, Illinois, stopped a parcel of New Testaments, as contraband, which was addressed to General (Bishop) Leonidas Polk's Army at Columbus, Kentucky. This may have been, however, because General Grant at that moment was beginning a movement in Kentucky which obliged General Polk to retire from Columbus, for later there was no further difficulty. Under the same system a goodly number of Testaments were sent directly to Richmond under flag of truce with the consent of the commanding officers of both armies. The Maryland Auxiliary reported in 1863 that it had sent to the South from the American Bible Society 86,424 volumes of Scripture during the year. Some five thousand of these volumes were sent, with the consent of the authorities, to prisoners of war in Richmond. All the difficulties which attended the plan to supply the South were removed, and by the middle of 1863 shipments of books in large quantities from New York were regularly forwarded under flag of truce by way of fortress Monroe to their destination. The books mentioned above sent by the Maryland Bible Society were in fifty-seven cases, which were forwarded to Richmond by way of Fortress Monroe and City Point under permit from the Secretary of War; and the United States Government and the Norfolk Steamship Company paid all expenses of transport. Such benevolent and picturesque courtesies under flag of truce were probably unparalleled in the history of wars. They could only occur where both of the contending governments and their generals had an inbred respect for the Bible and conviction of its power to benefit men.

Curiously enough, the grand old Virginia Bible Society did not at first respond to efforts made to supply its depository with Scriptures. In November, 1863, a letter was received from its Secretary which stated that after two years of war, having received no response to a reasonable request for grants of Scriptures, it had made other arrangements and therefore was no longer under necessity of applying to the American Bible Society. From the outbreak of the war until the date of this letter, 22,650 volumes of Scripture had been sent to the Virginia Auxiliary through the Maryland Bible Society. The cause of the misunderstanding was that the Virginia Society did not realise that these books coming from Maryland were sent by the American Bible Society. It, therefore, believing that the Society was not willing to supply its needs, sent the Rev. Dr. Hoge to London to obtain Scriptures from the British and Foreign Bible Society. The considerable grant which was made in response to Dr. Hoge's request had to take its chances of running the blockade. It does not appear that many of these books reached Virginia.   As to the famine of Bibles in the South generally, shortly after the books arrived from England, Rev. Dr. Thorne of North Carolina wrote that with all of these books and all which had been printed in the South and all which had been gathered up from churches and Sunday Schools, the supply was as a drop in a bucket as compared with the terrible destitution which existed.   In 1863 some of the prisoners of war in Richmond who had been supplied with Testaments from New York sold their Testaments in order to buy food.   The price at which they sold them at the doors of the Libby Prison was twelve or sometimes fifteen dollars apiece.   This fact impresses one with the famine of Bibles in Virginia.   After the matter was thoroughly understood by the Virginia Auxiliary, its officers made graceful expressions of appreciation of the spirit and practice of the Society toward the people and the armies of the South.

In 1863 the Rev. L. Thorne, pastor of a Baptist Church in Kingston, North Carolina, managed to send to New York by way of Baltimore a request for a grant of 25,000 Bibles and 75,000 Testaments for the North Carolina Board of Army Colportage.   The grant was made and the books received to the immense joy of Mr. Thorne.   He wrote to the secretaries his heartiest thanks for the gift.   A grant not strictly limited to army work in the South was 25,000 volumes of Scripture granted to the Southern Baptist Sunday School Board in the same year.   As the United States troops occupied more and more of the Southern territory, grants were made to the old Auxiliary Societies.   Thus the Memphis and Shelby County, Tennessee, Auxiliary received a grant of 20,000 Testaments for the Southern Army and 50,000 for the United States Army under General Grant, then occupying Memphis.   The books for the Southern troops were passed through the lines by order of the general.   After the occupation of Mobile, Alabama, a grant was made to the old Mobile Auxiliary for use among soldiers and citizens.

Nor were the Southern soldiers confined in various Northern States forgotten.   Some 35,000 volumes of Scripture were given to such prisoners of war.   Most of them welcomed the Bible men and their books; some, especially bitter against the Government, refused to take Bibles tainted by contact with "Yankees." Tens of thousands of prisoners of war exchanged during the four years carried south with them these pure tokens of Christian kindness shown by men whom they regarded as their natural foes. But these shipments of Bibles had a far greater effect in succeeding years.

If the government had not facilitated the despatch of Bibles to the South, the Southern people must have remained not only without Bibles, but without knowledge of the kindly wishes of Northern Christians for their highest welfare. A little later the Society had access to the devastated lands where the bitterness of strife and of financial strain long blocked intercourse with all other people from the North. The reason why an exception was made in regard to the Bible Society was the hearty good will shown during the war in the supply of Scriptures to troops and other destitute people in the South.

While the stress of war gave keen insight and foresight and intelligence of plan to the members of the Board and the executive officers of the Society, President Frelinghuysen and Secretary Brigham did not long participate in the labours of this strenuous time. Their great work was done in the years which prepared the Society to endure the test.

On the 12th of April, 1862, President Theodore Frelinghuysen finished his long and useful life. At the time of his death he was residing, as President of Rutgers College, at New Brunswick, New Jersey. A year before, he had presided as usual at the annual meeting of the Society and delivered an interesting and stimulating address upon the duty of the Society in the presence of the extraordinary disturbances then beginning to be felt throughout the country. During the sixteen years of his service as President of the Society he showed himself entirely devoted to its interests because of love for the Bible. In his private life he devoted a certain time every day to study of the Book in order to promote his own spiritual development. This habit so left its mark on his conversation and on his thoughts that he was a living epistle, known and read of all. When he was senator of the United States he joined with others in maintaining a weekly Congressional prayer-meeting, and he was also teacher in a Sunday School in Washington. When he was dying, one near to him asked, "Is it peace with you now?" "All peace," he answered, "more than ever before"; and in a few moments he had ceased to breathe. At Mr. Frelinghuysen's funeral, in New Brunswick, flags were at half mast, places of business were closed, the church bells tolled, and the Governor, the Chancellor, and the Chief Justice of New Jersey, with a number of other distinguished citizens, were his pall-bearers. And thus while cannon were thundering at Yorktown, Virginia, at New Orleans a thousand miles away, and at many other places between, his body was committed with all honour to the tomb.

Mr. Frelinghuysen had presided at every anniversary of the Society since his election as President in 1845, and the Board of Managers placed on record its deep sense of the loss which the Society, the church, and the community sustained in his death.[1]

Dr. Brigham's rugged health had shown signs of failing during a year or more before his death, but it was none the less a shock when he passed away on the 19th of August, 1862, in the sixty-ninth year of his age. During thirty-six years he had served as Secretary of the Society, for the first fifteen of these years enjoying the counsel and fellowship of the sturdy and noble senior Secretary, Rev. Dr. James Milnor. His character was so simple and sound that every one trusted him. He had the quickest sympathy with everything which concerned the welfare of mankind, and he lived with the one purpose of advancing the kingdom of God. The completeness and harmony of his qualities especially fitted him for the office of Secretary with its many delicate and difficult relations. Rev. Dr. William Adams in preaching the funeral sermon gave a remarkably graphic description of the duties of Corresponding Secretary of the Bible Society. Partly to remind the reader that this description of the Secretary's duties holds good to the present day, we quote this part of Dr. Adams' address:

"If any one has imagined that the whole duty of a Secretary of one of our national Christian Societies consists in

[1] Manager's Minutes, Vol. 9, p. 260.

writing and filing a certain number of letters, he has not caught the first idea of the service.   It is not asserting too much to say that the general success of the organisation will depend upon its Secretary.   He is ordinarily its chief executive officer; he is surrounded and aided by various committees giving him counsel and sharing with him responsibility, but he must devise, and arrange, and project, and accomplish.   Compute the many delicate questions certain to arise in a Society like the Bible Society; the many Agents and employees in all departments in every district of the country and the world; the changes of events which are to be observed and reported throughout the vast field which has no limit save that imposed by our own capacity in possessing and cultivating it; forget not the occasions, public and private, with manifold details which are to be improved for stimulating the indifferent, informing the churches — compute, I say, all these various interests, claims, duties, and services, and tell us what tact, expertness, justice, magnanimity, patience, gentleness, scholarship, and piety are needful in one invested with such an office and conducting it with complete success.   That our friend and brother attained this success is an honour of no ordinary kind."

CHAPTER XXXII

AFTER the death of President Frelinghuysen, the Hon. Luther Bradish, for many years a Vice-President of the Society, was unanimously elected President. Mr. Bradish had won the high regard of the members of the Board and of the Society by his genial simplicity of soul, attractive manners, and especially his matter-of-course Christian character. He was a member of the Protestant Episcopal Church, and as a liberal, warm-hearted Christian he extended the right hand of fellowship to all servants of Jesus Christ. In his early life, Mr. Bradish had served the government, having been sent by President Monroe in 1820 to visit countries lying about the Mediterranean Sea. His duty was to collect information on commercial conditions preparatory to the negotiation of treaties. He spent five or six months in Constantinople and prepared the way for a commercial treaty with Turkey, although meeting much covert opposition from the Ambassadors of European powers with the single exception of Russia. His advice as to the best method of procedure in negotiating a treaty with Turkey was followed with success under President Jackson. As Vice-President of the Society Mr. Bradish attracted attention to the qualities which had made him speaker of the New York Assembly and later Lieutenant-Governor of New York and presiding officer of the State Senate. His clearness of comprehension and statement, his courtesy to all, and his skill in advancing business were remarkable. The same qualities served him when presiding in the Board of Managers. To preside at such a meeting on the first Thursday of August, 1863, was his last public act. After the meeting he went to Newport, his usual summer residence, and on the 30th day of August his long life was quietly closed. It was noted at the time as a striking fact that the early presidents of the Bible Society all reached advanced age with dignity and usefulness. Boudinot died at the age of eighty-one, John Jay at eighty-four, John Cotton Smith at eighty-one, Theodore Frelinghuysen at seventy-five, Luther Bradish at eighty; and like the worthies mentioned in the Book of Hebrews, "these all had witness borne them through their faith."

On the death of President Bradish, James Lenox, Esq., a Presbyterian gentleman long and favourably known for his constant interest in the well-being of the Society, having become a member of the Board of Managers in 1837, and a Vice-President in 1852, was elected President of the Society. His election gave general satisfaction to those who had the interests of the Society at heart, and he presided over its deliberations during the two last years of the war.

Although war brings blight it may also bring needed stimulus. The great need of the armies engaged in fierce combat, and the decision to supply all soldiers with the Scriptures was a blessing to the armies and to the Society; to the armies North and South it was a blessing by influence upon individual soldiers and sailors to which an officer in the United States Navy testified when he said: "I am not a religious man myself, but my best men are." To the Society it was a blessing because in an enterprise of this magnitude difficulties seemed ever piling mountain-high, and such an environment has the effect of rendering the minds of men more alert and discerning.

Since the soldiers were young men of the teachable age, need was strongly felt to help them while separated from the restraints of home life. For young men left without moral restraint tend to degenerate; and perhaps it is more true of the young soldier than of other young men that when he begins to go down-hill plenty of people seem glad to speed his gait. So the Society was ruled by the highest possible motives. War does not annul Christ's command to spread the gospel.

To the people at home an important reason for taking the Bible to soldiers arose from the thought of their being ever in danger of sudden death and therefore naturally inclined to seriousness. But the imminence of battle rarely led the youthful soldier to turn to his little Testament. When battle impends the soldier's mind perceives little but the work before his eyes. Like the young man in serious ill-ness, asked if he had made his peace with God, the soldier must have done that long before, or he can never do it in the midst of struggle.

Men in the army are much like men out of the army. When there is no fighting and life runs like a song it is easy to forget God, for most men who are comfortable do not note what they owe to God's loving-kindness. Many of these soldiers were children of Christian parents having the habit of going to church and Sunday School, of Sab-bath-keeping, devoted to God and to reading his word. Many of the young fellows had a store of Bible verses which they liked to recall; such as " The Lord is my shep-herd," " Cast thy burdens on the Lord." Many knew that the Bible furnishes cheer and stimulus which is precious, but cannot be gained from comrades in the camp. Little by little, however, the soldier may forget his habit of reading the Bible. After a time his conscience forgets it, too. He thinks he means well and that surely is enough, even if he does make a mistake once in a while. In the camp the devil is always at work with obscene literature, with gambling out-fits, with sneers of hard-featured teachers of atheism, and where the camp is near a city, with unlimited liquor and the smiles of painted women.

In the trenches, where day after day to stand up or even to raise the head is sure death, there is a certain monotony which wears on the nerves. In the camp, too, while troops are waiting orders, monotony often becomes insufferable. There is absolutely nothing to do or to plan day after day, perhaps week after week. At such times the little book is taken up as a last resource, and is liked because it brings memories of home. Unexpectedly it stimulates thought, and it offers the marching orders of Jesus Christ as a direct and personal message most comforting to a lonely soldier-boy.

When the camps were filling with recruits and instruc-tions had gone forth from the Bible House for the supply of Scriptures to the soldiers as they were enlisted, the demand for books was so sudden and so great that the stock in the depository was completely exhausted. Orders came from all parts of the country at once and it was nearly impossible to fill them and keep any books in the depository. In the year ending March 31, 1861, the issues from the Bible House were 721,878 volumes. The issues of the following year were 1,092,842 volumes.

Meanwhile the directions to the Agents throughout the country were to "give these books freely to the destitute people of the Southern States as occasions offer in connection with the movements of our forces. The American Bible Society has seen no reason to depart from its old principles and practice as a national and catholic institution and such it will remain, by God's blessing. To all of our people, loyal or disloyal, we hold forth the Word of Life." The Society exists to give away what it has, and still to give away.

This continual giving caused the printing of books to become an immense enterprise. At the Bible House it was a time such as causes a business firm, like the rich man of the parable, to pull down what it has and build greater. The printing equipment at the Bible House was composed of sixteen power presses, and in the printing office, bindery, and shipping office together, over 300 persons were employed. Books were printed and bound at a rate never before known in the history of the Society. In the year ending March 31, 1862, 370,000 volumes more were issued than in the previous year. In the one month of September, 1862, 168,632 volumes were printed in the Bible House; a total equivalent to an average of seven volumes every minute of every working day. In 1863 the Board of Managers, with some hesitation, decided to print the New Testament in nine separate portions, small enough to go into a vest pocket. As an experiment, in April, 1861, the gospel of John, the Book of Psalms, and the Book of Proverbs had been separately printed in such volumes, and the demand for these books, amounting to 85,000 copies in two years, was decisive. Some members of the Board had held back from approving the plan, but they could not resist the evidence of the demand, especially from the Army and Navy. In 1864, it was announced that the issues during the three years of war had amounted to 3,778,105 volumes, which was more than the total issues of the first twenty-eight years of the Society's work. More than a million and a half of these books had been distributed in the last year, and so it came to pass that in 1866, on looking back, it was found that issues from the Bible House during the four years for home use alone amounted to 5,297,832 volumes.

In the supply of the Northern troops, at the very first the whole effort of the Society was directed to furnishing Auxiliary Societies with books enough to enable them to put the Scriptures into the hands of men as they enlisted. A second phase of this work of the Society was the undertaking to supply directly the troops in the field; and finally, when the Christian Commission had shown its remarkable ability to handle great questions of supply, the Society devoted its attention to furnishing the Christian Commission with all the books which it could distribute.

The Auxiliaries, as a rule, supplied the soldiers as they first enlisted, each one caring for the quota from its field. For instance, the New Hampshire Auxiliary Bible Society supplied eight regiments and individual companies as they were organised, giving them 6,000 New Testaments. The Vermont Bible Society gave ten thousand volumes to the troops from that state. The Massachusetts Bible Society supplied 40,000 volumes to the Army and Navy, besides making a donation of about $2,800 to the national Society for its general work. The Connecticut Society and eleven smaller societies in that state supplied twenty-eight regiments, and a large number of sick and wounded in hospitals. In the first two years of the war Auxiliaries purchased from the Bible House over one million copies of Scripture which, for the most part, were given to the soldiers and sailors. At the great military centres the Auxiliaries had to ask aid from the national Society. For instance, the Washington City Auxiliary asked for a grant of 18,000 volumes in 1864. It had supplied the Army of the Potomac itself with Scriptures before this, and this grant was asked for the hospitals and forts in the neighbourhood of Washington, and the flotilla upon the Potomac River. This Auxiliary reported upon the local religious opportunities of these soldiers. Among the hospitals and in the forts many Bible classes had been organised, and chaplains from the hospitals were in the habit of conducting such Bible classes.

The New York Bible Society did a splendid work among the soldiers passing through the city, from all parts of the country, and also among the crews of the vessels of war anchoring in New York Harbour; but like the Washington Bible Society, it was obliged to rely upon the national Society for aid in its work, sometimes calling for a grant of ten or twelve thousand dollars' worth of books in one year.

It is a matter of interest to see that in the year ending March 31, 1863, the national Society received $45,442.16 in donations from 284 Auxiliary Societies, and in the same year it received in payment for books $193,761.95 from 711 Auxiliary Societies; this circumstance showing to some extent the efforts made by the Auxiliaries, even when they were poor, to pay at least for the books which they used in their fruitful work for the army.

Meanwhile the United States Army assumed vast proportions. Call after call was sent out by the President, now for 300,000, now for 300,000 more, then for a draft or conscription of 500,000, and so on. The losses in the war were very great. Fully half of the soldiers who fought the scores of battles were under twenty years of age. It is sometimes difficult to realise the enormous extent of territory involved in these events. Armies along a frontier that measured literally thousands of miles, fiercely struggled for life; lost it; won it. The tremendous sweep of the murderous contest can be judged from the soldiers' diaries. Some of them during the terrible four years marched five or six thousand miles in order to win peace on the field of battle. These facts led the Board in February, 1863, to authorise the Committee on Distribution to issue for the army 475,000 Testaments and separate portions.

During the war there was great waste of Bibles and Testaments as of other articles of equipment. Battlefields swallowed up hundreds of the little books on the bodies of dead soldiers. Wounded men commonly lost all their belongings. Again and again, when troops were ordered suddenly to break camp, in the hurry of packing knapsacks and camp equipage, perhaps in the night, with other small articles these little books were unwittingly left behind, to the amazement of villagers who searched the vacant ground the next day. The book in a soldier's kit is like a seed in soil that may be parched by drought or flooded by cloudburst or become food for insects; yet these risks must be taken, for the world will starve if no seed is sown.

Let it not be imagined, however, that this seed was wasted or that the work of the Society for the army was not appreciated. In a company composed entirely of Roman Catholics half of the men took the Testaments with cordial thanks and almost all of those who refused did so because they could not read. Workers of the Christian Commission, writing from the bloody fields of Virginia, often expressed sincere belief that the soldiers are more accessible to the gospel than the young men at home. " The soldier's Bible seems to receive better care than anything else which he has." Rev. H. A. Reid, chaplain of the 5th Wisconsin Infantry, wrote, " The Bible is more read and reverenced by men in the army than by the same men at home. These men on the average are going to be better citizens than they were when they came out to take part in the war." A sick soldier at Jefferson Barracks, Missouri, showed his Bible to Agent Wright. It was torn, water-soaked, defaced by the rough usage of the campaign. " I love to read this book," he said, " ten times more than I did when my wife put it into my knapsack. When I feel lonely and cast down, I go off by myself alone and read a chapter in the Bible. Then I can pray and then all becomes bright again."

One of the Agents in the Southwest talked with a Roman Catholic Captain in General Banks' army. It was at the end of his second year of service. " Did the men take care of their Testaments?" he asked. " Yes, and they read them too!" " Could you see any good results from their reading the Testament?" " Yes, I've seen men who were of the lowest scum of humanity become sober, thoughtful, respectable fellows; and because this is so I want to do something to help send the New Testament into the army."

And the Captain insisted on giving the Agent ninety cents, which happened to be all the money he had. A Massachusetts pastor who served the Christian Commission in the army of the Cumberland centering about Chattanooga, Tennessee, said: " I have contributed to the Bible Society all my life, but I never knew its worth and power until to-day. The first collection I shall ask from my church will be for that Society to buy Testaments for soldiers, and the next will be for the Christian Commission to hand them over to the army."

The Christian Commission was organised in the Bible House by the Young Men's Christian Association. It aimed especially to foster the higher life of the soldier. It obtained from the Society at various times considerable grants of Bibles, Testaments and portions, which it received at the Bible House and carried to the troops in various parts of the country. It became a great distributing Agency in connection with all of the United States Armies and the various squadrons of the Navy. Its work of distribution reached soldiers and sailors in their camps, in the hospitals, and even on the battle-field. About fifteen hundred clergymen and laymen took part in the work of distribution and it was a wonderful success in accomplishing what it set out to do. As time went on, the supply of the soldiers and sailors was more and more systematised. The Board could not and did not throw off its responsibility for the proper use of grants made for the troops. It appointed capable Agents, one for each great Military District, and a wonderful work was carefully and thoroughly done through the Christian Commission. The whole number of Scriptures granted to the Commission and by it put in circulation during the war was 1,466,848 volumes. The value of the books granted by the Society for this great distribution through the Christian Commission was $179,824.59.

Mr. George Hay Stuart, President of the Merchants' National Bank, of Philadelphia, the President of the Christian Commission, wrote to the Board of Managers in March, 1866, " There are few homes in the land where a Union soldier has thrown off his knapsack without bringing back from the war a book from your press, and to many a home has the pocket-worn Testament found its way as the only memento of the one who will never return. Henceforth, that is the family heirloom."

Upon the Society and upon its future new forces were now acting. They sprang from the stress of the period of the civil war. The bonds uniting different elements in the Society and in the Auxiliaries grew stronger; tendencies to admit responsibility for the support of the Society became more marked among the people; the world-value of Bible work received new light. The executive officers and the Board of Managers could no more escape the constant pressure for large and effective action than a diver in his helmet can escape atmospheric pressure when he is fifty feet under water. But little occurrences showing how thoroughly the people sympathised in all great work taken in hand often brought encouragement and inspiration. At a Bible meeting in Arkansas the Society's Agent in his address mentioned the two mites of the widow who cast her all into the Treasury and a gift of sixty-eight cents from a woman in Turkey who sold her copper kettle to get it. The next morning a little girl came to him bringing a pair of new woollen socks. "Mother has no money," she said, "but she sends these. They are all that she has to give to help send the Bible to those who haven't any." The mother was a widow with four children. Such gifts of love for the poor which the Society received quickened the faith of those hard-pressed men at the Bible House.

The return of peace found the Society with larger resources at command and with broader and nobler aims than at any previous period of its history. Before the war was through the men at the Bible House learned that the burdens of war-time had been placed upon them for good by the providence of God Himself, and their hearts went out like the Psalmist, in prayer and thanksgiving: "For Thou, oh God, hast proved us; Thou hast tried us as silver is tried; Thou broughtest us into the net; Thou layedst a sore burden upon our loins; Thou didst cause men to ride over our heads; we went through fire and water, but Thou broughtest us out into a wealthy place!" [1]

[1] Psalms 66, vv. 10–12.

CHAPTER XXXIII

SOME FRUITS OF CHRISTIAN FEDERATION

THE surrender of the Southern armies in the first months of 1865 revealed their utter exhaustion. This brought to thoughtful people a beginning of realisation of the desolations which war had wrought in the South. In the northern and western parts of Virginia almost every grove was gashed by shells and every field seamed by the trenches of attack and defense. Military necessities had destroyed enormous quantities of property. Georgia had been desolated by many battles; and finally the march of General Sherman's Army from Atlanta to Savannah, when the troops fed from the country as they went, left a track from forty to sixty miles wide, stripped of everything that could be eaten, and of all fences and outbuildings which could be burned for cooking the soldiers' daily food. The main artery of communication, the Georgia Central Railroad, had been taken up rail by rail for three hundred miles, all the cross-ties burned, and the rails heated to redness in the fires of burning, and twisted around trees or telegraph poles lest some one should fancy that they might be relaid.

The same desolation scarred the fair face of South Carolina and North Carolina, where Sherman's army passed in its long, hard progress from Savannah to Goldsboro and Raleigh. Families had not been injured in their persons, and there had been no general destruction of dwellings; but all fit cattle had been devoured; every horse and mule in the path of the army had been impressed, old worn-out beasts being left in exchange. Wherever the armies marched during the terrible four years, desolation indelibly recorded their path. In a large part of the Southern States the people were reduced to a dead level of want. There were no favoured classes, for all classes were poor beyond understanding. A pitiful letter which came to the Bible House in New York in 1866 illustrates this general condition. A retired minister was living in an obscure village in North Carolina. He had been for several years a Life Member of the Society. He wrote that he was seventy-four years old and, much impoverished by the war, he had no means to buy candles by which to read his Bible in the evening. Hence he found it impossible to read the small type of an ordinary Bible. The light of his fire was too feeble. So he begged the Board to let him have a Bible with large print, for he would fain have the solace of reading in the evening hours. It is needless to say that this venerable saint received immediately a copy of the New Testament and Psalms in Great Primer type, the largest which the Bible Society possesses.

" When God shakes the nations He magnifies His own word. It moves right forward in the track of mighty providences, and leagues its powers with all the grand issues of the age. It has been so in every great struggle for progress, in the fall of Rome, in every world convulsion in modern history; it is to be so in the case of our own tremendous conflict." [1] The great religious question now before the Society was the same in essence as that which gave the Bible Society its existence: the necessity of encouraging religious life among isolated and cheerless families. Here the Society could give first aid. The feeling of all in the Bible House was that there should be no withholding of the priceless boon of the Bible to those willing to receive it. It was not a question of money, but of religion; not a matter of calculation, but of faith in God and service for His Kingdom. For the destitution in the South was vast, pitiful, appealing to the inmost souls of all members of the Society. The old stimulus of need to win multitudes left without the Bible applied with new force in this case; and with general approval it was decided in 1865 that among the works by which the Society should celebrate its jubilee year, a prominent place must be given to the re-supply of the South. In all those Southern regions the Society had

[1] Secretary Holdich in the Annual Report of 1863, page 95.

rendered comfort and solid encouragement to the disheart-
ened population. It could not give away its money. The
case was something like that of St. Peter at the temple gate
when he said to the cripple, " Silver and gold have I none;
what I have I give thee." The Board foresaw its immense
responsibility for aiding the restoration of all the devastated fields.

The Society's Army Agency on the old war area was continued for the supply of troops in many places east of the
Mississippi River and for some 80,000 soldiers who were
retained on the Western Plains and in Texas. This gave
an opportunity for the distribution of Scriptures in different
parts of the South without new machinery and it was found
that wherever the Board, the Auxiliaries and the Bible
Agents met need, efficient work was immediately done.
The work of these agents brought life to dead Societies as
well as strength to the Society.

Circumstances which demanded of the Agents the most
prompt supply were those of the lowliest of Christ's followers. In California the Society's Agent found an old
woman from Texas living in a ragged tent alone in an en-
campment of Southern people who had moved to the Pacific
coast after the war. She could hardly express her joy at
receiving a copy of the New Testament bound with the
Psalms and in type large enough for her feeble vision. As
the Agent left her he congratulated the woman on her hope
of a resting place some day in the " city which hath foundations." He said to her, as a contrast to her insecure
little tent: " There no rough winds nor stormy skies will
come to destroy our peace." The response of the old lady
sprang from her heart, and was not phrased in accordance
with the grammar of the schools. She joyfully said: " Nary
wunst ! "

Southern Christians responded to these kindly offices
like those who watch for the dawn. They also co-operated.
Rev. Mr. Gilbert, one of the Missionary Agents in the South,
speaking of some of the good people of Virginia wrote that
it seemed to him an omen for great good that " the first
fruit of benevolence coming out of the soil trampled by
the iron hoof of war, should be labour in behalf of that

inspired volume which lies at the basis of our liberties."
The overtures of the Bible Society in other states were
answered almost as soon as the cannon ceased to roar.
Gov. Brownlow, of Tennessee, and a number of leading
citizens of that state offered their services to help in Bible
distribution. The Society's Agent at Nashville wrote that
he never encountered people so anxious to buy family Bibles,
but there was absolutely no money in the country districts,
and so these eager people had to make the best of the
smaller and cheaper Bibles which the Society could give
them.

The Southwestern Bible Society, at New Orleans, voted
in 1865 to resume co-operation with the American Bible
Society so as to supply troops as well as families. Several
denominations in South Carolina took pains to inform the
Bible Society of their gratitude for help in supplying the
destitute with Scriptures. In North Carolina, in 1866,
fifteen Auxiliary Societies as well as a number of Bible
Committees assumed a share in the general supply of the
destitute which was recommended by the Society. Mississippi friends of the Bible were ready to co-operate with the
Society although no money could be raised and grants would
have to be asked from New York without present return.
In September of 1865 the Virginia and the Alabama Bible
Societies resumed Auxiliary relationship. Rev. Dr. Wood-
bridge, President of the Virginia Society, wrote to Secretary
Holdich, " We desire that the old relations shall be resumed
entirely as though the war had not been. This is the spirit
and the object of the Board of Managers of the Virginia
Bible Society." The Alabama Society created much surprise at the Bible House by announcing that it had in hand
$600 and would shortly receive $800 more, making $1,400
altogether which before long it would send to the Treasurer
at New York.

A year later the Virginia Auxiliary ordered $10,000 worth
of Scriptures for depositories in that state. The Society
sent the books charging only one-third of the actual cost. In
South Carolina where people were suffering in 1867 for
bread, applications for Scriptures came from thirty-one districts which were quickly supplied. In Georgia where the

COLORED COLPORTEUR AMONG THE STEVEDORES

white people were on the verge of starvation, 15,000 volumes were sent as grants to Auxiliary Societies desiring to distribute Scriptures. In Arkansas where a large part of the population were hungry all the time because there was no way of earning money, the Society granted, in 1867, $6,000 worth of Scriptures. Another incident of the same year, showing the eagerness of the Southern people to receive Scriptures in their terrible destitution, was that contributions of money were sent to the Society from Southern States which had not yet begun to recover from the losses of the war. There was great significance, however, in the fact that two years later the number of Auxiliaries in the Southern States had reached a total of 856. Cordial Christian sympathy had not been extirpated by the bitterness of the temporary estrangement.

During the later years of the period which ends with 1871, when the Southern States received full control of their own affairs, tremendous social and financial problems still rested upon the Southern people. Letters from South Carolina in 1866 mentioned depression and discouragement because of the unsettled condition of the country. In North Carolina friends wrote that money was more scarce than ever, because labour had not yet been regulated. In Missouri, a border state which had supplied men to both armies, the return of the discharged soldiers revealed, if it did not create, new antagonisms. Jefferson City, the capital of the State, had become a moral desolation; most of the churches had been closed and many church organisations had become extinct. These pressing problems were small, however, in the presence of the questions relating to freed slaves.

For years the Society had supplied such coloured people in the South as were able to read. In the later years of the war these grants increased. The Bible was everywhere welcomed by coloured people. Rev. Dr. L. D. Barrows Superintendent of Education among the negroes of South Carolina, Georgia, and Florida, wrote in 1866, asking Scriptures for coloured people. " To my mind," he said, " there is not one open door on this round earth where the Society can do so much good as by supplying coloured people just learning to read. I submit to you, no reader will you find who will thumb this book like these new readers, who may be seen in groups and squads on the streets and on the plantations reading and giving the benefit of their reading to others."

In the first year after the war it is estimated that at least 500,000 negroes learned to read. Rev. W. F. Baird, the Agent of the Society among the coloured people of the South, wrote in 1866 of a conversation with a negro forty-four years old who had stumbled through a recitation in English, and sensible of his failures had remarked, " If the Lord lets me live until to-morrow I *will* have that lesson right! " Another illustration of the eagerness to learn which he found among the coloured people was a man who worked for his physical life at his trade of making cotton-gins from half past six in the morning until five o'clock in the evening, who then gave himself to intellectual life, walked two miles to a night school, and after an hour in attendance there, every night studied until twelve or one o'clock. His idea was that he would like to be a well-equipped man.

Nevertheless, the case of the coloured people was most perplexing. During the last year of the war, especially while Sherman's army marched through Georgia and the Carolinas, great masses of coloured men, women and children, left the plantations and fled to the army for protection and support. The government, through the Freedmen's Bureau, tried to care for the blacks, their support, education, and their labour on the plantations under equitable contracts; but this government aid extended only through 1870, when the Freedmen's Bureau was given up. Throughout the years immediately after the war, the two great social questions before the nation were, first, the protection and restoration of political rights to the white population of the South who had staked and lost all; and second, the protection and education of the newly emancipated slaves.

It was interesting to discover that in some Southern States Auxiliary Bible Societies as they were re-organised, received coloured people to membership. From North Carolina in 1866 came many demands from Bible Committees for large type Scriptures for the use of coloured people who were not yet skilled readers. Of course, the newly emancipated people were included in the general supply of the South already ordered.

The question of money to meet these extraordinary demands was a serious one. Hitherto the Society had lived as did the Israelites in the wilderness who were fed by daily manna. A condition of the daily bounty was that the people might not make the gift an object in life. There must be no hoarding, no gluttony, there must be nothing which might diminish the sense of daily dependence upon the most gracious God. The Society had held to the principle of spending all its receipts. It had no invested funds, owned no stocks of any kind; its entire property was the Bible House and the plant for printing and binding. Nothing could have been done to meet the sudden demands upon the Treasury had not the school of the years of war taught the nation that this great work of Bible distribution calls for support as a benefit to the whole nation.

In 1862 a Committee was appointed to review the general operations of the Society in order to propose any possible economies. While this matter was under consideration, the British and Foreign Bible Society in a fraternal letter,[1] as an expression of Christian sympathy offered a donation of 2,000 pounds sterling to the American Society. In the meantime, however, Providence had placed the Treasury beyond need of this aid, but this did not diminish appreciation of the offer or the warmth of expressions of gratitude in the letter which declined the generous offer.

In 1863 the Finance Committee was able to announce the complete payment of the mortgage upon the Bible House. The building had been paid for without taking a cent from ordinary contributions for Bible work. Later considerable amounts were paid into the Treasury in connection with the Jubilee celebration. The Pennsylvania Bible Society, for instance, made a donation, as a jubilee offering, of $5,000 for printing the Arabic Bible, and $5,000 for supplying 20,000 Testaments and Psalms to be distributed in the

[1] February 2, 1862.

Southern States. Small amounts came from unexpected quarters. In 1864 the Rev. Dr. Van Dyck, translator of the Arabic Bible, sent fifty dollars to the Society as a thank offering for being spared to complete that great work which had occupied sixteen years. Among the many legacies received during this period was one from J. E. Worcester, the lexicographer, who bequeathed the copyright and income of sales of his great dictionary to the American Bible Society and the American Peace Society, each to have one half of the income. People in Turkey sent donations of over $1,000 to be used in giving the Bible to freedmen. Of this amount forty dollars was from a Mohammedan who was interested in the emancipation. Does any one ask why a Mohammedan, taught that slavery is ordained of God, should feel sympathy for American slaves? The answer is that American missions and Bible agents during a whole generation had been teaching Turkey the nature of gospel philanthropy. It was natural for a man subtly moved through the Bible, to send his gift for freed slaves to the Bible Society.

In 1865 the Board through such gifts found that it had more money than it immediately required and for the first time invested surplus funds for emergencies. In 1867 the receipts of the Treasury from thirty-nine states and territories amounted to $743,000. The people had rallied to the support of the Bible Society, and rescued it from serious embarrassment.

The greatest amount ever received in a single year as donations from Auxiliary Societies was $113,309 given in 1866. The largest sum received up to that time in a single year in donations from churches and individuals was $71,-874 in 1866. This sum was not exceeded in any year until forty years later. The total of donations from churches and individuals during the war period, (1861-1870) was $507,925; the total of Auxiliary donations was $814,517; and the total of legacies received during the same period was $865,252 — that is to say, aside from the receipts from sales of books $2,187,694 had been paid into the Treasury for the general work during this period of war and unparalleled expenditure. The stress of the times had aroused

the people to deny themselves in support of this great national enterprise. The receipts from sales during the same
period, amounting to $3,053,802, fully provided for the
large expenditure in the printing department. And so it
came to pass, in the good providence of God, that the Society was able promptly to do its considerable work for
the Southern States, without neglecting work abroad.

Not only upon the members of the Board of Managers
did the stress and burden of responsibility for this work
weigh in these times, but upon each of the Secretaries and
upon the Treasurer; each one encumbered by the magnitude
of the needs most closely before his eyes. All were haunted
at times by dread of overlooking needs, of failing to gauge
the quality of incessant demands for help, and of distinguish-
ing between trust in God and blind self-will when the fields
clamoured for help although the Treasury seemed empty
and no supplies in sight. Each of these men, however, was
fitted and furnished so that from the treasure of his godly
heart he could bring out things new and old for the inspiration and stimulus of his associates. So it came to pass
that these strenuous experiences tended to weld together
these men of different theological views through their elementary beliefs, hopes, and habits. Out of this time of stress,
then, the Society came forth a more efficient, more aspiring
institution, more than ever convinced of its divine mission.
Like the Israelites in their education as the chosen people
of God, it found its daily journey guided by the pillar of
cloud or of fire, it had its hungers, its thirsts, its tempta-
tions, perhaps, to give up so wearing a struggle, and its
repeated rewards of trust; but throughout its rugged path
its power was union in hope for the land to be occupied as
a province of the Kingdom of God.

This union in hope was not restricted to the Bible House.
Dr. Taylor, the Secretary immediately in charge of the
Society's affairs in the South, was very much interested in
1867 to receive a set of resolutions from the Lexington,
S. C., Auxiliary. From that state, which was the first to
raise the flag of secession came these welcome words: "We
hail the American Bible Society as an instrument in the
hands of God to unite us as a people — brothers of a com-

mon country and a common destiny — in all efforts for the evangelisation of the country and the world." This statement which was repeated in spirit again and again in Southern States may be said to emphasise the choicest fruit of the federation of Christians which the Bible Society represents, and of which the basis is need to combine for the world's good all forces, both visible and latent, among the servants of Jesus Christ. Wherever the Society has worked its daily experiences have disclosed the replacing of cold courtesy by cordial love, the growth of fraternity, the concentration of powers, and a new efficiency in advancing the Kingdom. In this feature of its organisation the Society exhibits a method of Christian activity at once fruitful and sane. Such a federation is possible only through laying aside purely personal preferences and repugnances so that the wish and the command of the Redeemer may have richer fruition in the world. Such a federation of denominations exerts an attraction upon unbelieving cynics whom organic union of churches could not startle. One great result most clearly brought into view through the stress of the war period was, in short, the increase of a sense of brotherhood tending to actual union of all hearts through conformity to the image of the First Born among many brethren.

CHAPTER XXXIV

THE PULSE OF LIFE

GENEALOGY enthralls many students of history. From the point of view of the influence of parents upon the children and their descendants there is rich suggestion and a certain satisfaction in tracing worthy characteristics, sturdy purpose, and noble achievement which are linked together from generation to generation. Though names are modified or obliterated, though individuals are removed by death, deeds remain belonging to the family as it follows its allotted course, unmistakably a unit from first to last. Change, even deaths from year to year may affect the outward aspects of an institution such as the Bible Society; but like an influential old family its distinctive principles and its permanent qualities remain through the years.

The services to the Bible Society of a number of distinguished men were terminated by death during this period. The Rev. Dr. Lyman Beecher, who was a Secretary of the Convention at which the Society was organised, Rev. Dr. Eliphalet Nott, Gen. J. G. Swift, the distinguished surgeon, Dr. Valentine Mott, the Rev. Dr. John McDowell of Philadelphia, renowned for his interest in Sunday Schools and Bible classes in the Presbyterian Church, Rev. Dr. G. H. Sayre, Rev. Dr. T. S. Biggs, and Chief Justice (N. J.) Hornblower, all of whom were members of the Convention of 1816 (the last named being a Vice-President of the Society), all passed away in this period. Among other Vice-Presidents of the Society, Judge McLean of the United States Supreme Court, died in April, 1861. Vice-President George Douglass of Long Island, died in February of the same year.

When the close of the war brought the Society into direct relations again with its friends in the South, the Board expressed its regrets in a fraternal memorial on the death during the war of Vice-Presidents Samuel Rhea of Tennessee, J. B. O'Neall of South Carolina, and C. C. Pinckney, also of South Carolina. The wide range of the interests of the Society was illustrated by the circumstance that the first of these distinguished gentlemen was a Presbyterian, the second a Baptist, while the third belonged to the Protestant Episcopal Church.

One of the first of the friendly greetings received from the South after the close of the war was a message of confidence and good cheer from General John H. Cocke of Virginia, Vice-President of the Society since 1844. He died in 1866, greatly beloved, maintaining his interest in all good things, with mental faculties wonderfully preserved to extreme old age. Vice-President William B. Crosby, connected with the Society since 1816, and elected member of the Board in 1830, died in 1865, leaving a vacant niche hard to fill.

In 1867 the Hon. J. H. Lumpkin, Chief Justice of Georgia, and the Hon. J. A. Wright, once minister of the United States to the Court of Prussia, both Vice-Presidents of the Society, passed away. In the same year Vice-President Freeborn Garretson, and Vice-President Heman Lincoln of Massachusetts died. Mr. Lincoln was a warm friend of the Society who had held the office of President of the Baptist Home Missionary Society and had filled other positions of responsibility in connection with Baptist missionary operations. Vice-President Peletiah Perit died in 1864, and Vice-President Benjamin L. Swan in 1866.

In April, 1868, Vice-President W. W. Ellsworth finished his course. The son of the Hon. Oliver Ellsworth, second Chief Justice of the United States, he was worthy of his distinguished parent. He was an earnest supporter of the Society from its organisation, and was elected Vice-President in 1848. Another Vice-President of long and well-tried fidelity was Thomas Cock, M.D., of the Society of Friends. He became a member of the Board of Managers in 1834, and in 1839 was made a Vice-President. The Board of Managers mourned the removal of one so endeared to them by his many virtues, his gentle manners, and his earnest Christian spirit.

In 1869 the Board suffered loss again in the death of Henry Fisher, Esq., for sixteen years Assistant Treasurer of the Society. His complicated duties during the Civil War were performed with indefatigable industry, a zeal which absorbed him, and a love for the work which made it completely successful. Millions of dollars passed safely through his hands during his long incumbency. He was prompt, earnest, exact, conscientious and thoroughly consecrated — an honour to the Protestant Episcopal Church of which he was a member. A. L. Taylor, Esq., was elected Assistant Treasurer in November, 1869.

The services of the Rev. Samuel L. Tuttle entitle his name to a place in this record of the great family of the Society, although he had not official relation to the Board. Appointed in 1863 assistant to the Secretaries, he performed duties assigned to him from day to day. He was prudent, tactful, energetic, and worked in the office up to almost the last day of his life, the 16th of April, 1866. During the Civil War it had not seemed necessary to employ three Secretaries at the Bible House, but on Mr. Tuttle's death the intricate questions arising from the reorganisation of the Society's work in the Southern States made it necessary to appoint a third Secretary, and in 1866 the Rev. T. Ralston Smith, D.D., well-known as an esteemed pastor in New York City, was called to office of Corresponding Secretary.

As James Russell Lowell observes, " In times of struggle we have our Sinais and our talks with God in the bush." This spiritual value of trials must be recognised as a main element of the permanence of the Society's eminence. Throughout the period from 1861 to 1871 the Secretaries of the Society were spurred to utmost activity. They were under strain, whether at the desk, or walking, or eating, or dreaming in sleep. The growth of population through its natural increase as well as through immigration, demanded immediate discovery of new methods of distribution, for as the nation grew the work must grow. The completion of the Pacific railroad in 1869 brought a renewal of pressure upon the men at the Bible House. It laid upon the Society new responsibilities, for in the vast regions thus opened villages and towns were springing up in a night like mushrooms. Every difficult phase of the steady increase of demands from the home field caused the Bible House to throb with life and activity.

The distinctiveness of the Society's bearing under such strains in some degree depends upon continuity in the office of Secretary. As has been noted, Secretary Brigham had the advantage of the counsel and advice of Secretary Milnor for several years, and in the same way Secretary Holdich, the senior Secretary of the Society after Dr. Brigham's death, could look back with satisfaction to twelve years of association with Dr. Brigham in his work as Corresponding Secretary. In the whole of the first fifty years of the Society's history one or the other of these three men had direct connection in some way with almost every important action. To take the place of Secretary Brigham the Rev. W. J. R. Taylor, D.D., of Philadelphia, was elected Corresponding Secretary. Dr. Taylor was an able and efficient man whose talents gave him special power in dealing with the many problems presenting themselves in the Southern States at this time, but after eight years of service he felt obliged to return to the pastorate and resigned in October, 1869, to become pastor of the First Reformed Church of Newark, N. J.

On the resignation of Secretary Taylor the Board divided the whole work of the Society into two sections, that at home and that abroad; placing Secretary Holdich in care of the work abroad and Secretary Smith in charge of the work at home. By this means responsibility for each branch of the work would be concentrated under the management, it being understood that an assistant to the Secretaries, and additional clerical aid as necessary, would be provided. The kindly service of the Society for the army was a general missionary enterprise as truly as that which commanded the services of William Carey or Gordon Hall. So the Secretaries as well as the Board were fully prepared to press forward the Bible cause in the home land.

The members of the Board were always close to the public affairs of the country. In 1865 they were smitten when the bullet of a madman killed President Lincoln, one of the Life Directors of the Society; and they passed a resolution of grief, for he had been struck down at the very fruition of the policies in which he had led the nation. In 1869 when General Grant took his seat as President of the United States in Lincoln's place, the Board of Managers presented him with a finely bound Bible. Three Vice-Presidents of the Society visited him with this book: Vice-President Salmon P. Chase, Chief-Justice of the United States, Vice-President Frederick T. Frelinghuysen, United States Senator, and Vice-President George Hay Stuart, the President of that great Commission which had co-operated with the Society in the supply of the armies which had been like pieces on a great chess-board in the hands of General Grant. It was immediately after General Grant's inauguration that the simple ceremony took place, and the book was accepted with kindly words of appreciation.

As the life of a living, growing body throbs in all its members, the Auxiliary Societies, too, showed themselves alert and active in these critical years. Each was independent in affairs of its own field. But through the fellowship of co-operation with the body which they regarded as a "parent Society" they were all participants in its gains — and its pains. During all of this period the Auxiliaries were stimulated to great efforts and many of them reached a degree of efficiency which was amazing.

In the South the Auxiliaries for some time after the war were offered help from New York to do their allotted work. To be put in general circulation in Georgia the Society in 1867 granted over 15,000 volumes to the Auxiliary Societies of that state. Thirty-three Auxiliaries in Alabama organised or revived by the Society's Agents were supplied with books for sale and free distribution. In Mississippi it was not possible to revive the old Auxiliaries so speedily, only seven having taken up active work during the first year after the war. In Louisiana the Southwestern Bible Society of New Orleans threw good-will and energy into its general work. Its principal sources of supply were obliterated during the war, and in 1867 the Pennsylvania Bible Society made a special contribution in order to have the Board send 6,000 Testaments and Psalms for distribution among the poor of New Orleans. In Arkansas no traces could be found of the former Auxiliary Bible Societies, and in 1867 about $6,000 worth of Bibles were sent to the state to be distributed by volunteer Agents who worked without pay during the general re-supply among the most destitute of the people. In Missouri, also, the Auxiliary Societies not being re-organised for a long time, the Society had to make many grants of books for distribution by local committees. In Tennessee, which was early occupied by the national troops, signs of recovery of ability appeared soon after the close of the war; yet here, too, it was clear that gratuitous help of the national Society would be necessary for some years. The sure response of these Societies to the measures adopted by the Board was well represented by the comment of the Louisville, Kentucky, Bible Society upon the decision to supply soldiers of both armies. " No better method could be adopted," it said, " for quieting the billows now raging over our once happy land than to let the voice of Him who stilled the storm when upon earth, be heard through His word."

In the Northern States the situation of the Auxiliary Societies was very different. In Ohio fifty-three Auxiliaries were able to do something, but only twelve of them commenced resupplying their fields immediately after the decision of 1866. A considerable number of " Sunday School Branches " of the Auxiliaries helped in the work. In Illinois Auxiliaries suffered less from the distractions of wartime than in many other states. In 1861 the Auxiliaries and their branches in Illinois made a total of 1225. Fifteen hundred ministers co-operated. In the year ending March 31, 1867, Illinois Auxiliaries remitted to the national Society somewhat more than $82,000. About half of this sum was in payment for books used by the Auxiliaries in their local work, and donations for the general work of the national Society made up the rest. Only the Auxiliaries in New York State did more in that year than those of Illinois in the way of remittances to the Society. The New York Bible Society sustained an arduous work of supplying Scriptures to the Army and Navy, paying the whole expense of the distribution and part of the cost of the books.   It received during the four years of war grants of books from the National Society valued at $37,684. These grants were made because the work was really national in character.   The New York Female Bible Society, busy with its special work of sending women to read the Bible to the poor, contributed $1,008 to the general Society. The Massachusetts Auxiliary Bible Society during this same period made a generous donation of $5,000, specially designated for the publication of the Arabic Bible.

In the midst of this period of unaccustomed labors, the Annual Meeting in 1866 decided to mark the beginning of a new half century by undertaking a third General Supply of destitute families throughout the United States. It was a great undertaking, but it was energetically carried out.   In 1871 the Society reported that 2,990,119 families had been visited, 228,807 families supplied, and 218,839 persons not included in the destitute families.   By 1870 it had learned that the vast regions newly opened to settlement since the war, could not, in the nature of things, be fully supplied by any merely local effort.   Direct distribution by the Society must supplement such efforts.   This necessity increased the labour, the cost and the duration of the General Supply ordered in 1866.

The Auxiliaries in general were, as ever, eyes and arms and nerves of touch to the Society in all parts of the home field.   In 1870 the reports of the Society ceased to contain a separate department of work for the South, the wounds having partly healed which had made such a department desirable.   At that time there were 7,125 Auxiliaries and Branches in the United States.   That a goodly number of these local societies were doing the work which falls to members of the Society is clear.   For these local Societies had in the field 194 County Agents with 110 paid colporteurs and 24,949 unpaid Bible distributers seeking the destitute willing to be supplied with Scriptures.   None can deny the influence upon the nation of such a force circulating God's word.

Because the poor are handicapped in the struggle for a worthy life, it seems that God must have a special blessing for those, like the Society's Agents, who are occupied in helping the execution of His purpose for the poor. The people with whom the Agents dealt were frequently half-pagan, ignorant people. Some poured a pan of dish water on the Agent to drive him away, and some treasured a verse from the Bible as a revelation and a marvel. Christians of education and intellect advised with the Agent, imparting refreshment and encouragement. As a result of making known his experiences among the destitute, a by-product, so to speak, of the Agent's work, too, was promotion of a spirit of fraternity among the churches of different de-nominations and between members of the church when drawn into a common line of labour. The Society had in 1870 about forty Agents in the home field aided by twenty Assistants. They were established in every state of the Union excepting those in which Auxiliary Societies main-tained agents of their own. The Agents were men of devo-tion, activity, experience and insight. Upon them the Man-agers at the Bible House relied for tireless labours in be-half of individuals destitute of the Scriptures. The Agent was the voice of the Board, reaching to needy people in the most destitute parts of the country. To the lonely homesteader the Agent's presence and kindly sympathy was like a breeze from the mountains in a sultry valley.

The Agents superintended the work of the Auxiliary Societies, animated Bible distribution, audited accounts, gave lessons in book-keeping, and distributed Scriptures from shack to shack in thinly settled regions where Auxiliaries had little reach. Within their own districts they watched over all the interests of the Society; as an incidental mat-ter trying, as far as possible, to increase contributions. The essential in the character of the Agent was likeness to Jesus Christ in utter devotion to the purpose of the Al-mighty, and in immeasurable sympathy for all the suffering.

Among the more ignorant settlers in the new districts commercial book agents acted on the theory that people wish to be deceived, selling gaudily bound Bibles on the instal-ment plan to poor people who paid ten dollars or more for the book. Sympathy was at once aroused for those duped by such men. A negro in Kentucky exhibited with some

pride one of these Bibles to an Agent of the Society, having bought it for twelve dollars. The Agent asked the
negro if he could read it. " No," he said. " Is there any-
body in your family who can read it?" " Nary one," he
said. " Then what are you going to do with the Bible?"
" Oh," he said, " my little Mary is being teached to read,
and when she larns how she'll read it to us." It was an
unmixed pleasure to offer to people so eager to get the Bible
a clearly printed, neatly bound volume for fifty cents, giving at the same time comfortable words of sympathy along
with the Book of all comfort.

As a matter of economy, in 1869 the Society's Agents
were withdrawn from Vermont, Virginia, and Rhode Island.
In each of these states a strong Society seemed well fitted to
handle by itself the needs of the state. This was really
a piece of optimism concerning Auxiliaries which was hardly
justified by experience. Of these three Societies the Virginia Bible Society alone proved itself able to work without aid from an Agent supported by the National organisation.

This chapter opened with a list of changes in the person-
nel of the Society. The facts set forth impress one with
the solid permanence of the life of the organisation. By
the grace of God the Society's initiative and activity per-
sist although its membership is mortal. Needs of the home
land in no way diminished appeals to the Society from foreign lands. We shall see in other chapters that this period
was also a time of tension abroad. In the year ending
March 31, 1868, more books were provided for the foreign
field than the whole number issued from the Bible House
in any single year of the first thirty-five years of the Bible
Society's work.

While the Bible House was occupied seemingly to its full
capacity with the publication of Scriptures for use at home,
it was preparing plates for several important versions to be
used abroad. In 1864 while demands from the home land
upon the Society seemed to absorb the whole of its resources,
the Board was so moved by the destitution of millions in
South America that it appointed a permanent Agent in the

region now known as Argentina. This was the beginning of the fruitful La Plata Agency of the Society, and in fact a turning point of the Society's enterprises followed by efficient and energetic action in South America not before known.

THE following pages contain advertisements of a
few of the Macmillan books on kindred subjects.

Three Religious Leaders of Oxford and Their Movements: John Wycliffe, John Wesley, John Henry Newman

By S. PARKES CADMAN

Cloth, 8vo, $2.50

This book deals with three great Englishmen, great Christians, great Churchmen, and loyal sons of Oxford, who, in Dr. Cadman's opinion, are the foremost leaders in religious life and activity that university has yet given to the world. "Many prophets, priests and kings," writes Dr. Cadman, "have been nourished within her borders, but none who in significance and contribution to the general welfare compare with Wycliffe, the real originator of European Protestantism; Wesley, the Anglican priest who became the founder of Methodism and one of the makers of modern England and of English-speaking nations; Newman, the spiritual genius of his century, who reinterpreted Catholicism, both Anglican and Roman."

THE MACMILLAN COMPANY
Publishers   64-66 Fifth Avenue   New York

Why Men Pray

By CHARLES LEWIS SLATTERY
Rector of Grace Church, New York City

Cloth, 12mo, 75 cents

Dr. Slattery defines prayer roughly as "talking with the unseen." In his book he does not argue about prayer but rather sets down in as many chapters six convictions which he has concerning it. These convictions are, first, that all men pray; second, that prayer discovers God, that, in other words, when men become conscious of their prayer they find themselves standing face to face with one whom in a flash they recognize as God; third, prayer unites men; fourth, God depends on men's prayer; fifth, prayer submits to the best; and sixth, prayer receives God.

THE MACMILLAN COMPANY
Publishers   64–66 Fifth Avenue   New York

Henry Codman Potter

Seventh Bishop of New York

By GEORGE HODGES

Cloth, 8vo, Illustrated, $3.50

It will be a source of gratification to Bishop Potter's many friends to learn that the preparation of the official biography of Dr. Potter has been entrusted to Dean Hodges of the Episcopal Theological School. Long conversant with the large essentials of Dr. Potter's life, his training and sympathy have been such as to qualify him to do the task well. The biography that he has written describes Dr. Potter's career throughout his ministry, especially as rector of Grace Church and as Bishop of New York. The great public services of Bishop Potter are also dealt with at length.

THE MACMILLAN COMPANY

Publishers   64–66 Fifth Avenue   New York

The Man of Nazareth

By FREDERICK LINCOLN ANDERSON, D.D.

Professor of New Testament Interpretation in Newton Theological
Institution

Cloth, 12mo, $1.00

There is nothing in English just like this book. Written
not for theologians, but for the average man and woman, it
nevertheless grapples fearlessly and independently the most
important modern questions about Jesus, his development,
and his career, including many matters which are only rarely
discussed. Yet the whole book is remarkable for its simplicity
and clearness. While there is no display of ponderous learning, the author shows that he is at home in all the recent
literature of the subject.

Dr. Gifford says, in *The Watchman-Examiner:* " Small in body, this
book is great in spirit. It deals with a great subject in a great way. It
is clear in analysis, simple in style, and profound in thought."

Columbus Journal: " We can conceive of no argumentative biography
more convincing. Quite the sanest thing in the way of popular theological literature."

The Standard (Chicago): " It gives one the impression that it was
written at white heat. The mood is so reverent that it may be used for
devotional purposes."

Men's Classes are already using it.

The Drama of the Spiritual Life: A Study of Religious Experience and Ideals

By ANNIE L. SEARS

Introduction by JOSIAH ROYCE

Cloth, 8vo, $3.00

The basis of this book is an empirical study of the prayers,
hymns and general religious poetry and other expressions of
religious experiences. In the opening chapter it is stated
that " man is incurably religious " because as human man is
idealistic. Religion is, therefore, close to the common life,
yet in religious idealism a problem is involved. This problem religious mysticism attempts to solve. In the second
chapter the author seeks to make clear what are the universal elements of religious experience, and in the succeeding portions of the volume she traces the story of religious
experience through its differences, oppositions, tensions, conflicts, compromises, and reconciliations. The problem of the
work is to discover whether the conflicting elements and
forms of religion can be harmonized and whether a significant
spiritual experience results.

THE MACMILLAN COMPANY

Publishers   64–66 Fifth Avenue   New York